Merry christmas

with love

Gwen charlie & Grant

Historic Sites of Northumberland
& Newcastle upon Tyne

Glen Lyndon Dodds

Albion
Press

Albion Press
40 Park Parade Roker Sunderland Tyne & Wear
©2000

http://members.tripod.co.uk/albionpress

Access the Albion Press Website to view many
of the photographs found in this book in colour

ISBN 0 9525122 1 1

British Library Cataloguing in Publication Data.
A catalogue record for this book is available from the British Library

Book and jacket design by Gavin Dodds

Printed and bound in Great Britain by
Biddles Limited Woodbridge Park
Guildford Surrey GU1 1DA

Contents

Preface 5
A Brief History of Northumberland
& Newcastle upon Tyne 7

Alnwick Castle 18
Aydon Castle 28
Bamburgh Castle 33
Belsay Castle and Hall 40
Blackfriars, Newcastle upon Tyne 46
Brinkburn Priory 49
Chesters Roman Fort 53
Chillingham Castle 59
Corbridge Roman Site 65
Cragside 72
Dunstanburgh Castle 79
Etal Castle 85
Hexham Abbey 88
Housesteads Roman Fort 96
Lindisfarne Castle 104
Lindisfarne Priory 109
Newcastle upon Tyne Castle 115
Norham Castle 121
Prudhoe Castle 130
Seaton Delaval Hall 136
Vindolanda Roman Fort and Settlement 141
Wallington Hall 149
Warkworth Castle 158
Some Other Sites of Interest 166

Glossary 172
Bibliography 175

For my mother and father

PREFACE

Northumberland has to be one of England's most enchanting counties. It is a fascinating place, with much to excite anyone interested in history and its charm is enhanced by the fact that many of the historic sites are set in beautiful surroundings.

As far as I can recall, the first historic monument in the county I visited was Chesters Roman Fort, where I went as a child, accompanied by my parents and brothers. Some of my fondest recollections of time spent in Northumberland date from 1975 and 1977 when my family and I visited places such Holy Island and Alnwick Castle, accompanied by my grandparents, who were on holiday from war-torn Rhodesia where they lived on a remote farm with the ever present risk of being attacked by bands of roaming terrorists. They were very impressed with Alnwick and with Northumberland in general, and were amazed by how much of the county is rural. I share the enthusiasm they felt. In short, Northumberland is one of my favourite counties and I hope that my affection for it is reflected in the text of this book.

I wish to thank Sir Humphry Wakefield for reading and commenting on the chapter on Chillingham Castle. Thanks, too, must go to Dr Robin Birley for doing likewise with the chapter on Vindolanda. I also wish to thank my brother, Shaun, who has taken most of the photographs that accompany the text, a task that often required waiting patiently until clouds had passed by and the sites in question were bathed in sunlight, thereby making the photographs more vibrant than would otherwise have been the case. Unless stated otherwise, the photographs are all by Shaun Dodds.

Glen Lyndon Dodds
Sunderland, 25 October 1999

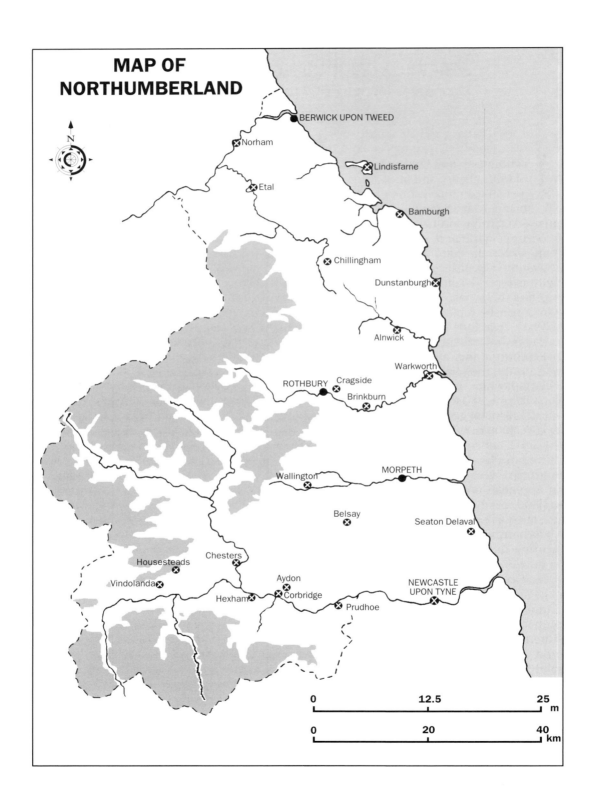

A BRIEF HISTORY OF NORTHUMBERLAND
AND NEWCASTLE UPON TYNE

Northumberland, England's northernmost county, contains much of interest in terms of both history and landscape. The county is bounded on the west by the Pennines, a chain of mountainous country stretching from the Peak District of Derbyshire to the Scottish border and known as the 'backbone of England.' The Pennines provide wild and windswept terrain and panoramic vistas that delight the eye, as do the Cheviots, a range of hills occupying much of north-west Northumberland. Indeed, the Cheviots form the highest ground within the county, with the Cheviot itself rising to 2,676ft (816m). Elsewhere, particularly along the coast to the east, one finds a completely different landscape, low-lying and heavily exploited land that contains the county's best farming country. The coast itself comprises rocky headlands and magnificent sandy beaches that stretch into the distance.

To a considerable degree Northumberland's landscape is man-made, but the earliest inhabitants had little impact on their environment. They were prehistoric Stone Age hunter-gatherers who evidently led a nomadic existence, primarily it seems living along the coast (the Bamburgh area appears to have been particularly attractive), but at times venturing inland up the river valleys to exploit resources such as the annual run of salmon and trout to their spawning grounds, and to hunt deer that had moved from the lowlands to their upland summer pastures. Such upland hunting, however, appears to have been limited.

Pastoralism began during the most advanced phase of the Stone Age, the Neolithic Period (c.4000-c.2000 B.C.), and was subsequently followed by the commencement of small-scale cultivation. The pollen record shows that limited woodland clearance thus occurred in places such as the Milfield basin in the far north of Northumberland, evidently the principal area of Neolithic activity in the county, where Neolithic folk were responsible among other things for erecting a fenced droveway associated with a large enclosure at Coupland. Neolithic communities have also left traces of their former presence in other ways, such as pottery - found for instance at Thirlings and Yeavering - and burial mounds such as barrows.

During much of the subsequent Bronze Age (c.2000-c.700 B.C.), which witnessed the introduction of bronze artifacts and a gradual increase in their availability, a proportion of the dead continued to be buried in or under such mounds, in some cases utilising ones dating from the Neolithic period. Moreover, the Milfield basin remained an important area of human activity, as is attested for example by the presence of several broadly contemporary hengiform monuments dating from the first half of the second millennium: in southern Britain the construction of henges commenced towards the close of the Neolithic period and some henges in the Milfield basin may likewise have been erected in late Neolithic times.

The population in the county apparently expanded during the Bronze Age, with areas hitherto neglected such as parts of Tynedale witnessing settlement, and at least some of Northumberland's population lived in unenclosed groups of huts known to have existed on the Cheviots and elsewhere. In the closing centuries of the Bronze Age the climate deteriorated, becoming both wetter and colder than that of today. This resulted in the abandonment of many upland sites and an apparently increasingly insecure society in which weapons became more plentiful, likely due to growing competition for land and livestock.

Early in the following Iron Age (c.700 B.C.-A.D.79), palisaded enclosures are known to have been established, and such sites may have existed in the closing centuries of the preceding epoch. They consisted of timber-built huts surrounded by wooden enclosures, and at least some such doubtless had a defensive function. Soon after the middle of the 1st millennium B.C., a number of the palisaded settlements developed into hillforts, with substantial defences in some instances, and most of the hillforts lie north of the River Wansbeck. Although none is in the first league of British hillforts, a few of respectable size do exist in the county, such as at Lordenshaws, Harehaugh and Yeavering Bell. The latter, near Wooler in the Cheviot foothills, is the largest hillfort in Northumberland. Within its defences, enclosing an area of 13½ acres (5.5 hectares), the traces of over 130 huts have been located. Contemporaneous with the hillforts, were further palisaded settlements and enclosed homesteads.

It was probably during the Iron Age that Celtic-speaking peoples arrived in Northumberland. What is certain is that by the 1st century A.D. at the latest, Celtic was spoken by the region's inhabitants, as was evidently the case throughout Britain.

The most powerful people in the north of England for much of the 1st century AD, and possibly for quite some time before that, were the Brigantes, centred on Yorkshire. It is generally thought that the north-eastern frontier of Brigantia lay along the Tyne. Some scholars, however, believe that the frontier may have lain further to the north, perhaps along the River Coquet for example. What is clear is that at least the northern half of the present county was largely if not entirely the territory of a tribe known as the Votadini, whose territory extended northwards far across the Tweed where the tribal centre was evidently located at Traprain Law in Scotland.

It was in the 1st century A.D. that the inhabitants of Northumberland were faced with the might of Rome, for the Romans were determined to conquer Britain and turn it into a province of their empire, a process that began in A.D. 43 when a formidable army landed in what is now Kent. In A.D. 78, a soldier named Julius Agricola was appointed to govern the province and rapidly succeeded in gaining the submission of the Brigantes, who had already been softened up by a predecessor. He then pressed on deep into Scotland, most probably via a route west of the Pennines, although Roman forces also advanced northward by way of Northumberland, skirting the territory of the Votadini, who had perhaps become clients of Rome.

Under Agricola and his successors a network of roads, supply-bases and forts was established in the region. This included Dere Street, the main northern artery, running north from York to Corbridge in Northumberland, and then on into Scotland. It left Northumberland at Chew Green, an isolated upland military installation. Another major road, now known as the Stanegate, branched off Dere Street just after it had crossed the Tyne, and ran west from Corbridge towards Carlisle.

The most notable reminder of the Roman presence in the county is of course Hadrian's Wall, by far the most famous relic of Roman rule in Britain. Commenced in A.D. 122 or 123 on the orders of Emperor Hadrian (117-38), and running 73 miles (117 km) across the Tyne-Solway isthmus, sections of the Wall were 7 to 10ft (2.13 to 3m) thick and as much as 15 to 20ft (4.57 to 6.1m) high. Moreover, a ditch was dug along the northern side of the Wall, save where it occupied the edge of precipitous high ground. Hadrian's Wall marked the northern frontier of the province, for the Romans had abandoned Scotland by A.D. 105 at the latest.

It is generally believed that the Romans initially intended that the main garrisons for the Wall would be located a short distance to the south along the Stanegate, from where they could advance if needed to support troops manning small fortlets (milecastles) located approximately every 1620 yards (1481m) along the Wall, and between which were pairs of turrets serving as observation posts. According to this view, while work on constructing the Wall was underway, a change of plan was decided on - to move the main garrisons forward to the Wall itself, where a number of major forts were thus included along its length. However, it has been recently argued that the provision of forts was an integral part of the Wall programme, not an afterthought, though this view is unlikely to become dominant.

While construction work was in progress, a large ditch flanked by banks and known as the *Vallum,* was dug behind the line of the Wall in a strip of cleared ground, save for along the Wall's most easterly stretch between Newcastle and Wallsend, where no trace of the *Vallum* has ever been found.

The *Vallum* could be crossed via causeways at forts and traffic through the Wall was permissible. Initially it passed through the milecastles, but following the provision of the *Vallum* it did so via forts. Some of the latter, moreover, partly projected from the line of the Wall and had gates that enabled members of the garrison to have ready access to the land beyond the frontier where outpost forts existed at places such as Risingham and High Rochester.

2. Hadrian's Wall near Vindolanda

Although mostly built by legionaries, the Wall was usually garrisoned by auxiliaries, men drawn from various parts of the empire who could look forward to being granted Roman citizenship following 25 years of service.

In A.D. 139, Emperor Antoninus Pius decided to reoccupy southern Scotland. As a result the frontier became the Antonine Wall, a turf structure erected between the Clyde and the Firth of Forth. But in around 163 this was abandoned and Hadrian's Wall resumed its role as the province's northern frontier. In the early 3rd century, southern Scotland was once again briefly occupied before the frontier reverted for the final time to Hadrian's Wall, though as in the past, Northumberland north of the Wall remained within the Roman sphere of influence. The outpost forts, though, were evidently abandoned in the early decades of the 4th century.

During the Roman occupation of Britain many impressive towns and villas were built. However, in common with other far northern counties, Northumberland differed markedly from what prevailed further south, for as noted it was a frontier zone throughout most of the Roman occupation. It is perfectly true that urban settlements developed outside forts but it is equally true that none of these deserves to be called a town with the exception of Corbridge, which developed into a town in the late 2nd and early 3rd centuries after the military presence at the site had been reduced. The only town in the county, Corbridge was far less extensive and impressive than ones found elsewhere in Roman Britain. Furthermore, villas were evidently absent. None has been found in Northumberland.

While a proportion of the residents of the urban settlements were of native origin, the vast majority of the indigenous population remained rural dwellers and although some acquired goods from traders within the settlements, their lifestyle remained essentially the same as it had been in the days of their forefathers. However, the greater level of security that generally existed during the Roman period led to less emphasis on defence: it is not uncommon to find the ramparts of hillforts partially overlain by the huts of settlements inhabited during this period.

It was in the early years of the 5th century that the Romans abandoned Britain. According to Germanic tradition, this event was followed - from 449 onwards - by the arrival of large numbers of warlike Anglo-Saxons from northern Germany and adjacent areas who transformed much of post-Roman Britain into Germanic England. Archaeological finds in England attest to significant Anglo-Saxon settlement, (which evidently commenced before the Roman withdrawal), as does for instance the fact that sooner or later the English language replaced the Celtic tongue - something Latin had failed to do.

The Teutonic people primarily involved in the conquest and settlement of the North were the Engle - or Angles - who originated directly or indirectly from Schleswig-Holstein and southern Denmark: those who settled in Northumberland were evidently the descendants of people who had already settled in Britain. Although archaeological traces of these folk (after whom England is named), are common in much of the country this is not the case north of the River Tees, where Germanic settlement occurred later and less intensively than it did in many other parts of England. Evidently, the Tyne was a point of entry for Anglian settlers. Indeed, it may well have witnessed the first English settlement in Northumberland. Another early focus of Anglian activity - and often said to have been the first - was the Bamburgh area which was reportedly seized by a Germanic warlord named Ida in the mid 6th century, the founder of a line of kings.

One of Ida's grandsons was named Aethelfrith, who reigned c. 592-616. The Northumbrian historian, Bede, (c.673-735) states that this king overran a great deal of territory, 'exterminating or enslaving the inhabitants, making their lands either tributary to the English or ready for English settlement.' Additionally, he gained control of another Anglo-Saxon state, Deira, in Yorkshire. Thus the extensive kingdom of Northumbria was created, extending north from the Humber into southern Scotland and as far west as the Irish Sea. During the remainder of the 7th century, three of his successors were the most powerful rulers in Britain.

Despite the Anglian takeover, Northumberland's population doubtless remained of predominantly native stock. As J.E.A. Jolliffe has commented, in later periods there were 'so many parallels to Celtic custom' in this region that one has to accept a marked degree of 'historical continuity.' This view is supported by other factors. For example, there are stronger traces of the Celtic language in place-names, and more particularly in the names of natural features, than is the case in much of England. Names of Celtic origin are numerous in the upland areas, and Northumberland's river names are all Celtic.

The 7th century witnessed the permanent arrival of Christianity, which had existed to some degree prior to the arrival of the Anglo-Saxons, who were pagan. Indeed, in 635, Aidan, a monk from Iona off the west coast of Scotland, founded a monastery and a bishopric on the tidal island of Lindisfarne (also known as Holy Island). A key figure in the Northumbrian church was a person of humble birth, St Cuthbert, a man of great charm, sincerity and strength of character, who served for some years as Prior of Lindisfarne before becoming a hermit on nearby Farne Island. In 685 he reluctantly accepted his election to the bishopric of Lindisfarne and served as bishop for two years. Previously he had undertaken preaching work in remote and mountainous parts of the kingdom 'which others feared to visit', thereby 'guiding the peasants heavenward', and as bishop he did likewise, albeit accompanied by a retinue befitting his position. He subsequently retired to Farne Island, where he died on 20 March 687, leaving behind a great reputation for sanctity.

By the close of the 7th century, Northumbria's days of political greatness were over and in the 10th century the once mighty kingdom - which had experienced occasional Viking aggression in the interim - was absorbed by the expanding kingdom of England.

In 1066 England was invaded by William of Normandy, who was crowned within months of his victory at Hastings. But further campaigning was required before he could truly regard himself as England's master. Indeed, it has been said that his son, William II (1087-1100), should really be viewed as 'the Conqueror' as far as Northumberland and the far north of England in general is concerned. Certainly, during William II's reign the North-East was more securely in Norman hands than previously, although the settlement of the region through the creation of baronies and knights' fees primarily occurred in the days of his brother and successor, Henry I, (1100-35).

The Norman Conquest was not followed by a considerable influx of settlers from Normandy: the newcomers only formed a minute fraction of the population. Hence the speech of ordinary folk remained essentially English: the Normans spoke French. On the other hand, Norman personal names such as William and Geoffrey gradually came into vogue among the native population, which was mostly engaged in working the land.

With royal sanction, during the Middle Ages some areas in Northumberland, as elsewhere in the country, were liberties or franchises - places where government was in the hands of private individuals or institutions and where officers of the Crown were normally excluded. This was true, for example, of territory in the east and north-east of what is now

Northumberland. The land in question comprised Bedlingtonshire, Norhamshire and Islandshire, tracts of territory that formed part of the palatinate of Durham (centred between the Tees and Tyne), land in which the bishop's writ, not the king's, ran.

Pastoral farming was an important facet of the medieval economy, especially in upland areas. Large flocks of sheep and herds of cattle existed in many places. The Umfravilles, for example, lords of Prudhoe and Redesdale, had substantial numbers of such livestock grazing on the moors of Otterburn and Redesdale. Arable farming was also practised, particularly in lowland areas, and witnessed expansion during the 12th and 13th centuries (in line with events nationally) as more and more food was required for a growing market, entailing the extension of cultivated land into areas of waste, scrub and woodland, a process that resulted in the creation of new settlements. But from about 1300 deteriorating weather conditions - the climate became colder and wetter - led to a contraction of arable farming in the upland areas and ploughland returned to grass.

Among key players in the agrarian development of the county were monastic houses: monasticism had been revived in the region in the late 11th century after dying out because of Viking activity. Notable in this regard were the Cistercian monks of Newminster near Morpeth, a monastery founded beside the River Wansbeck in south-east Northumberland in 1139 by monks from Fountains Abbey in Yorkshire on land granted by the lord of Morpeth. With characteristic Cistercian zeal, they ran a number of far-flung outlying farms or granges in mid Northumberland, transforming substantial areas of upland into sheep-grazing, thereby selling significant quantities of wool.

Wool was Northumberland's principal export during the Middle Ages and was mostly shipped from Newcastle, the most important town in the county. Newcastle came into existence after William the Conqueror's son, Robert, established a castle beside the Tyne in 1080, some twelve miles (19km) upstream from the coast. The castle, rebuilt in stone by Henry II and John in the second half of the 12th century and the early years of the 13th, dominated an expanding community outside its walls, a community that had evidently become established early in the 12th century.

Newcastle expanded rapidly. By the close of the 13th century - at which time Newcastle was in the process of erecting impressive town walls approximately two miles (3.2km) in circumference - it had easily outstripped Corbridge, relegating it to second place in the county's hierarchy of boroughs. At this time Newcastle's population may well have been in the region of 10,000 people, in which case only Bristol and York would have been more populous provincial boroughs.

Primarily, Newcastle's development was due to seaborne trade. Cargoes such as wool, coal and lead were shipped down the Tyne to a large number of destinations both home and abroad, with most of the vessels involved being foreign. Imports were probably more varied in nature than exports and included iron, corn, furs, woad, wooden boards and wine. Not surprisingly, Newcastle's foremost export during the medieval period was wool, and in the early 14th century Newcastle ranked sixth among English ports engaged in this trade. In 1334, its overall economic growth had been such that it was ranked fourth in wealth, surpassed only by London, Bristol and York.

On 23 May 1400, a long process towards self-government ended when Newcastle became an independent county, with its own sheriff and six aldermen as well as a mayor: Newcastle had had the right to elect a mayor since 1251. However, the area of the royal castle remained part of Northumberland.

3. A section of Newcastle town wall near Black Friars

In the meantime, the 14th century had generally proved a time of woe for Northumberland, a time when many of the gains of the preceding two centuries were overturned, a time when fear pervaded the county, fear partly induced by natural disaster such as the Black Death - which first struck Northumberland in 1349 - but more often than not due to Anglo-Scottish raids, for England and Scotland were frequently at war from the late 13th century onwards.

How many people in Northumberland died as a result of the Black Death in 1349 is unknown. But the number of deaths was doubtless high. It is known that on 28 townships belonging to Durham Cathedral Priory the overall death-rate of tenants was just over 50 per cent. Admittedly, most of these villages lay in County Durham but two, Willington and Wallsend, were in southern Northumberland and they suffered severely: Willington's tenant death-rate places it among townships in the sample with between 50 and 59 per cent of their tenants killed, whereas Wallsend's death-rate was over 60 per cent.

Turning to Scottish invasions, they were not an entirely new phenomenon. In 1138 for example the canon, Richard of Hexham, recorded depredations wrought in the vicinity of his monastery by a Scottish army 'more barbarous than any race of pagans'. But the 14th century witnessed more frequent incursions, either by armies or raiding bands, something that in the short-term had a devastating effect on local society as a whole. Speaking of the early decades of the century when Robert Bruce was King of Scotland, Jean Scammell comments: 'Life could only continue within the immediate Border area with the Scots' permission. Even the garrisons of Alnwick and Bamburgh treated with them; and at least two attempts were made from the latter to negotiate for the preservation of some nearby holdings.'

In the late 15th and 16th centuries great lawlessness existed in remote North Tynedale and Redesdale, on the bleak western margins of the county. It was the domain of border reiving clans such as the Charltons, Dodds, Milburns and Fletchers who, as a result of the decline of law and order in the area largely brought about by the Scottish wars, essentially became a law unto themselves. In addition to feuding among each other, they raided comparable groups resident on the Scottish side of the border, (who responded in kind), and stole from other inhabitants of Northumberland living in the more civilised parts of the county. In 1554, the Merchant Adventurers of Newcastle agreed, among other things, that they would not apprentice anyone 'to serve in this Fellysshype of non suche as is or shalbe borne or brought up in Tyndall, Ryddisdall, or anye other suche lyke places' because they were dishonest. By the close of the century, tighter control by the agents of the Crown had brought the reivers to heel.

By this date Berwick upon Tweed, the northernmost town in Northumberland, had been provided with superb defences, the best early modern town defences in Great Britain. Berwick had had a chequered history. In the 13th century it had been the wealthiest town in Scotland. During the subsequent Anglo-Scottish wars it had changed hands repeatedly, before finally passing permanently into English control in 1482. Work on the Elizabethan defences, comprising a wall 20ft (6.1m) high, set behind a ditch 150ft (46m) wide, and complete with projecting bastions and artillery, began in 1558, when a Scottish invasion was feared. It continued until 1569 when it was abandoned before the scheme had been completed: the south and west sides of the town continued to use a town wall dating from medieval times. (An earth embankment was added behind the Elizabethan wall in the years 1639-53, much later than intended: it was an integral part of the design).

Other notable events during the 16th century included the closure of Northumberland's monasteries in the 1530s, part of Henry VIII's programme of abolishing monasticism in England, and the emergence in the second half of the century of coal as Northumberland's principal export in succession to wool. Coal had been shipped from Tyneside since at least the mid 13th century but only gradually achieved preeminence in the local export market. The amount of coal shipped from the Tyne subsequently increased dramatically, rising for instance from 32,950 tons or so per annum in the mid 16th century to 452,625 tons in 1633-34, dwarfing exports from other North East ports such as Sunderland in County Durham. The coal was mostly bound for London.

Shortly after this, in the 1640s, England was rent apart by civil war but Northumberland witnessed little fighting. The most serious military activity occurred in early 1644 when a large Scottish army crossed the border to assist the ailing war effort of the Parliamentarians against Charles I and his adherents - Charles was of course also the Scots' king, for his father James VI of Scotland had succeeded to the English throne in 1603. The outnumbered Royalist forces in the county withdrew before them and the Scots duly appeared before Newcastle, which was held for the king. Finding it too well defended, they pressed on southward, following some skirmishing, to join their allies. But later in the year, after the defeat of a Royalist army at Marston Moor in Yorkshire, they retraced their steps and joined another Scottish army that in the meantime had entered the region, and both besieged Newcastle. The town surrendered in October, whereupon parliament proceeded to lift an embargo on the region's coal and salt exports enforced since the beginning of the previous year.

Turning to the rural scene, during the 17th and 18th centuries the open fields of many villages on the coastal plain and in the Tyne valley were enclosed by consent and divided up into individual consolidated farms. As Leslie Hepple comments: 'The enclosure of open land allowed better husbandry, and the introduction of sown-grasses, clovers and turnips encouraged new crop rotations, increased yields, and provided winter feed for the sheep and cattle, so solving one of the major problems of medieval agriculture.' Comparable developments followed in the upland areas. In about 1729 the antiquary John Horsley observed that enclosure was for instance underway near Elsdon.

Growth and improvement occurred in Newcastle, especially in the latter half of the 18th century. For example, fine residential squares such as Clavering Place were constructed for the wealthy. Moreover, traffic-flow was rendered more easy in the old parts of the town and, increasingly, land beyond the town walls (which began to be dismantled) was developed. Culturally, too, it was a time of advancement. Educational facilities were more numerous than had been the case - there were several good private academies - and a number of literary, scientific and humanitarian societies. On the other hand, poverty and disease were endemic in working class quarters of the town.

John Wesley, the much-travelled Methodist preacher, expressly visited these areas to preach to their inhabitants. His first visit was in May 1742, and he was not impressed by what he found: 'We came to Newcastle about six, and after a short refreshment walked into the town. I was surprised: so much drunkenness, cursing and swearing (even from the mouths of little children) do I never remember to have seen and heard before, in so small a compass of time.' However, after preaching in the Sandgate district, 'the poorest and most contemptible part of the town', many responded to his message in a positive manner, displaying 'love and kindness'. That December, under Wesley's direction, work on constructing the first Methodist preaching house in the North East commenced in what is now Northumberland Street, Newcastle. It was only the second purpose-built Methodist chapel erected.

The 18th century also witnessed the expansion of the coal industry. Collieries opened at Byker, Jesmond, Wylam, Longbenton and elsewhere. A network of wagonways consisting of tracks of parallel wooden rails, laid on sleepers, along which horses drew wagons, was established to transport coal to the Tyne or coast. Coal was, for instance, shipped from Seaton Sluice where, in the years 1761-64, a gentry family, the Delavals, excavated a new harbour entrance to improve their coal shipping facilities, and in 1777, 177 ships left the harbour laden with coal. As in the past though, most coal was shipped from the Tyne.

Coal continued to be of great importance in the local economy during the 19th century and was mined at deeper and deeper levels. The early decades of the century also saw the conversion of wooden wagonways to iron rails, and the introduction of steam locomotives. In this context, it is worth noting that George Stephenson, a pioneering figure in railway history, was a native of the county, for he was born at Wylam in 1781 and while employed at Killingworth Colliery, built and tested his first locomotive in 1814.

Another industry that expanded during the 19th century was Tyneside's glass industry (which dated from the early 17th century) and produced a wide variety of glassware. Iron manufacturing, too, witnessed growth. Prior to 1800, iron foundries existed in Northumber-land (Corbridge, for example, was a centre of ironworking in the Middle Ages) but their number now increased, largely due to the demand for iron rails and steam locomotives. As the century progressed, though, increasing competition from elsewhere had a devastating effect on the local glass industry - it largely disappeared - and resulted in the marked contraction of the iron industry. Conversely, the latter half of the 19th century saw the significant growth on Tyneside of shipbuilding, (something that had occurred on a small-scale since the Middle Ages) and the establishment of a dynamic armaments industry. By the close of the century Tyneside was world famous for both.

Economic growth brought migrants to Northumberland and Newcastle, significantly contributing to population expansion. In 1871, for example, a fifth of Northumberland's population had been born outside the boundaries of Northumberland and County Durham, 31 per cent of them in Scotland, and three years later Newcastle's Medical Officer of Health claimed that only Liverpool, Manchester and Bradford had a higher proportion of Irish in their population. Migration within Northumberland itself also occurred. Rural decline took place as farm labourers forsook the countryside in the hope of making a better life for themselves on Tyneside or elsewhere.

Meanwhile, the 1830s had seen a massive redevelopment programme in central Newcastle, the brainchild of the builder and property developer Richard Grainger, who employed the services of a number of talented architects. The programme resulted in the creation of nine streets - the finest of which became known as Grey Street in 1836, in honour of Earl Grey of Reform Bill fame - and many new buildings in the classical style such as the Theatre Royal and a splendid Central Exchange. In short, Newcastle was transformed into the best designed Victorian town in England.

Grainger's development contrasted starkly with conditions in the poor parts of Newcastle such as the Quayside, where overcrowding and squalor were commonplace. In

4. Grey Street, Newcastle, by J. W. Carmichael

1845 a survey conducted on behalf of the government found 33 streets near the Quayside without either drains or sewers. Not surprisingly, disease was frequent: typhus, for instance, was endemic and when cholera periodically struck it claimed a higher toll than in the more prosperous parts of the town. Slum clearance ensued - to make way for commercial development, a process facilitated by destruction caused by a major fire in 1858 - and better residential accommodation was provided in the Scotswood, Elswick and east Byker districts of Newcastle.

The 20th century, too, witnessed mixed fortunes. During World War One, for example, many families in the region were adversely affected by the bloodshed in France and elsewhere: thousands of Northumbrians perished. On the other hand, the war was a boom period for the shipyards and armaments industry. Recession followed in the 1920s, bringing hardship and unemployment, and worsened during the Depression years of the 1930s. By the late summer of 1932 unemployment had reached its greatest extent. To illustrate the point, in North Shields and Willington respectively it stood at 48 and 74.6 per cent.

In line with events nationally, and indeed internationally, the latter half of the 1930s witnessed significant economic recovery. The government's policy of strengthening the armed forces in view of the growing power of Nazi Germany contributed to this process. The Walker Naval Yard, which had closed in 1928, was one of the places that benefited. It re-opened in 1935 to build vessels such as the battleship *King George V*.

Following the Second World War - in which Tyneside was subjected to limited German air raids - living standards for Northumbrians improved. Nevertheless, the region's economic growth lagged somewhat behind the national rate and therefore, as in past generations, migration to more prosperous areas such as the South East happened.

The 1960s was a bad decade for the region's traditional heavy industries. A marked decrease in demand for coal resulted in the closure of pits, while increasing competition from Germany and Japan adversely affected the region's other major heavy industry, shipbuilding, with the result that yards likewise ceased to exist. Today, shipbuilding and coalmining have virtually ceased on Tyneside and in Northumberland, contributing to high rates of unemployment.

Since 1974 Northumberland's boundaries have been slightly smaller than previously. As part of a national reorganization of local government, the new Metropolitan County of Tyne and Wear was created that year. Its major conurbations are Newcastle and Sunderland, and it includes within its boundaries places such as Tynemouth, Whitley Bay and Gosforth that were formerly part of the south-east of Northumberland, a county which, as the foregoing paragraphs indicate, has a long and fascinating history stretching back well into prehistoric times.

ALNWICK CASTLE

Alnwick Castle, a favourite location for film-makers, stands majestically on the south side of the little River Aln and is truly impressive, outwardly giving an impression of former feudal might while the interior is that of a sumptuous stately home.

It was founded as a motte and bailey castle with wooden buildings in the Norman period - the exact date is unknown - and was subsequently rebuilt in stone. The oldest parts of the fabric date from the days of a baron named Yvo de Vescy, who acquired Alnwick (pronounced 'Annick') in the mid 1090s, and the stronghold was described as 'very strongly fortified' shortly after his death in around 1134. Further construction work ensued in the days of Vescy's successor, his son-in-law Eustace Fitzjohn, who was killed while fighting in Wales in 1157, by which time the motte had been reduced in height and was crowned by a shell keep.

Eustace was in turn succeeded by his son, William, who assumed the name Vescy as the bulk of his possessions came through his mother's line. It was during William's days as lord of Alnwick that Scotland's king, William the Lion, invaded the North East. He unsuccessfully besieged Alnwick in 1173 and returned the following year to invest the castle again, where-upon an English force advanced from Newcastle and fell upon his camp at daybreak, taking him prisoner.

During the early 13th century, William's successor Eustace, played host at Alnwick to King John, a much-travelled monarch who visited the castle more than once while engaged in Anglo-Scottish affairs. John came under increasing pressure from disaffected members of the baronage opposed to his heavy-handed rule and Eustace was one of his critics. John therefore confiscated Eustace's estates and, in 1213, ordered the destruction of Alnwick Castle, although he seems to have soon changed his mind for the stronghold survived. Presently, the king became reconciled to Vescy but it was not long before Eustace was once again prominent among his opponents and played a leading role in compelling John to sign Magna Carta in June 1215. Civil war followed - in late 1215 John burnt Alnwick - and in 1216 Eustace was killed while besieging Barnard Castle in County Durham, the seat of an adherent of King John.

In the mid 13th century England was again rent by civil war, one waged between Henry III and the supporters of Simon de Montfort, Earl of Leicester. The head of the Vescy family, John, (a grandson of Eustace), fought on the side of the rebels. He was at Lewes in 1264 when an outnumbered rebel army routed that of the king and was at Evesham the following year when the tide turned decisively in Henry's favour. Vescy was wounded and made captive. He was allowed to go free but his possessions, including Alnwick Castle, were confiscated. In 1266, he responded by leading a revolt in which he seized the castle. But Henry III's son, the future Edward I, marched north with a formidable army and compelled him to surrender unconditionally. Yet again, his life was spared. Indeed, he was pardoned and allowed to regain his estates after paying a fine.

John de Vescy died in 1288 and was succeeded by a brother, William, who followed him to the grave in 1297, leaving an illegitimate son who was killed at the Battle of Bannockburn in 1314. By this date, Alnwick Castle had passed into the hands of the Percy family. In 1309

5. Alnwick Castle (Professor Norman McCord, University of Newcastle upon Tyne)

Bishop Antony Bek of Durham, into whose hands Alnwick had passed, sold the castle and the barony of Alnwick to Henry Percy, a senior Yorkshire baron.

It is frequently asserted that this transaction was dubious; that Bek was not the owner of Alnwick but was rather holding the estate in trust for the family of William de Vescy. On this point, however, J.M.W. Bean, an authority on the Percies, comments: 'It is clear that some contemporaries believed that in selling Alnwick to Henry Percy . . . Bek . . . was breaking the trust reposed in him by William Vescy and was acting dishonestly: but the deeds and charters which have survived suggest that there was no foundation for this belief.'

The acquisition of the barony made Percy one of the most powerful men in the country. Like many people, he was a critic of Edward II, an irresponsible king devoted to a favourite named Piers Gaveston, (we are told that 'the king would speak to no one save in his presence'), and in 1312 Percy was prominent in seizing and executing the hated royal favourite. As a result, his estates were confiscated. But they were soon restored and in 1314 Percy took part in Edward's invasion of Scotland which ended disastrously at Bannockburn, where Percy was captured. The following year he died at Alnwick, which had been substan- tially rebuilt during his brief period of ownership. He had for instance reconstructed the keep in the form of seven semicircular towers ranged around an irregular-sided courtyard, and strengthened the curtain wall by the addition of towers.

In 1368, the 26-year-old great-grandson of the first Percy lord of Alnwick, became the fourth baron. Likewise named Henry, he initially raised the family to new heights of wealth, power and prestige. Like his forebears, he was prominent in the military sphere, serving both at home and abroad. In 1378 for example, (the year after he had been created Earl of

Northumberland), he besieged and captured Berwick Castle and put all its defenders to the sword. During the siege, his young son, a youth of 12 also named Henry, conducted himself with such gallantry that he was given the nickname 'Hotspur'.

In 1399 Percy, the head of the most powerful family in Northumberland and Cumberland, sided with Henry of Lancaster against Richard II and played a leading part in overthrowing the king in favour of Lancaster, who became Henry IV. However, relations with the new monarch soon soured. So much so, that in 1403 the Percies rose in revolt. Hotspur led an army south to effect a junction with other opponents of the king, but was soundly defeated and killed near Shrewsbury. Following this reverse, Northumberland surrendered to Henry IV at York and was briefly imprisoned. Upon his release, he proved far from reconciled and revolted unsuccessfully again in 1405. He fled to Scotland and Alnwick subsequently surrendered to the king. The earl's turbulent life ended in 1408 when he was slain at Bramham Moor in Yorkshire, still an adversary of Henry IV.

The first Earl of Northumberland's extensive estates had been forfeited through his treason. In 1416, however, the bulk of this property, including Alnwick Castle, was restored to the family by Henry V who granted it to the first earl's grandson.

Further vicissitudes befell the Percies as the 15th century progressed. The second and third Earls of Northumberland, for example, died fighting on the Lancastrian side during the Wars of the Roses - wars fought between rival branches of the royal family, the Houses of York and Lancaster. The second earl was slain at the First Battle of St Albans (1455) whereas his son and successor perished at Towton, (1461).

Following Towton, Yorkist forces under the Earl of Warwick moved against strongholds in Northumberland such as Alnwick, which were held for the Lancastrian, Henry VI and his queen, Margaret. By mid September, Alnwick had submitted (the other Lancastrian strongholds likewise soon yielded) and a Yorkist constable was appointed to hold Alnwick with a garrison of 100 men. But during the winter of 1461-2 the castle was retaken by a Lancastrian, Sir William Tailboys, and was held for that cause until July 1462 when it surrendered following a siege by Yorkist troops.

On 25 October 1462, Queen Margaret (who had journeyed to France to enlist the support of her kinsman, Louis XI), landed near Bamburgh at the head of a small army and proceeded to lay siege to Alnwick, which soon capitulated owing to a lack of provisions. Warwick presently came north again to deal with the situation. But on 5 January 1463, while he was before Alnwick, a substantial enemy force arrived in the vicinity. He thus raised the siege, whereupon the garrison abandoned the castle and headed north into Scotland, with the result that Alnwick was again garrisoned for King Edward IV.

However, in May, Sir Ralph Grey, the deputy commander of Alnwick, handed the castle over to the enemy: it is said that he had been piqued at not being placed in command of the garrison by Edward. Alnwick remained in Lancastrian hands until 23 June 1464 when its garrison, demoralized by a Yorkist victory near Hexham, capitulated as Yorkist troops marched against it.

John Neville, Lord Montague, a younger brother of Warwick, had played a prominent part in suppressing Lancastrian resistance in Northumberland and, on 27 May, just prior to the fall of Alnwick, Edward IV rewarded him by granting him the Percy title of Earl of Northumberland and almost all the Percy estates in the county. Neville held the title and estates until 1470 when Edward restored the earldom to Henry Percy, a son of the third Earl of Northumberland.

The 16th century witnessed a determined effort by the Crown to strengthen royal authority in the border region, something that entailed undermining Percy dominance. Cardinal Wolsey, for instance, Henry VIII's famous minister, fostered the growth of a Crown party in Northumberland consisting of local gentlemen who looked to London and not the Percies for advancement.

The Crown also intervened in the love life of Henry, the sixth Earl of Northumberland, a weak, thriftless character plagued by ill-health, who held the title in the years 1527-37, during which he dissipated his inheritance. As a young man, he fell in love with Anne

6. Alnwick Castle from the north

Boleyn, but was compelled to renounce her by Wolsey after Henry had set eyes on her himself. When Anne fell from royal favour, Northumberland was appointed a member of the commission to try her but avoided the unpleasant task by pleading sickness.

The sixth earl, who became estranged from his family, died childless in 1537, where-upon his remaining estates passed into the hands of the Crown, to whom he had agreed to leave them. They remained in Crown hands until 1557 when the earldom of Northumberland was restored to the family by Mary Tudor. Thomas, the seventh earl, (whose father had been executed for treason by Henry VIII), spent some of his time at Alnwick but mostly lived elsewhere. This was not unusual - at no time during the 16th century was Alnwick used by the Percies as one of their normal residences.

The seventh earl died violently in 1572. He was executed at York for his part in a revolt against Queen Elizabeth. His successor, a brother, soon incurred the mistrust of Elizabeth and her ministers and was required to live in the south of England. His chief residence was Petworth in Sussex - a property acquired by the Percies in 1150 - and which was now to serve as their main residence for nearly two hundred years. In 1584 the earl was imprisoned in the Tower of London by the government, which doubted his loyalty. The following year he was found in his prison quarters, shot through the heart. It was maintained that he had committed suicide, but he may well have been murdered.

One of the most interesting members of the Percy line was Henry, the ninth earl, who succeeded to the title at the age of 21 in 1585. He participated in military ventures, such as the defeat of the Armada and was known as 'the Wizard Earl' on account of his fascination with chemistry and astronomy. In 1605, his kinsman, Sir Thomas Percy, an unsavoury character whom he had appointed constable of Alnwick Castle in 1594, was one of those who planned to blow King James I and parliament to kingdom come in the Gunpowder Plot. Sir Thomas was killed following the plot's discovery, while Northumberland found himself in the Tower of London under suspicion of having been party to the conspiracy. He remained in the Tower for seventeen years where he had his own servants, dined on his own food, built himself a bowling alley, and enjoyed the company of several individuals who shared his penchant for experimentation and scholarship, such as Sir Walter Raleigh, a friend of long-standing who had been confined to the Tower two years earlier.

The ninth earl died in 1632. It is likely that he never visited Alnwick, and although he is known to have taken an interest in his northern estates, the castle suffered neglect. In 1622 much of it was described as being 'very ruinous and in great decay.' When Charles I arrived here in May 1639 during the days of the tenth earl, the castle was too ruinous to receive him and so he lodged in Alnwick Abbey.

In 1670 Josceline Percy, the eleventh Earl of Northumberland, died, leaving an only daughter, a four-year-old named Elizabeth. She married the Duke of Somerset in 1682 and followed her father to the grave in 1722. Her son, Algernon, served as Lord Lieutenant of Northumberland, (his father repaired and refurbished part of Alnwick Castle to serve as his son's residence), and Algernon was thus the first member of the family for over a century to live at Alnwick.

He died in 1750, not long after succeeding to the dukedom of Somerset. He had, moreover, been created Earl of Northumberland, and upon his death the latter title passed to his son-in-law, Sir Hugh Smithson, a Yorkshire baronet who assumed the surname of Percy and proceeded to thoroughly overhaul the Northumberland estates, making them more profitable by for instance using up-to-date farming methods. He also employed the noted architect James Paine to make alterations to the castle and Robert Adam to design new interiors: Jill Allibone has suggested that Paine may have decorated the Dining Room and the Drawing Room, the latter of which was recast by Adam. Moreover, 'Capability' Brown was engaged to enhance the adjacent park and provide a terrace immediately to the north of the keep. In 1766, Hugh was created Duke of Northumberland, partly for his political activities such as serving as Lord Lieutenant of Ireland.

Algernon, the fourth duke, who held the title in the years 1847-1865, travelled extensively and had a great admiration for Italian art and decoration of the 15th and 16th centuries. In 1854, he initiated a major phase of alteration work at Alnwick, a programme that was still in progress at the time of his death. Among those engaged in this task were Anthony Salvin (a leading northern architect), the celebrated Italian architect and archaeologist, Luigi Canina, Director of the Capitoline Museum in Rome, and Giovanni Montiroli.

Among other things, the work entailed adding the Prudhoe Tower to the north-west end of the keep, (a Salvin tower substantially higher than the others), and removing virtually all Adam's work in the keep's interior and replacing it with rooms betraying the fourth duke's love of Renaissance Italy. Only Adams' Breakfast Room was retained 'to show the style of decoration which had been adopted throughout the building', but was subsequently gutted in 1887. Moreover, a school of woodcarving was created at Alnwick, where pupils were taught by the brilliant young Florentine carver, Anton Bulletti, whereas Carrara marble fireplaces and other artifacts were produced in Rome and transported to Alnwick.

In 1940, during the retreat to Dunkirk, George Henry Percy, ninth Duke of Northumberland, was killed at Pecq in Flanders while serving with the Grenadier Guards. He was only 27 and had held the title for a decade.

The present head of the family is Ralph George Algernon Percy. Born in 1956, he became the twelfth Duke of Northumberland in 1995. Of the castle, he comments, 'it is . . . a wonderful family home and I have always loved it . . . . As children, my brothers, sisters and I treated it as a huge playroom, not appreciating the priceless paintings and furniture that were often targets for water pistols and arrows!'

Description

Alnwick Castle occupies an area of 7 acres (c. 2.8 hectares) and is entered from the west via an impressive barbican and gatehouse dating from about c.1310-20: they are sometimes erroneously said to date from about 1440. The barbican, described by the late Sir Nikolaus Pevsner as 'the best in the country', projects 56ft (17m) from the gatehouse and above its entrance arch is the Percy lion carved in stone, while the battlements are adorned with several carved figures, as are those of the more lofty gatehouse: the figures date from the 18th century but no doubt replaced original ones. At its outer end, the barbican is vaulted but beyond this it is open to the sky, with high walls to the left and right, and formerly contained a drawbridge over a dry moat that was filled up in the 16th century. Beyond the drawbridge, further protection was afforded the gatehouse by a portcullis and great double doors. Either side of the passage through the gatehouse are guardrooms in polygonal flanking towers.

From the gatehouse, one enters the outer bailey. Directly ahead lies the heart of the castle, the majestic keep, reached by a pathway that skirts southward, passes through a gateway into the inner bailey, and turns north towards imposing semi-octagonal towers that flank the keep's entrance. Directly in front of the entrance is a wooden bridge, occupying the site of a former drawbridge.

The semi-octagonal towers date from the mid 14th century and were erected by the second Lord Percy. Their battlements are adorned with several carved figures. Below the battlements, and beneath a string-course on each tower, is a row of shields bearing the armorial devices of families connected with the second Lord Percy.

On entering the gate passage, the groove of a portcullis is visible. Moreover, a door on the right side of the passage opens to a dungeon, lit only by arrow slits. Prisoners were

7. The barbican and gatehouse

incarcerated here via a trapdoor. Also noteworthy, is a Norman arch at the inner end of the passage and partly ornamented with two orders of chevron.

Beyond lies the inner courtyard, which is enclosed by the keep and contains a well dating from the early 14th century complete with the original wooden pole and wheels for winding up the buckets.

A doorway on the north side of the courtyard opens to an entrance hall - known as the Lower Guard Chamber - a simple room of modest proportions. It has a plain stucco ceiling and walls festooned with a display of arms and armour, mostly the equipment of the Percy Tenantry Volunteers, a unit formed in Napoleonic times.

From here, one progresses to the foot of the Grand Staircase - work on which commenced in 1861 - an imposing spectacle, a foretaste of what is to come. Part of the magnificence is provided by panelled coloured marbles on either side and groin-vaulted ceilings. The steps themselves are of freestone, with each step comprising a single piece of stone 12ft long (3.66m) quarried at Rothbury several miles from Alnwick. The overall effect is one of great spaciousness and light, contrasting markedly with that of the entrance hall.

The stairs lead up to the Upper Guard Chamber. This serves as a vestibule to the state rooms and is magnificent in its own right, 30ft (9.14m) square and 26ft (7.92m) high. It has a marble mosaic floor made in Rome, while the walls and coffered stucco ceiling are mostly white with gold highlights. The walls are adorned with a number of paintings, including a fine harbour scene by Claude Lorrain and works by Canaletto. Among the portraits, is one of the tenth Earl of Northumberland by Van Dyck, portraying him in his capacity as Lord High Admiral. The earl supported parliament during the Civil War, but opposed the execution of Charles I and played a part in bringing about the restoration of the monarchy in 1660. Another wall contains niches with marble statues by Giuseppe Nucci representing Justice and Britannia. Moreover, a frieze runs around the room just below the level of the ceiling and incorporates four paintings by Francis Golzenberg depicting scenes from the martial *Ballad of Chevy Chase*, a poem celebrating the Battle of Otterburn.

From the Upper Guard Chamber, one enters the Ante-Library (which contains a number of important works of art, including paintings by Titian) en route to the Library, occupying an entire floor of the Prudhoe Tower. The Library contains thousands of volumes in bookshelves of light oak inlaid with sycamore, and as the room is 23ft (7m) high, the topmost books are reached via stairs and a gallery. Among objects on display are marble busts of Francis Bacon, William Shakespeare and Sir Isaac Newton, located above the room's three fireplaces.

8. The Upper Guard Chamber (the Collection of the Duke of Northumberland)

To the east of the Ante-Library is the Saloon (sometimes referred to as the Music Room), the first of a sequence of interconnecting state rooms. Here, the dominant colours are red and gold. In common with the Upper Guard Chamber, the Saloon contains work by Canaletto, including a painting of Alnwick Castle and another of the Percies' former London residence, Northumberland House. Also noteworthy, are a portrait of Charles I's wife Henrietta Maria by Van Dyck and a splendid triple portrait by Van Dyck's contemporary William Dobson, the finest English portait painter of his generation and a man who deserves to be better known. The painting reflects his characteristic robust realism. Dobson himself is one of the gentlemen portrayed. The room also contains fine furniture, such as two pairs of 19th century Boulle cabinets made in Paris. The marble fireplace was carved in Rome by Giovanni Taccalozzi and has figures of Dacian slaves by Nucci. The ceiling, the most eye-catching part of the decor, was inspired by decorations in St Peter's, Rome. It consists of a number of sunken and richly decorated panels, some of which are star-shaped.

The Red Drawing Room, whose walls are covered with red damask ornamented with a gold pattern, is the next state room entered, and is slightly larger - it measures 46 by 34ft (14 by 10.36m) - and is also more sumptuous. Indeed, it is the most sumptuous room in the castle. It likewise has a marble fireplace by Taccalozzi, with caryatids by Nucci, and this is flanked by a pair of ebony cabinets mounted with 'pietra dura' panels made in 1683 by Domenico Cucci for Louis XIV of France, the founder of Versailles. They were purchased by the third Duke of Northumberland in 1822. Paintings include a portrait of a Venetian nobleman by Tintoretto, a self-portrait by Andrea del Sarto, and *The Temple of Jupiter Panhellenios, Aegina* by Turner. Once again, there is an elaborate coffered ceiling, consisting of polygonal panels.

The Red Drawing Room is located in the north-east corner of the keep. Immediately to the south, and occupying the site of the medieval Great Hall, lies the Dining Room. Here, too, red is the predominant colour. The room measures 60 by 24ft (18.3 by 7.3m) and is thus not only longer than the former hall but also longer than any of the other state rooms. It has a superb marble fireplace that was exhibited in Italy by Taccalozzi before being sent to Alnwick, and which again is supported by two figures, in this case, one by Nucci, the other by Strazza. Above the fireplace hang portraits of the first duke and duchess. The room, which has a splendid carved frieze and a coffered ceiling of ungilded pinewood with cedar panels for the background, contains a number of other portraits and items such as silverware. Most notable, however, are two great 18th century Meissen dinner services.

Next comes the Breakfast Room. a much less imposing room whose wall covering is heavily embossed paper that imitates leather. On either side of the fireplace are paintings attributed to the late 17th century artist, Peter Hartover. One depicts Alnwick Castle, whereas the other is of Warkworth, the Percies other great castle in Northumberland.

The tour of the castle's interior concludes with a stroll along the Picture Gallery. Corbelled out over the inner courtyard and built as a service corridor by Salvin, this leads back to the Upper Guard Chamber and the Grand Staircase.

A circuit of Alnwick's outer defences, which include several towers, reveals that the fabric dates from different periods. Sections of the masonry date from the 12th, 14th and 15th centuries, but much too is post-medieval, having been reconstructed in more recent times.

One of the towers is known as the Constable's Tower. It stands east of the keep and looks northward towards the River Aln, running through the vale below. Built in the early 14th century by the first of the Percy line to own Alnwick, it served as the residence of the castle's constable. It now houses the Percy Tenantry Volunteers Exhibition, which includes some of the unit's equipment and accoutrements as well as models depicting members of the force, raised in 1798 by the second Duke of Northumberland.

From here a section of curtain wall that contains 12th century masonry runs westward to the Postern Tower, (again built by the first Lord Percy of Alnwick), situated closer to the keep and formerly connected to it by a length of no longer extant curtain wall running south-west. The tower contains a small gateway or sally-port: in medieval times this was the only entrance or exit for the castle other than that through the barbican and gatehouse. The northern face of the keep was not enclosed by the curtain wall. The Postern Tower was thus erected to help defend the keep, not only by enabling flanking fire to be directed at an enemy, but by allowing defenders to sally out via the postern to attack the flank of anyone assaulting the keep. The tower now serves as a museum containing displays of archaeological artifacts.

9. The keep from the inner bailey, looking west

To the west, and formerly connected to the north-west end of the keep by the curtain wall, stands the Falconer Tower which likewise afforded protection to the northern face of the keep: the present structure is however a rebuild by Salvin.

Between the towers, and thus running along the north side of the keep, is a broad terrace that provides lovely views of the River Aln and parkland beyond. It dates from the mid 18th century but was reconstructed in 1864-65. Upon it stand several pieces of artillery from the 17th and 19th centuries.

In the north-west corner of the castle's perimeter stands the early 14th century Abbot's Tower, said to owe its name to the fact that the Abbot of Alnwick Abbey was allowed to reside in it during times of danger. Today, the building houses the regimental museum of the Royal Northumberland Fusiliers and is open to visitors to the castle.

One of the towers along the castle perimeter is located opposite the entrance to the keep. The tower gives access to gardens lying to the south-east of the castle. In the days of the fourth duke, an Italianate garden was developed here to a design by the eminent Victorian gardener, William Andrews Nesfield. In the 1950s, the garden site became a forestry nursery, but a programme of redevelopment is currently underway, the brainchild of Jane, the present Duchess of Northumberland. The innovative scheme, to which several eminent garden designers have contributed, will, it is claimed, provide visitors with an experience in 'garden architecture' unparalleled elsewhere in the country.

AYDON CASTLE

Aydon Castle, one of the finest examples in England of a 13th century manor house cum castle, is enchanting and occupies an impressive position a short distance to the north of Corbridge.

It was built in the late 13th and early 14th centuries by Robert de Reymes, a wealthy Suffolk merchant who acquired Aydon and other property in the area in 1296. In that year he is mentioned as being resident at nearby Shortflatt, and at about this time he set to work building himself a residence at Aydon, already the site of a manor house but one that was likely in a rather dilapidated state.

In 1296 prolonged conflict with Scotland commenced and de Reymes participated in campaigns north of the border in 1297 and 1298 and was to do so again in the years 1309-14. Indeed, in the latter year he was captured, presumably at Bannockburn. The following year the custodian of Aydon, Hugh de Gales, immediately surrendered it to a Scottish army that arrived on the scene and the Scots occupied Aydon for a while before burning it and destroying or stealing goods. In view of the destruction wrought, Reymes subsequently turned to Edward II for assistance and among other things in September 1317 was granted an annuity for life of £10.

But his troubles were not over. That December, Reymes' former custodian, de Gales and a party of rebels, (associates of one of Reymes' neighbours, the freebooter Sir Gilbert de Middleton), seized Aydon and ravaged the area for a month during which time they did damage to Reymes' furniture and household goods to the value of £200.

In 1324 Robert de Reymes died. Since acquiring Aydon, expenditure on the castle and the financial losses inflicted as a result of the Scottish wars and the consequent lawlessness had greatly affected his fortunes, rendering him impoverished.

He was succeeded by Robert de Reymes II, who also served against the Scots and was a knight of the shire for the parliament of 1346. In that year a formidable Scottish army under David II, who was 'right jolly, and desirous to see fighting' according to Andrew Wyntoun, invaded the North. It sacked Lanercost Priory in Cumbria and then headed east into Northumberland and plundered Hexham, whereupon the 'fortalice of Aydon hall' was surrendered to David on condition that none of the garrison would be harmed. The following year Robert de Reymes served as the Sheriff of Northumberland. He died in October 1349, a victim of the Black Death.

He did so indebted to the Crown and possession of Aydon and the rest of the de Reymes' estates was only restored to the family by the Crown in 1377, following a prolonged legal battle. The head of the line at this date was called Nicholas - he was the third son of Robert de Reymes II - and had been imprisoned in Corfe Castle, Dorset, for providing shelter and assistance to the murderers of an unpopular governmental official in the region, Sir John de Coupland, who was cut down in December 1363.

After gaining possession of his inheritance, Nicholas played a role in both local and national politics. As Philip Dixon comments: 'He had clearly become established as an important man in the area, but his early wildness remained, for he frequently figures as a defendant, being sued for recoveries of debts by both individuals and institutions.' In 1385, when he made his way to London to attend parliament, he was arrested, imprisoned, and compelled to agree to pay a debt to the Exchequer and a fine.

28

10. Aydon Castle: the photograph was taken in the outer courtyard. The entrance to the inner courtyard is on the left, the kitchen wing is in the centre, and the adjoining hall block on the right

Nicholas de Reymes died in 1394. Future heads of the family were less prominent figures who let Aydon to tenants (Nicholas' son and successor Robert Reymes IV, who died in 1416, lived at Flotterton near Rothbury) and Aydon suffered from neglect. Indeed, in 1450 it was described as 'a certain castle in ruinous state.'

In 1541 Robert Reymes IX, who lived at Shortflatt, which had been the family's seat for several generations, granted Aydon to Sir Reynold Carnaby of Hexham, the younger son of a local gentry family whose seat was Halton Castle, in exchange for land near Ponteland. Upon his death in 1543, Carnaby left Aydon to his younger brother, Cuthbert, who came to live at Aydon and was no doubt responsible for a major programme of alteration and restoration of the fabric. By 1579 Cuthbert had moved to Halton, which he had inherited, but one of his sons lived at Aydon until 1600 when he in turn inherited Halton Castle.

Aydon remained in the hands of the Carnaby family until 1654 when it was sold for £653 as a result of financial hardship caused by the Civil War. The purchaser was from the former enemy camp, a Parliamentarian, Captain William Collinson.

In 1702 Collinson's son, Henry, (the last owner-occupier of Aydon) sold the property to a lawyer named William Douglas who had previously bought the Carnaby estates and so now owned all their former property. Following its purchase, Aydon became a farmhouse, with part of the buildings evidently being used for storage.

In 1966 the Blacketts of Matfen, (a gentry family into whose hands Aydon had passed by marriage to Douglas' granddaughter in 1751), entrusted Aydon to the Ministry of Works and as a result major repair work was undertaken for the first time since the mid 16th century. Since then, the majority of post-medieval fittings etc have been removed.

Description

Aydon Castle stands in an isolated position on the fringes of a wood. Strong natural protection was provided immediately to the north, east and south, where the ground falls away steeply into a deep ravine through which flows the Cor Burn.

The castle is approached from the north-west. As first built by Robert de Reymes I, it was simply a manor house consisting of a hall block, adjoined at right angles on a north-south axis by a chamber block with a small wing containing latrines projecting eastward. The chamber block was evidently constructed first and is sometimes dated to around 1280, prior to de Reymes' days at Aydon. On this point however Philip Dixon, who attributes the chamber block to de Reymes, states: 'The pattern of ownership and occupancy of the manor . . . makes it very improbable that any of its lords spent time or money on the house at least since the death of Peter de Vaux in 1256.'

By about 1315 substantial additions had been made. In addition to furnishing the existing buildings with battlements - de Reymes obtained permission to fortify Aydon in 1305 - two wings had been added to the west end of the hall range, one extending westward, the other running north. Moreover, from the north-east end of the latter an embattled wall ran eastward to link up with one running north from the north-west end of the chamber block, thereby forming a small courtyard. An outer courtyard had also been created by building a curtain wall from the west end of the building running westward from the hall, around to the east end of the latrine wing. Subsequently it appears that a D-shaped tower was constructed in the northernmost angle of the curtain wall, apparently c.1350.

The first feature one notices upon approaching the castle is the remains of this tower, projecting somewhat from the curtain. A short distance beyond this is a simple arched gateway opening to the outer courtyard. On either side of the entrance and running along the inner face of the curtain wall were lodgings, though generally the outer courtyard, which measures about an acre (0.4 hectare) appears to have been devoid of buildings.

To the south-east of the entrance stands the core of the castle, entered via a simple archway at the west end of the inner courtyard's north wall. The south side of the inner courtyard is bounded by the hall range,

11. The outer courtyard, looking north-east towards the D-shaped tower

whose principal chamber is of course the Great Hall. This occupies much of the first floor and is reached via an external flight of stone steps parallel to the block, steps once sheltered by a lean-to covering.

The steps lead to a screens passage at the west end of the hall. The walls here date from the 16th century and have replaced screens framed in timber. The Great Hall itself is a commodious room open to its 16th century timber roof, (the original roof was probably more steeply pitched), and the lord's table stood at the east end, with light provided by a two-light window on either side of the hall: the splayed window recesses have chamfered stone seats. There is no fireplace. Warmth would have been provided by a fire on a hearth or a portable brazier, with the smoke escaping through a louvre in the roof. It is probable that the walls were plastered white and ornamented with painted scenes or friezes, at least towards the east end.

A doorway in the east wall opens to the adjoining chamber block, whose first floor is occupied by what is known as the great chamber. It has a small attic room above its southern end: the upper room dates from the 19th century but there was an earlier chamber at this level. The remainder of the great chamber was a lofty room open to the roof, which was steeper and higher than that of today. It is thought probable that the great chamber was subdivided by a timber parti-

12. The hall block from the inner courtyard

tion, with the smaller, less lofty southern portion, perhaps serving as an anteroom to the northern chamber which doubtless served as the solar of the de Reymes family.

The great chamber's most notable feature is a large stone fireplace. It is on the west side of the room but was initially located on the opposite wall and was moved to its present position during the 16th century, at which time it was set in the wall about 1ft (30cm) lower than had been the case opposite, thus accounting for its rather squat, heavy appearance.

The east wall has a doorway opening to the small latrine wing which contains a garderobe at its east end, as well as a wall cupboard and a basin. The fireplace in the west wall is a 16th century addition.

Stairs dating from the 19th century lead down from the great chamber to the ground floor, occupied by a rather intriguing room whose function evidently altered over the years. The room can also be entered from the ground floor of the hall block or directly from the inner courtyard, but initially access was solely via stairs from the chamber block's first floor. The room was thus the most secluded at Aydon, and on its east side is a fireplace with what is the most decorated chimneypiece in the castle: its hood is ornamented with face masks,

13. The south wall of the hall block, showing the chimney that served the fireplace of the lower hall

dogtooth and foliage. Moreover, a door in the east wall opens to the latrine block. It seems reasonable to conclude that the room was intended to serve as the most private of the de Reymes' chambers. If so, its function evidently soon changed following the provision of access from the inner courtyard via a doorway inserted in the north-west corner, for the room appears to have then served as a hall for the lord's personal servants. In the days of the Carnabys, it was the kitchen of their house.

From here, one enters the ground floor of the hall block, much of which was occupied by a hall of comparable size to the Great Hall on the floor above: the partition walls that subdivide the room probably date from the 16th century. The lower hall may have been used by servants or attendants of the de Reymes and was heated by a massive fireplace towards the west end.

Originally, Aydon's kitchen lay to the west of the screen's passage on the first floor of the hall block. But it was soon superseded by a larger kitchen at the north end of the first floor of the north-west range (whose ground floor contained storerooms). In the latter kitchen one can still see wall cupboards, a large sink and spout, and a large fireplace at the north end of the room.

An opening in the kitchen's north-east corner leads out on to the wall-walk of the inner courtyard: the parapet is embattled and the embrasures have holes for swinging shutters while some of the merlons are pierced by arrow-slits.

Upon returning to the inner courtyard itself, one will note a doorway in its east wall. This opens to an orchard, an enchanting part of the castle and one that provides fine views of the exterior of the chamber block and the latrine wing.

Another doorway, this time in the curtain wall that partly encloses the orchard, opens to the edge of the ravine of the Cor Burn. A short walk from here leads around to the south face of the hall range and one of the most interesting features of the castle; the outer projection of the massive fireplace located in the lower hall. It terminates below the eaves line of the range in a semicircular attached shaft from which the smoke escaped through lancet openings.

Aydon Castle is in the care of English Heritage.

BAMBURGH CASTLE

Bamburgh Castle is the most spectacularly sited castle in Northumberland. It stands majestically on a basalt outcrop overlooking the North Sea and is one of the largest castles in Northumberland, popular with tourists, film-makers and students of history alike.

The earliest fabric of the castle dates from the 12th century, but the site has a history stretching back to the late Iron Age when a hillfort probably existed here. During the subsequent Saxon period, Bamburgh was the seat of a fort and royal palace. In the late 11th century, a castle is known to have occupied the summit and featured in a revolt against William II led by Robert de Mowbray, the Earl of Northumberland.

William reacted energetically to the conspiracy. He marched north at the head of an army drawn from all parts of his kingdom and besieged Mowbray's castles in Northumberland, the strongest of which was Bamburgh. William himself was not able to prosecute the siege to a conclusion for he had to leave to deal with a Welsh threat, but left troops to continue the task.

During his absence, Mowbray left the castle under the cover of darkness at the head of a party of knights and sailed southward in a vain attempt to enter Newcastle. Having been

14. Bamburgh Castle, viewed from the south-east

thwarted by his opponents who promptly responded to his flight, he fled to Tynemouth where he was duly captured by William's troops and escorted back up the coast to Bamburgh which was still holding out under Mowbray's doughty wife, Matilda, and his nephew Morel, Sheriff of Northumberland. They were forced to yield when it was threatened that Earl Robert would be blinded unless a surrender was immediately forthcoming.

William II's successor, Henry I, subsequently granted Bamburgh Castle to Eustace FitzJohn, lord of Alnwick. Eustace's tenure of the castle came to an end in the late 1130s during the reign of Stephen who doubted his loyalty and took Bamburgh into royal hands. It subsequently passed into the control of Henry, the son of David I of Scotland, who held the earldom of Northumberland for much of the mid 12th century, but returned to the English Crown in 1157 during the reign of Henry II.

Owing to its exposed position, Bamburgh suffered from the elements. In the mid 1230s for instance, its commander, Hugh de Bolbec, informed Henry III (for whom Bamburgh was subsequently held during the civil war known as the Barons' War), that damage had been wrought to the fabric by 'violent gales that have again been prevalent in these parts.'

In November 1307 Edward II, who had just ascended the throne, granted custody of the castle to Isabella de Vescy, widow of John de Vescy of Alnwick and subsequently a member of the household of Edward's queen. Edward's reign witnessed major discord between the monarch and the bulk of the baronage and in parliament in August 1311, Isabella was one of those censured by opponents of the unpopular king, most likely primarily because she controlled Bamburgh Castle, a fortress of strategic importance. Edward's Gascon favourite, Piers Gaveston, an ambitious and highly unpopular individual was sheltering in the castle at the time, having been expressly left at Bamburgh by the king while en route south to face his critics in parliament where Gaveston was accused, among other things, of leading Edward into evil ways. Gaveston was therefore sentenced to banishment. It was also decreed that custody of Bamburgh Castle should be taken away from Isabella. Hence, on 18 December 1311, Edward appointed Henry de Percy custodian of Bamburgh. Isabella defiantly refused to hand over the stronghold to him. Finally, on 28 May 1312, she was commanded by the king to give up the fortress.

Despite its strategic position, Bamburgh Castle was not always well maintained. On Saturday 8 September 1330, following an inspection of the fabric, it was reported that the castle's condition was such that if repairs were not speedily undertaken the whole place would become 'a heap of ruins.' Partial repair work evidently ensued and in 1333 the castle withstood a siege during a period of Anglo-Scottish conflict. An English army under Edward III was besieging the town of Berwick upon Tweed further up the coast. In an attempt to make the English lift the siege, a large Scottish army under the command of Archibald Douglas invaded the North East and moved against Bamburgh Castle, where Edward's young wife Philippa of Hainault - described as 'a paragon among English queens' by the late May McKisack - was then resident. Doubtless the resolve of the defenders was strengthened by her presence. What is certain is that the Scots were repelled.

On occasion, a number of important prisoners were held at Bamburgh. The most notable was David II of Scotland, captured at the Battle of Neville's Cross in 1346 while engaged on an invasion of England. He spent a few months at Bamburgh (barber surgeons were brought to the castle from York to remove an arrow that had struck the king at Neville's Cross) and remained here until early 1347 when he was conducted to the Tower of London where he was to stay until 1357.

The last major phase of building work in the medieval period commenced in the mid 1380s under Sir John Neville, during the reign of Richard II. Among other things, this included the construction of a new hall, 66ft (20.1m) long and 34 ft (10.36m) wide.

In the 15th century, Bamburgh Castle featured prominently in the Wars of the Roses. Following a crushing defeat in Yorkshire in March 1461, the Lancastrian Henry VI and his queen, Margaret, fled to Scotland through Northumberland, where Bamburgh numbered among castles garrisoned on their behalf. But later in the year, Yorkists under the Earl of Warwick gained the submission of the Lancastrian strongholds in the county for Henry's rival, Edward IV.

Bamburgh was entrusted to the keeping of Sir William Tunstall. His brother, Sir Richard, was however a Lancastrian and in the autumn of 1462 he headed a successful plot that enabled him to gain control of the castle. In Wales on 1 November, a member of the Paston family wrote as follows: 'Syr Wylliam Tunstale is tak with the garyson of Bamborowhg and is lyke to be hedyd, by the menys of Sir Rychard Tunstale, is owne brodyr.'

Meanwhile, Margaret had enlisted French support and, on 25 October 1462, landed near Bamburgh at the head of troops. The castle opened its gates to her, as did the castles of Alnwick and Dunstanburgh shortly thereafter. Edward IV assembled a strong force to deal with the situation and Margaret thus sailed from Bamburgh to Scotland. Not long after her departure, Warwick was entrusted with the task of subduing the Lancastrian castles in Northumberland. On Christmas Eve, Bamburgh's garrison surrendered conditionally, (as did that of Dunstanburgh further down the coast). It is often said that shortage of supplies had reduced the garrisons to eating their horses. That this was so, is first mentioned in John Stow's *Annales*. But Dorothy Charlesworth has sensibly questioned whether this was really the case, and suggests that Stow (whose account dates from the 16th century) may have been embroidering what really occurred.

Following the surrender, one of the principal defenders, Sir Ralph Percy (who was constable of Dunstanburgh, but is said to have been in Bamburgh), was escorted to Durham. There, he swore allegiance to Edward and was placed in command of both Dunstanburgh and Bamburgh, one of the conditions of the terms of surrender. He soon proved false. In March 1463 he allowed a Franco-Scottish force to occupy the castles and by the close of the year, if not before, Henry VI was based at Bamburgh although Margaret and their son, the young Prince of Wales, had sailed to France. Henry was soon joined by a die-hard Lancastrian, the Duke of Somerset - who had been present in Bamburgh during the siege of late 1462 - and other staunch supporters. Early 1464, therefore, found Bamburgh serving as a base from which the Lancastrians conducted various military undertakings in Northumberland, in one of which Percy was killed. That May, however, Somerset was captured in battle near Hexham and put to death, whereupon Henry VI fled from the county and was eventually captured in Lancashire.

In the meantime, the Lancastrian castles in Northumberland had fallen to the enemy. Bamburgh's garrison proved the most determined. The castle was subjected to a battering by royal ordnance (the first time in the Wars of the Roses that artillery was used in the region) and stormed. Sir Ralph Grey, Bamburgh's commander, who had been seriously wounded during the siege, was later tried and executed at Doncaster.

Bamburgh Castle subsequently suffered from neglect. In 1538 it was described by its constable, John Horseley, as 'sore in ruine and in suche decaye that in all the sayd chastell there is neyther lodgyng for man or horse, doore, wyndowe or howse that is drye.' Its sorry state continued and the castle was in a ruinous condition when Lord Crewe, the Bishop of Durham, purchased Bamburgh in 1704 from the impoverished Forster family, (to whom he was related by marriage) which had held Bamburgh since the early years of the 17th century.

Crewe died in 1721, having bequeathed the castle for charitable purposes. His trustees subsequently began a lengthy programme of restoration that commenced in the 1750s and continued into the early years of the 19th century. The keep was made habitable once more.

15. The castle as seen from the village of Bamburgh

Other work included the rebuilding of apartments located along the south side of the inner ward, extensive rebuilding of the curtain walls, and the construction of a windmill at the west end of the castle.

In around 1813 a visitor observed that a large room had been 'fitted up for educating the boys of the neighbourhood' and that a suite of rooms was allotted to two mistresses and 'twenty poor girls, who, from their ninth year, are lodged, clothed, and educated, till they be fit for service.' Among other things, the castle also possessed an infirmary serving the needs of the local populace.

In 1894 Bamburgh Castle was purchased by the first Lord Armstrong of Cragside, a leading northern industrialist who wished to convert the castle into a convalescent home to honour the memory of his wife who had died the previous year. Although this scheme did not come to fruition, Armstrong had much of the castle remodelled to his taste, employing the services of C.J. Ferguson of Carlisle. Lord Armstrong died in 1900 and was succeeded by a great-nephew, William Henry Watson-Armstrong, who was subsequently created first Lord Armstrong of Bamburgh and Cragside and spent some of his time at the castle. On 1 October 1987 the third Lord Armstrong of Bamburgh and Cragside, (who moved to Bamburgh from Cragside in 1977), died, leaving a widow and an adopted son and an adopted daughter. The title thus became extinct. The Trustees of the last Lord Armstrong now own Bamburgh Castle.

Description

Bamburgh Castle occupies a site of 8 acres (3.2 hectares) and consists of a sturdy keep and three baileys or wards. It is entered from the south-east through a gatehouse that is partly of Norman date. Rounded angle towers with arrow loops flank the entrance, a tunnel-vaulted archway. Progressing through this, a sunken road flanked by high walls briefly heads northward before curving westward towards an inner gateway. The latter has a 12th century vault but is largely of 19th century date. From here, and again continuing in a westerly direction, the road heads up sloping ground until the wall to one's left ceases and the keep is visible, built near the curtain wall on the southern, landward side of the castle. An open space, partly enclosed by buildings to the east of the keep, is the inner ward, while to the west of the keep is the east ward, beyond which lies the west ward. The ruins of a 12th century chapel lie towards the east end of the inner ward: it had a nave, square chancel and apse. Internally, the apse had shafts between the windows which were likewise shafted.

16. The entrance

A tour of the interior of the castle begins near the chapel, with rooms ranged along the south side of the inner ward. The first room entered is the lofty museum; formerly a kitchen with three fireplaces. It was largely restored in the mid 18th century by Dr Sharp, one of the Crewe trustees, and served as the main classroom of the Charity school mentioned above. Among items on display are oil paintings and watercolours by Thomas Miles Richardson, and his son, T.M. Richardson junior, as well as a portrait of Cromwell by Robert Walker.

From here, one progresses westward to a room with a pointed tunnel-vault: the museum has a timber ceiling. Among objects on view are Italian spode, coalport china, and an 18th century oak tridarn cupboard. A doorway at the far end of the room opens to a smaller chamber, again with a pointed tunnel-vault. Sevres porcelain, late 18th century biscuit porcelain, and Crown Derby ware are some of the items displayed.

A door in the north side of this room, opens to another chamber with a pointed tunnel-vault and in common with the preceding rooms this room is likewise not sumptuous. Here, among other things, is an Anglo-Flemish oak cupboard dating from the late 17th century and further coalport.

On the west side of the room is a doorway through which one enters the King's Hall, the most imposing room at Bamburgh. One does so at the 'low' end of the hall, and the doorway just mentioned dates from medieval times and is the northernmost of three service doors located at this end of the hall: the others are blocked.

The King's Hall almost entirely dates from the late 19th century and is located on the site of a great hall built in 1384-90. It has a musicians' gallery at the low end and a false hammerbeam roof carved from teak at Cragside by a local craftsman, Thomas Worsnop, while panelling around the lower stages of the walls is again of teak, with decorative panels of pollard oak. Above the panelling, the walls are of exposed sandstone and are adorned with displays of weaponry and a number of portraits such as one of Dr Sharp by Benjamin West, another of Charles II as a boy, (a studio copy of a painting by Van Dyck at Windsor), and one of the first Lord Armstrong by Hermann Schmiechen. Among items displayed in the King's Hall are suits of armour and firearms.

Off the far end of the King's Hall, and separated from it by a large archway, is the Cross Hall which is partly adorned by superb Flemish tapestries portraying the life of Emperor Justinian. Over the fireplace is a good early 17th century painting by either T. Rombouts or Honthorst depicting men playing cards.

From the north-west end of the Cross Hall one heads through a porch - whose stone vaulting is carved to imitate knotted rope - and up some steps to what is known as the Faire Chamber, which contains a Dresden dessert service and various other items, including Louis XV and Louis XVI furniture. Progressing westward from here is a corridor that leads to the keep, only part of which is open to visitors.

Records show that expenditure on the keep occurred in 1164, but the amounts in question are not large and the keep was doubtless already almost finished by this date, perhaps having been started in the 1150s. It measures 69 by 61½ft (21.1 by 18.9m) and is 78ft (23.7m) high. Externally, it has a high moulded plinth, walls strengthened by buttresses, and a square turret at each corner. The principal entrance is at ground floor level near the north end of the east face and is not wholly original: its two orders of colonnettes have been renewed. Access to keeps was not normally achieved at this level and testifies to the sense of security enjoyed by the garrison of Bamburgh on their well-nigh impregnable rock. Internally, much of the keep was changed during the 18th century.

The corridor mentioned above, from the Faire Chamber, terminates in steps that ascend to the Armoury, on the south side of the keep's first floor. The Armoury may originally have been two rooms, for the west part has a groin-vault whereas the east end is tunnel-vaulted. Here, too, one finds a slight apse, giving rise to the suggestion that this part of the Armoury once served as a chapel. The Armoury houses a selection of armour and firearms, such as late 18th century English flintlock muskets.

On its north side, a door opens to a large room with views of the sea. This is the Court Room, which measures about 32 by 23ft (9.75 by 7m), and may originally have served as a guardroom. Among paintings that hang here is one of Dorothy Forster by Sir Peter Lely; another of Lord Crewe by Jonathan Richardson; and a superb one of Lady Armstrong (wife of the third Lord Armstrong of Cragside and Bamburgh) by the late Pietro Annigoni, a celebrated Italian portrait painter whose sitters included President Kennedy and Queen Elizabeth II. Lady Armstrong died in March 1999.

A doorway in the south-east corner of this room, opens to a flight of straight stairs in the keep's east wall that descend to the ground floor and end near the medieval entrance: the vaulting of the stairway is original, whereas the steps have been renewed.

Like the first floor, only part of the keep's ground floor, whose walls are 9-12ft thick (2.74 - 3.66m) is open to the public and this consists of a large room whose vaulting is partly supported by large rectangular piers without capitals. Towards the south end of the room is a well, with a modern head. The well dates from Saxon times and was thus incorporated in the keep when the latter was erected centuries later. Bored to a depth of 140ft (42.7m) through sandstone and basalt, it was mentioned as being 'of a marvellus grett dypnes' in 1538 by Richard Bellasis.

One exits this room at its south end and, after passing through service rooms such as kitchens, a tour of the interior concludes with the 'dungeon', which houses a display of what conditions were like for people unfortunate enough to be incarcerated and ill-treated in such a place.

Finally, in the west ward, is a museum with objects associated with the first Lord Armstrong, such as hydraulic machinery, and exhibits devoted to aviation and shipping.

17. The Norman keep

BELSAY CASTLE AND HALL

B elsay has much to offer the visitor. Here, only a few miles north-west of Newcastle, one can explore a fascinating medieval tower-house castle, see an early 19th century Grecian mansion, and stroll through an exotic garden located within a quarry from which stone for the hall was won.

Belsay is chiefly associated with the Middleton family, which is known to have been in possession of the manor since at least 1270 when it was held by Sir Richard de Middleton, the Lord Chancellor of Henry III in the years 1269-72, and thus a figure of national importance.

In 1278, during the days of Sir Richard's successor, the Middletons' residence at Belsay - which no longer exists - was deemed suitable to accommodate Edward I. Subsequently, in 1318 during the troubled reign of Edward II, Belsay was forfeited through treason, but at some point between 1371 and 1396 the Middletons regained possession of the estate, and it is thought by some that Belsay Castle was erected at this time, though others favour an earlier date of around 1340. What is certain is that the castle was in existence by 1460 for the heraldic details of wall paintings are associated with Sir John de Middleton VI, active in the years 1439-60.

In 1614, Thomas Middleton built a two-storey range against the west side of the tower-house: there is reason to believe that the range replaced a medieval structure occupying the same site and likewise adjoining the tower-house. Thomas served as Sheriff of Northumberland in 1618 and 1634 and supported parliament during the Civil War era, during which time he acted as a commissioner for sequestering the estates of Royalists and as a commissioner for taxes.

He was succeeded by a nephew, who was created a baronet in 1662 and died in 1690. His son and successor, Sir John, married the granddaughter of one of Cromwell's generals, Lambert. Sir John died in 1717, having provided additional accommodation by erecting a large block against the west end of the early 17th century range. He probably did so in 1711.

Another member of the family, Sir William Middleton, the third baronet, served as a member of parliament from 1724 until his death in 1757 and under the Duke of Cumberland against the Jacobites in 1746. He also enhanced the setting of Belsay Castle by planting substantial belts of woodland, including Bantam Wood to the west, while his wife planted snowdrops in the woods.

Sir William Middleton, fifth baronet, who succeeded to the title in 1768, had been severely wounded nine years earlier at the Battle of Minden while serving in the Royal Horse Guards during the Seven Years War. He made a number of changes and additions to the estate. For one thing, he diverted a road that ran on an east-west axis just to the south of the castle, created a circuitous drive from the north, and erected a folly known as Bantam Castle.

Upon his death in 1795 he was succeeded by a 16-year-old son named Charles Miles Lambert Middleton, his third son, the elder sons having died in childhood. Sir Charles was obliged to change his surname to Monck in order to inherit an estate in Lincolnshire that had belonged to his maternal grandfather.

In the years 1804-6, Sir Charles spent a prolonged honeymoon abroad, partly in Germany - where he saw and sketched a number of neo-Classical buildings such as the Brandenburg Gate - and in Greece where he was greatly influenced by the architecture of ancient Greece and met a member of the Cambridge Hellenists, Sir William Gell.

18. Belsay Hall

Following his return to England, and enthused by what he had seen, Sir Charles decided to build a Grecian mansion at Belsay to a design of his own (over 200 drawings for the project exist in his own hand) although he may have been influenced to some extent by Gell. It is sometimes said that John Dobson, a young man at this date, contributed to the plans but this is not certain. Construction work began on 25 August 1807, when digging the foundations commenced, and continued for several years. On Christmas Day, 1817, work was sufficiently advanced for the Middletons to move from Belsay Castle into the hall.

Furthermore, Sir Charles demolished the village of Belsay, which dated from medieval times (the villagers' former presence is attested by ridge and furrow in the vicinity of both the hall and castle) and between 1831 and 1860 rebuilt it out of sight further to the east. Among other things, he also provided a lake to the south of the hall, beyond which, on a hillside, he planted trees such as Scots pines and exotic conifers; to the west of the house he transformed the quarry from which the building stone for his new residence had been dug, into a garden; and removed formal walled gardens that existed south of the castle.

In the late 19th and early 20th century Sir Charles Monck's grandson, the seventh baronet, Sir Arthur Middleton (who succeeded to the title in 1867 and resumed the name of Middleton in preference to Monck in 1876), partly extended and altered the garden created by his grandfather and introduced a number of new species of plants that had been introduced to Britain such as rhododendrons.

Although the park and estate are still the property of the Middleton family, they ceased residing at Belsay in 1962.

Description

Visitors approach Belsay up a drive from the east, which terminates just to the north of the hall. After progressing through a stable block, one arrives at the entrance front on the east side of the house.

Belsay Hall is a highly unusual, severe, but nonetheless impressive building in the Doric style. It is built of beautifully dressed honey-coloured sandstone flecked with iron ore. One hundred ft (30m) square, it is six bays long, seven deep, and like a Greek temple, stands on a podium of three steps. With the exception of the four-storeyed north front, (the service side of the hall which rises no higher than the rest of the house), there are two main storeys plus a further floor at attic level whose windows all face a central light-well and are thus not visible from the exterior.

In the centre of the east face is a recessed entrance dominated by two great fluted Doric columns. This leads into an entrance hall. Here, a doorway on the north side gives access to an east-west passage associated with the service rooms, while another doorway opens to a drawing room on the south side of the entrance hall. A third doorway leads straight from the entrance hall to an oblong two-storey central hall occupying the heart of the house below the light-well.

The central hall is surrounded by well-executed fluted colonnades consisting of Ionic columns at ground floor level, and Roman Doric columns above, between which are fine brass railings with acanthus scrolls. Stairs behind the colonnade on the north side of the room lead up to the first floor.

The principal rooms lie on the south side of the house. One of these has already been mentioned: the Drawing Room, entered from the entrance hall and occupying the south-east angle of the ground floor. In common with the other rooms at Belsay, it is now devoid of furniture. It originally served as the Dining Room.

The largest room, the Library, lies immediately to the west of the Drawing Room and can be entered from it or from the far end of the central hall. The Library occupies the four central bays of the south front and has a fireplace of yellow scagliola and marble, while the ceiling, like those of the other main rooms, is coffered and ornamented with friezes. The Library served as the main living room.

Beyond the Library, and in the south-west angle of the house, is a room that was initially planned to be the Drawing Room. Instead, the room remained an empty shell until 1909 when it was made into the Dining Room, at which time, among other things, a wooden chimneypiece with fluted Doric columns was installed. Immediately to the north is an ante-room created in 1909: as originally planned, this space would have been part of the Drawing Room. Owing to dry rot, the anteroom's floor was removed in 1980 and not replaced. So, too, was the floor of the next room to the north, (the housekeeper's room from the late 1880s), and both rooms are now shells.

Beyond these rooms lie the scullery and the kitchen. The latter, in the north-west angle of the house, was once the housekeeper's room. It became a kitchen in 1888 when Sir Arthur Middleton fitted it up as such: previously, the kitchen had been located in a two-storey wing projecting from the north side of the house. Located to the east of the kitchen, and thus along the north side of the hall, are rooms such as the former servants' hall, butler's pantry and estate office. From the east-west passage mentioned above, stairs lead down to the basement, which is well endowed with vaulted cellars.

On the first floor, bedrooms on the west and south sides of the house are open to the public. They are all ornamented with friezes and, apart from the central bedroom on the south side - the principal bedroom - have white marble chimneypieces: the main bedroom has one of grey marble with white veins. The two rooms on the west side are nearest the top of the stairs and have wallpaper dating from the 1880s (likely produced by Morris and Co.) whereas the wallpaper in other bedrooms is thought to be of rather more recent date, perhaps around 1909 in the case of that of the principal bedroom.

Upon leaving the house via the front door and walking around to the exterior of the south side, one comes to two terraces. The upper terrace is merely grassed over, whereas the lower terrace, supported by a massive arcaded ha-ha, is ornately laid out with a geometrical design and contains a variety of shrubs and plants. The terraces provide good views southward to a rhododendron garden created by Sir Arthur Middleton (it is not open to the public) and through which the lake referred to above can be glimpsed.

Off the west end of the lower terrace lies the magnolia terrace, which is flanked by trees and where, among other things, various species of magnolia can be seen: in summer, the general colour scheme is one of pinks and purples. Here, a path heads westward towards the winter garden which includes a pair of sunken croquet lawns, azaleas, and a 92ft (28m) Douglas fir planted in 1830, a variety of tree introduced into Britain from North America only a few years earlier.

At the far end of the winter garden is a doorway located in a high sheltering wall dating from the days of Sir Arthur Middleton, and through which the path heads en route to what many will doubtless regard as the most enchanting part of the gardens at Belsay - the quarry garden and the adjoining west quarry: the latter is again the work of Sir Arthur. The quarry gardens have a

19. The Quarry Garden (David Dodds)

20. The castle from the south-west

wilder, more natural aspect than the gardens nearer the hall and deep shadows are cast in places by the enclosing rock faces. A variety of unusual trees, shrubs and ferns adorn the quarry garden, while snowdrops, primroses and purely native plants lie in the west quarry. Upon exiting the north side of the quarry garden, Belsay Castle can be seen lying in parkland a short distance away.

It will be recalled that a two-storey range was built against the west side of the castle by Thomas Middleton in the early 17th century, and that in turn this was subsequently adjoined by a large wing erected in about 1711. While the latter was demolished in the 19th century (only low walls remain) Thomas Middleton's range still stands, albeit roofless: in 1872 it was partly rebuilt by the seventh baronet.

It is from within this range that one enters the castle proper, which is 14th century in style. Belsay Castle is not large and does not occupy a position of great strength, but has nevertheless been described as one of the most impressive in Northumberland by Pevsner. It is a tower-house, oblong in plan, with the recessed entrance on the west face flanked by two short projections or wings at the north-west and south-west angles. It is built of honey-coloured sandstone and at the top of each corner is a bartizan with machicolated parapets. Three of the bartizans are of uniform height, but that at the south-west angle rises higher and is the most eye-catching feature of the exterior. Furthermore, machicolation also exists along the battlements between the bartizans.

The entrance opens to a lobby. Off this, to the north, are two small chambers; the first of which was perhaps a porter's lodge while the latter room, which is unlit, may have been a storeroom. A doorway on the south side of the lobby opens to a newel staircase and to the south of which, in the south-west corner of the tower, is a small chamber, the first of six arranged vertically in this part of the castle. On the other hand, another doorway in the lobby gives access eastward to a large pointed tunnel-vaulted chamber, the kitchen. This has a well - formerly 17ft (5m) deep - and a huge fireplace that has been partly filled in.

Access to the upper floors and the roof is via the newel stair. Upon ascending the stairs, en route to the Great Hall, the second and third of the six small chambers just mentioned are reached. The third room, at the same level as the Great Hall, has an opening on its north side near the doorway through which it is entered. The chamber's function is uncertain. It has been suggested that the opening was a squint and that the room was thus a tiny chapel, but this is not universally accepted. An alternative proposal is that food cooked on the ground floor was arranged and ornamented here before being passed through the opening to servants who then carried it into the adjacent Great Hall.

The Great Hall is located above the kitchen (which it exceeds in scale) and has single two-light windows in the south and north walls, complete with stone window seats where pursuits such as reading and needlework doubtless occurred, making use of the light provided. The room was heated by a large fireplace on the east side, and has faded remains of mural decoration dating from the 15th century. Rows of stone corbels are visible. These supported the floor of a chamber situated above the Great Hall.

A doorway near the north-west corner of the Great Hall opens to a room with a fireplace, two windows and, on the north side, access to a latrine: a comparable chamber occupies the space above and was entered from the room over the Great Hall.

Upon returning to the newel stair, one can ascend to the roof. Here, three of the corner turrets each contain a vaulted closet. On the other hand, the larger and taller south-west turret contains a more substantial chamber that was reached from the roof of the tower via an open stair. This room, the highest of the six located in the south-west angle of the tower, is larger than those below for it extends over the vault of the stairs.

Belsay Hall, Castle and garden are in the care of English Heritage.

BLACK FRIARS, NEWCASTLE UPON TYNE

During the early decades of the 13th century, orders of friars began to establish themselves in England. One such was the Dominican Order, also known as the Black Friars, which arrived in the 1220s. By 1239 at the latest, they had a presence in Newcastle upon Tyne with a friary in the north-west sector of the medieval town, a friary founded by Sir Peter Scot, a wealthy merchant.

Although their houses closely resembled monasteries, friars were not monks and worship featured less prominently in their daily routine. Instead, they were clerics who initially lived solely by begging. Moreover, they were mostly located in urban areas. For instance, all five of the orders of friars that existed were represented in medieval Newcastle.

The Dominican Order was the first of these mendicant brotherhoods to come into being. Its founder was Dominic of Osma, (died 1221), who began recruiting members in Spain shortly after 1200 after being alarmed at widespread heresy, heresy he wished to combat by sending out into the world intellectually vibrant individuals well-schooled in logic and theology; men committed to a life of poverty; men determined to preach the true faith to the multitudes.

The Dominicans' first house in England was established at Oxford and was followed by many others up and down the country. St Dominic had forbidden his friars to own buildings and land but such property was held in trust on their behalf, albeit on a small-scale. Newcastle's Black Friars for instance had, in addition to the seven acres (2.83 hectares) or so of ground upon which their friary lay, two gardens and four small closes that yielded them a paltry revenue.

In 1250 the prior was censured by the order's general chapter, (attended by representatives of the whole order) for architectural extravagance, and fabric dating from this period can still be seen among the ruins of the friary, located on Friars Street.

During the 14th century the friars accommodated royalty on more than one occasion. Indeed, in 1334 both Edward III of England and Scotland's monarch, Edward Balliol, were present with their retinues, and on 19 June Balliol did homage to Edward III for the kingdom of Scotland in the church.

The friary ceased to exist on 10 January 1539 when it was closed as part of the government's programme of dissolving the regular religious orders in England. It was subsequently sold to the mayor and burgesses of Newcastle who, apparently in 1552, leased it to nine of the town's guilds such as the Bakers and Brewers, the Fullers and Dyers, and the Saddlers and Tailors, though it is unclear when the '9 crafts' took possession of Black Friars: it was not until 1569 that they were recorded as paying 44s annual rent for their property. Sooner or later, the companies adapted the two-storey claustral ranges to suit their requirements. On this point, Barbara Harbottle comments: 'Though there is . . . no precise date for the initial adaptation of the three claustral ranges, the rather sparse architectural evidence suggests that the work was carried out in the late 16th or early 17th century.'

Further work followed between 1709-39, during which much of the surviving medieval fabric was destroyed. This was especially true of much of the upper storey of the claustral ranges. Among other things, the remodelling entailed the provision of new windows and

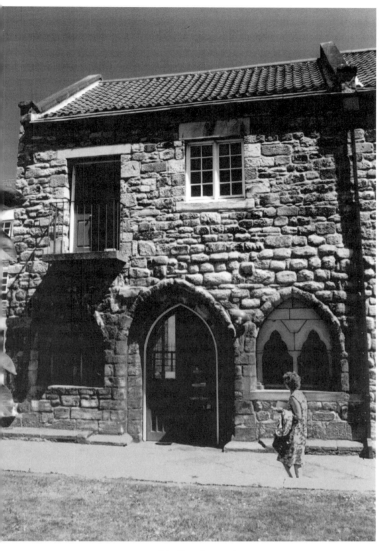

21. The chapter house

the alteration of floor levels: some of the floors at ground level for example were raised owing to the rise in the ground level of the cloister, partly as a result of the dumping of household rubbish. The Tailors and the Cordwainers were not involved in this process. The former had taken to meeting at a house they owned in Manor Chare, but returned to Black Friars later in the century and almost entirely rebuilt their former meeting house here in 1787-88. On the other hand, the Cordwainers, who had left Black Friars in 1729, met in a number of places elsewhere in Newcastle before returning in 1844.

From at least the 17th century until the 19th century, the various meeting houses at Black Friars were well used. As the companies only met quarterly their rooms were usually let for other purposes: first floor rooms, for instance, served as schoolrooms or in some other capacity, whereas ground floor rooms normally served as dwellings, in some cases those of people employed by the companies. In certain instances occupants were deemed to be deserving of charity and lived rent free.

During the 19th century, some of the properties at Black Friars began to suffer significant neglect and started falling into a state of dilapidation, a sad state of affairs that continued into the 20th century. 'It is a blot on the fair reputation of Newcastle', commented J. Douglas Mitchell in the mid 1920s, 'any longer to leave these ancient buildings in their present mouldering condition.' Indeed, in 1937 the Saddlers' property was condemned as unfit for human habitation and was duly let for warehousing.

Newcastle Corporation subsequently acquired Black Friars in the early 1950s. The

Tailors, for instance, sold their house to the Corporation in 1951. Later in the decade, and in the early 1960s, it seemed as though Dominicans would resume residence at Black Friars but this proved not to be the case. Although the Tailors had sold their meeting house to the Corporation they continued meeting at Black Friars until 1974 and were not alone in so doing.

In 1975, following a report commissioned by Newcastle's Planning Committee, restoration work commenced and was completed in 1981. Black Friars now houses, among other things, a restaurant and craft shop.

Description

Only the claustral buildings remain - in the Middle Ages the cloister consisted of an open garth approximately 69ft (21m) square, bordered on each side by a 10ft (3m) wide covered walk. The church of the friary was located along the north side of the cloister and projected beyond the claustral ranges. It was floored with alternate yellow and green-glazed tiles, and the nave housed laity who had come to hear the friars preach. The church was demolished in the 16th century, as was the north end of the east range.

The principal room in the east range was the chapter house. The west part of this still stands and now forms the north end of the east range. It dates from the late 13th century and has an arched doorway, flanked by two-light windows with cusped tracery, facing the cloister: one of the windows is a restoration. What remains of the chapter house is only partly medieval. For instance, the east and south walls date from a programme of remodelling in the late 19th century. The section of the east range immediately south of the truncated chapter house likewise contains medieval and Victorian fabric. Beyond this, the former Smiths' premises at the south end of the range, is thought to have originally been the friars' warming house. The masonry is essentially medieval and has three lancet windows in the south wall facing Friars Street.

At the east end of the south range a passage connects the cloister with the street. Much of the fabric of the south range is post-medieval. In the days of the friary the range housed the refectory, some of whose lancet windows have survived.

Rather more from the Middle Ages exists of the west range and includes a trefoil-arched lavatorium. The southern part of the range formed the guest house.

BRINKBURN PRIORY

Brinkburn Priory lies in an enchanting position beside a loop of the River Coquet in the heart of Northumberland, and was founded in about 1135 during the reign of Henry I by William de Bertram, Lord of Mitford, one of the county's most important barons. In founding Brinkburn, Bertram declared that he was doing so 'for my soul and my parents, for the remission of my sins, for my lords living and dead, for my wife and sons and my faithful followers.'

Brinkburn was an Augustinian house, and the original complement of canons likely came from Pentney Priory in Norfolk. The Augustinian canons, popularly known as the Austin canons, or Black canons on account of their black outdoor cloaks, lived by a Rule based on a letter written in the 5th century in which St Augustine of Hippo had given advice and regulations to a newly established religious house in North Africa. Although their lifestyle was monastic, Augustinian canons were not monks and their Rule was less demanding. For a start, religious observance was less time consuming, although it still occupied much of the canons' routine. Furthermore, food and drink were less restricted and there was more freedom to converse and to go beyond the bounds of the monastery into the world outside. For instance, they ministered in parish churches, which had been granted to their respective houses.

22. Brinkburn Priory viewed from the south-east: the manor house is on the left of the picture

49

The Augustinian canons' first house in England was established at Colchester in the early years of the 12th century. Others soon followed. Indeed, the order proved very popular with lay society and by 1135 - the end of Henry I's reign - forty houses had been established in the country. Further growth ensued. By 1350 there were 218 Augustinian monasteries in England, almost all of them being of modest size.

Little is known of the history of Brinkburn Priory, which was never a wealthy house. In around 1322, by which time Anglo-Scottish conflict had become a marked feature of life for the people of this region, the prior and canons petitioned Edward II hoping to obtain financial assistance in view of losses they had sustained. The 15th century also witnessed troubled times. In 1419 thieves stole chalices, vestments and other goods, whereupon the Bishop of Durham, within whose diocese Brinkburn lay, threatened those guilty with excommunication if the stolen articles were not returned within twenty days.

Meanwhile, in the 14th century the canons had built a chamber above the aisle of the nave. Another addition to the church, and possibly contemporaneous with the chamber, was a room erected above the chancel. Their function is uncertain.

Brinkburn Priory survived until 1536 when it was dissolved during the Dissolution of the Monasteries during the reign of Henry VIII. Following the suppression of the priory, the church remained in use as a place of worship serving local people: laity had previously had access to the west part of the nave. It remained in a decent state of repair until the close of the 16th century, but thereafter began to decay: the roof fell in during the 17th century and regular services ceased in 1683.

In the mid 19th century a programme of restoration occurred during the days of Cadogan Hodgson Cadogan, the then owner of Brinkburn, and among other things entailed rebuilding the collapsed south-west angle of the nave, the most extensively damaged part of the fabric, and removing the added chambers above the nave north aisle and the chancel so that the original roof profiles could be restored. He employed the services of a Newcastle architect, Thomas Austin. Care was taken to make the restoration as authentic as possible. Of the work, which began in 1858, A.B.E. Clark comments: 'Considering how many churches were heavily restored during the 19th century, the very sensitive and restrained manner in which the work was carried out does credit to both owner and architect.'

Description

Brinkburn Priory is approached from the north down a wooded path from which fine views of the Coquet can be seen flowing through low fields to the west. Suddenly, to the south, one catches a glimpse, framed by trees and rhododendrons, of

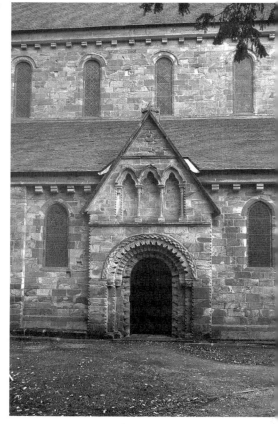

23. The north entrance, a mixture of Norman and Early English work

the church below, occupying a position of perfect seclusion, partly encompassed by the river and overlooked by high ground.

The church, a fine example of northern Transitional architecture, measures 130ft (40m) in length and was likely begun c.1190, with construction work lasting into the early decades of the following century.

It is entered through a door located in a slight gabled projection on the north side of the nave. The doorway is well endowed with Norman ornament, such as chevron and beakhead, while above it the gable has an Early English arcade of three trefoiled-pointed arches on detached shafts.

The nave is six bays long and has a north aisle, whose arcade consists of octagonal piers carrying pointed double-chamfered arches. The triforium has, above the piers, openings which each consist of twin round arches within an arch of the same form, while at clerestory level are round-headed windows located above the arches of the arcade. The north aisle contains evidence of vaulting: for instance on the north wall there are corbels, several of which carry two or three voussoirs of the vaulting ribs. However, as William Henry Knowles has observed, 'the corbels and springer stones vary so greatly - some chamfered and others moulded - and are so irregularly placed as to warrant the conjecture that the vaulting was never executed.' In common with other Augustinian houses, there is no south aisle. The south wall has five lofty round-headed windows and doorways that opened to the no longer extant east and west walks of the cloister.

East of the nave lies the crossing, surmounted by a low tower that hardly rises above the level of the ridges of the adjacent roofs. The piers supporting the tower have three shafts on each face, of which the central one is keel-shaped whereas the others are cylindrical. Of the shafts in question, those in the nave descend to a height of 14ft (4m) above ground where they terminate so that the canons' stalls could be placed against the piers, whereas those in the transepts descend to ground level. In the chancel, the central shaft terminates at the same height as do the shafts in the nave.

The transepts both have a rib-vaulted east aisle whose octagonal piers have very plain moulded capitals, (as do the crossing piers) while the triforium and clerestory are the same as in the nave. The aisles once had wooden screens - the beam holes can still be seen - and served as chapels. The north transept contains a large wooden sculpture, *The Risen Christ*, a recent work by Fenwick Lawson, whereas the south transept houses an organ built in 1868 by William Hill, perhaps the most important English organ maker of the 19th century. It was donated to the church by Sir William Armstrong, the owner of the nearby Cragside estate. The south wall of the south transept has a wheel window in the gable but this is not a medieval feature for it dates from the period of restoration: the original gable had collapsed leaving no evidence of its details.

The east wall of the chancel is the most imposing of the church and has three tiers of windows; the lowest two are lancets while the uppermost consists of smaller, round-headed, windows. Blank arcades with pointed arches run along the chancel's north and south walls and above these each wall has a tier of lancets and then one of round-headed windows. A blocked doorway can be seen in the north wall. It was inserted when a sacristy was built against the north side of the chancel. Of interest, too, is the grave cover of Prior William, (who was also a suffragan Bishop of Durham) and who died in 1484. It is decorated with a fleur-de-lis, a mitre and a crozier and is located on the north side of the chancel. The high altar dates from 1898. Some of the floor tiles beneath it are medieval: almost all the tiles in the church date from the 19th century.

In the west wall of the south transept a doorway with waterleaf capitals opens to the site of the cloister. The cloister is gone, although a blind arcade of trefoiled arches runs along the outer face of the south wall of the nave, while, built into the exterior of the south transept's west wall, is an opening that served as a book cupboard. Almost nothing remains of the east claustral range, whose upper floor contained the dormitory: adjoining the south side of the transept are the fragmentary remains of a vaulted passage that was perhaps the vestibule of the chapter house, little of which survives.

Nothing remains of the west claustral range. Indeed, it is possible that one was never built. On the other hand, much of the south range has been incorporated within a manor house, the eastern end of which mostly dates from 1810, whereas the western part of the house was rebuilt in the 1830s by John Dobson. The house, now an empty shell, has recently been opened to visitors and contains many rooms, some of which enjoy fine views of the Coquet. In places, medieval fabric is clearly visible. This is true for instance of the arch of the lavatorium recess - the south range housed the canons' refectory - which can be seen in a passage on the north side of the house. In 1952 occupation of the house ceased.

In 1965 H.A. Cadogan Fenwick placed the buildings at Brinkburn in the guardianship of the Ministry of Public Building and Works. The site is now in the care of English Heritage.

24. An interior view of the church, looking east from the nave

CHESTERS ROMAN FORT

Chesters Roman Fort, known in Roman times as *Cilurnum*, lies in a picturesque setting on a terrace above the North Tyne, which flows past the site to the east and south. Built in the A.D. 120s as part of the Hadrian's Wall frontier programme, Chesters was intended to guard the point where the Wall crossed the river. Initially, Hadrian's Wall ran right through the site, but the section in question was soon demolished when it was decided to place the fort here, with approximately a third of its area projecting northward beyond the line of the Wall.

Roman forts were built to a standard plan, although variations are known. They were shaped like a playing card, were surrounded by one or more defensive ditches and had a gate in each of the four straight sides, angle towers in the rounded corners and other internal towers at intervals between.

The perimeter walls of stone forts were about 4 to 5ft (1.21 to 1.52m) wide and approximately 12 to 15ft (3.66 to 4.57m) high to the level of the walkway, and were backed by a rampart of turf or earth and clay that likely rose to the same level as the wall-walk, thereby not only strengthening the wall but also providing a wider platform from which members of the garrison could repel assailants. The rampart was interrupted by the gates and the corner and interval towers and by the provision of other structures such as bakehouses and latrines.

Between the rampart and the rest of the interior was a road running around the whole circuit and within this a fort was divided into three main areas. One such, across the fort's width, comprised a central range of official and administrative buildings. This included the commanding officer's residence and the headquarters building. The latter, the nerve centre of the fort, lay at the junction of the two main roads, the *via principalis* and *via praetoria*. The former, from which the headquarters was entered, ran right across the width of the fort while the latter ran straight towards the headquarters from the fort's front gate. The remainder of the fort was occupied by rows of barracks, stores and workshops.

It is sometimes said that Chesters was garrisoned by an approximately 500 strong cavalry unit. Mounted units were certainly connected with the site. One such was a regiment of cavalry ('named "Augusta" because of its valour') believed to have formed the initial garrison. However, a document of AD 146 suggests that by then Chesters was garrisoned by an infantry unit. Among other units associated with Chesters were the First Cohort of Vangiones from the upper Rhineland - thought to have been present in the latter half of the 2nd century - and the First Cohort of Dalmatians from the Balkans, which may likewise have been at Chesters sometime during the same century. What is certain is that by 184 during the governorship of Ulpius Marcellus, a cavalry unit originally raised in Spain, *Ala II Asturum,* was based at Chesters (an aqueduct is known to have been built at Chesters by the regiment at this time) and the unit seems to have remained the garrison for the remainder of the fort's active service.

The daily routine for soldiers based at Chesters, as elsewhere, doubtless included exercise and training. Time, too, would have been spent on tasks such as guarding the fort, patrolling a section of Hadrian's Wall or territory to the north, and escorting supplies in

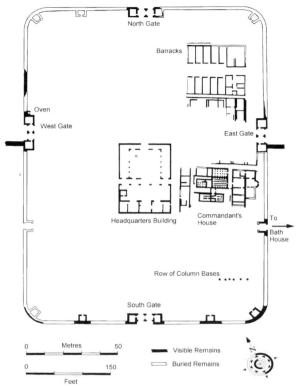

25. A plan of Chesters Fort (after English Heritage)

transit. Administrative staff would have been engaged on various duties in the headquarters building, dealing with such matters as the soldiers' pay and savings.

The diet of Roman soldiers included fruit and vegetables, bread, soup, meat, shellfish and, less frequently, fish. Among other things, garlic, spices and salt and pepper were used to add flavour to food and the main meal of the day was in the evening. Liquid refreshment included cheap wine and it seems probable that much of the wine consumed by soldiers on the northern frontier was produced in the Rhineland.

In common with most other Roman forts, Chesters was associated with a civil settlement that developed outside its walls, a settlement located to the south and southeast of the fort, heading down towards the Tyne. Here members of the garrison would have relaxed and spent part of their wages at places such as taverns, shops and, presumably, brothels. Prior to the early 3rd century, when Emperor Septimus Severus allowed Roman soldiers to marry, members of the garrison would no doubt have had unofficial wives and families resident in the settlement.

In later centuries, Chesters was levelled and mostly grassed over by a local landowner who purchased the property in 1796 and wished to create a parkland setting for his country house. But in 1832 he was succeeded by his son, John Clayton, who was passionately interested in Roman history, so much so that he undertook excavations at Chesters and elsewhere along Hadrian's Wall. John Clayton was responsible for establishing Chesters as a popular archaeological site and fittingly his portrait can be seen in the site museum which was completed in 1896, six years after his death, to house and display a collection he had amassed from Chesters and several other sites such as Housesteads and Vindolanda.

Description

The remains of the fort, which covers an area of 5.7 acres, (2.3 hectares) are approached from the north and Chesters, like other Roman forts, was essentially built to the standard plan mentioned above. But like some other forts along Hadrian's Wall, it was provided with two extra gates that served the Military Way, a Roman road running along the south side of the Wall. Moreover, in common with a number of Wall forts, three of Chesters' main gates lie beyond the line of the Wall.

The fort's north wall lies buried, but the fragmentary remains of the north gate are visible. In common with the other main gates, access through the north gate was via two slightly recessed passageways with round-headed arches. On their outer sides the passages were flanked by towers with guardchambers, while above the passages and between the towers was a central upper chamber. The west portal was blocked during the Roman period, and as its threshold is hardly worn it appears that this occurred early in the fort's history.

The west gate is better preserved than the north gate. Its thresholds are unworn, again testifying to the fact that for some reason the passages were blocked at an early date. A stone platform exists in the north guardchamber and it has been suggested that this may have supported a large water tank into which water was discharged via a small aqueduct carrying water down the hillside to the west. 'From here', states J.S. Johnson, 'the highest point on the site, a distribution system could have supplied water to those parts of the fort which required it, and, ultimately, to the bath house lower down nearer the river.'

Immediately to the north of the west gate, in the angle formed by the north guard-chamber and the perimeter wall, are the remains of an oven, while at the opposite end of the west gate the south guard tower is adjoined by a fragment of Hadrian's Wall.

The south gate - the only one of the main gates behind Hadrian's Wall - faced towards the site of the civil settlement that developed on lower ground towards the river. Its west portal was blocked up by the Romans, again it seems at a fairly early date. Here an aqueduct

26. The east gate

channel, covered with flat slabs, can be seen making its way through the portal: likely the aqueduct carried water from the supposed settling tank in the west gate to the civilian settlement or down to a bath house near the river. During its period of use, the road surface of the east portal rose by about 3ft (1m).

Several interval towers existed along the length of the curtain wall and the remains of some of these are visible. Two such lie along the south side of the fort, one either side of the south gate. That to the east stands over 6ft (1.8m) high, as does an angle tower in the south-east corner of the fort: nothing can be seen of the other angle towers.

Upon progressing northward along the fort's east perimeter one comes across a secondary east gateway, located approximately halfway between the south-east angle tower and the main east gate. Its single carriageway opened to the Military Way, and a comparable gateway in the west wall on the same alignment served the same purpose.

The east gate itself is relatively well preserved, making it one of the finest fort gateways on Hadrian's Wall, which adjoined its south guardchamber. Sooner or later its dual passageways were blocked off. Given the unworn nature of the thresholds, it is often asserted that the gate went out of use early in the fort's history. But it may well have been the case that the gate was seldom used - movement eastwards was after all restricted by the North Tyne - and that the decision to block the gate was taken later than is sometimes supposed. Either way, the east gate was blocked up, as was of course the west gate. Hence the only means of entering or exiting the fort from beyond the line of Hadrian's Wall came to be the north gate, or to be precise, its east portal.

Most of the remains of buildings located in the fort lie buried under grass. Of those whose remains are visible, one first comes across two barrack blocks located in the north-east part of the fort. One of the blocks lies to the north of the other, from which it is separated by a road. In addition to an officer's quarters at the east end, each contained separate compartments for the troops (only some of the compartments can be seen), and these lay side-by-side alongside a verandah and under a single roof. Each compartment housed several men and was subdivided into a living area and a small dormitory at the rear. The accommodation provided in the barracks was not generous: conditions would have been cramped when fully used. Frequently, however, the number of men present was doubtless reduced by the absence of members of the unit performing various tasks.

Immediately to the south of the second barrack block mentioned, and formerly facing on to the main east-west road bisecting the fort, are the remains of another barrack block, in this case one that appears to have been divided into entirely separate units.

On the opposite side of the road lie the remains of the commanding officer's residence, which was altered frequently during the fort's history and whose remains are thus complicated. The visible remains are thought to be those of three suites of domestic rooms - some of which were provided with hypocausts - ranged around a central courtyard that was subsequently encroached on by additional building. Late in its history, moreover, the building was provided with an eastward extension that projected into the space of the internal road running around the perimeter of the fort's defences, thereby obstructing movement at this point. The extension contained a separate small suite of baths with semicircular ends.

To the west of the commanding officer's house, beyond an elongated workshop, stable or store, lie the remains of the headquarters building or *principia* in the centre of the fort. Together with the fort's defences, and parts of a bath house yet to be discussed, the headquarters is apparently the only Hadrianic feature visible at Chesters and thus pre-dates the barrack blocks and commandant's house.

27. The remains of the bath-suite of the commanding officer's residence

Here, a central north doorway opened to a paved courtyard surrounded on three sides by colonnades. The courtyard contains a well, near which one of the stone slabs of the partially extant paving bears a carved phallus intended to bring good luck. To the south, the courtyard and flanking colonnades were bounded by a hall on an east-west axis. The hall, aisled on its north side, had a variety of functions, including the dispensation of justice - the foundations of the tribunal from which the commander gave judgment can be seen located at the west end of the body of the hall. Located along the south side of the hall are the remains of five rooms, the central one of which was the shrine (the others were occupied by administrative staff) where, among other things, regimental standards and a statue of the emperor would have been placed. A stone staircase here leads down to a partly sunken strongroom that was added to the headquarters building at a later stage in the fort's history, and greatly encroaches on the space of the first of the offices located to the east of the shrine, perhaps indicating that the office had gone out of use.

Heading south from the headquarters, one can see a row of columns in the south-east corner of the fort, doubtless relics of the verandah of a barrack block.

Upon leaving the fort by the lesser of the east gateways, and walking down towards the North Tyne, the remains of the garrison's bath house are encountered close to the river bank. The baths can also be reached from the east gate, although in Roman times this would of course not have been possible owing to the presence of the Wall.

The bath house is one of the most well preserved on Hadrian's Wall. It contains fabric from different periods, for it was extended and modified over the years and ultimately provided bathers with a variety of treatments. In Roman times, the floor-level of much of the building was about 3ft (1m) higher than that of today, owing to the presence of an underfloor heating system in which hot air from several furnaces circulated beneath floors supported on pillars.

The bath house is entered through a small porch on its north side. This opens to a large changing room, with a row of seven niches in its west wall that most likely housed statues, perhaps ones representing the days of the week. Off the east end of the changing room lay the latrines, where wooden seats were located over a deep channel along which effluent was carried down to the river.

On the other hand, off the south-west corner of the changing room is a lobby giving access to various treatments. For instance, it is adjoined to the west by an anteroom associated with hot dry treatment comparable to a sauna. In the anteroom the bather, (wearing sandals to protect his feet from heat generated by the underfloor heating system), would have spent time building up a sweat before progressing into the adjoining small hot dry room to the north, built against the changing room. Here, in addition to the floor, the room's hollow walls were also heated.

From here, to cool off, wash away sweat and close the pores of his skin, a bather returned to the lobby en route to a cold plunge bath located in a room to the east. Initially it appears that the plunge bath lay in a chamber off the far end of an anteroom entered directly from the lobby: the anteroom had a douche, the base of whose basin survives in the centre of the room. Subsequently, however, this bath seems to have gone out of use and was replaced with a smaller one in a corner of the cold room, as the former antechamber is known.

A door in the south wall of the cold room opens to the first of two rooms that provided steam heat treatments. A doorway in the west wall of the southernmost of these rooms, led

28. A view of the changing room of the garrison's bath house

into hot steam rooms where bathers would have perspired vigorously: the doorway was subsequently blocked and access to the rooms was thus only possible via the lobby. In an annexe off the west side of the hottest of the hot steam rooms, (the southernmost), are traces of pink mortar on the walls. The annexe contained a hot bath below a small window.

Finally, close to the bath house are the remains of Roman bridges that spanned the North Tyne. The first bridge was Hadrianic, but was replaced by a much larger structure in the early 3rd century and most of the surviving fabric belongs to this period. The river has shifted course somewhat since Roman times - it has encroached into the Chesters bank - and so the fragmentary remains of the bridge abutment here are normally not visible. In contrast, the impressive remains of the east abutment constitute one of the finest masonry structures to be found along Hadrian's Wall and can be approached via a footpath from the vicinity of neighbouring Chollerford Bridge.

CHILLINGHAM CASTLE

Chillingham Castle lies near the River Till in undulating country several miles south-east of Wooler and enjoys views of the distant Cheviot Hills. It was built in the mid 14th century by Sir Thomas de Heton, who had acquired Chillingham in the 1320s, a property whose earliest known owners were the de Vescy lords of Alnwick who had settled in Northumberland in Norman times and of whose barony Chillingham was a part. By the time Heton acquired Chillingham, however, it had passed through various other hands.

In September 1255 Henry III is known to have stayed at the then residence at Chillingham while returning south from the border. Later still, in 1296, Chillingham was likely destroyed by Scottish raiders who penetrated Northumberland that year when a period of Anglo-Scottish warfare commenced. What is certain is that on 1 July in 1298 Edward I was at Chillingham prior to invading Scotland, an invasion that resulted in the defeat of a Scottish army at Falkirk on the 22nd of that month.

As stated, Sir Thomas Heton acquired Chillingham in the 1320s. He was a prominent figure in Northumberland and in late 1317 had been one of the principal captors of a celebrated outlaw, Sir Gilbert de Middleton, who was seized at Mitford near Morpeth and subsequently put to death in London.

At Westminster, on 27 January 1344, Edward III issued Heton a licence to fortify Chillingham - or 'Chevelyngham' to use the contemporary spelling - and as a result Chillingham Castle was created, a structure that is generally thought to have incorporated already extant fabric. On this point, for example, the late Sir Nikolaus Pevsner commented that the south-west tower 'is at least partially a survival from an older' residence. Northumberland at this date was beset by unrest caused by Anglo-Scottish conflict and Chillingham was not the only castle erected in the county at this time: it is for example contemporary with Bothal Castle near Morpeth. Moreover, like a number of other 14th century castles such as Bolton in North Yorkshire and Lumley in County Durham - both of which it predates - Chillingham is rectangular in plan. Construction work was completed by 1348, in which year Heton granted the vicar of Chillingham and his successors quarters above the castle gateway as well as stabling for two horses.

As first built, Chillingham Castle evidently comprised four roughly square towers, standing at the corners of an enclosure and linked by a curtain wall. The entrance is believed to have lain on the south side of the castle or towards the south end of the west side. Sooner or later however, and most probably at an early date, ranges of stone buildings were erected against the curtain wall.

Sir Thomas Heton's eldest son predeceased him and so, in 1335, he decided to leave Chillingham to an illegitimate son, Thomas the bastard. However, a legitimate son named Alan objected to this and resorted to law in order to have the settlement overturned. He won his case and duly inherited Chillingham in 1353. The neighbourhood was far from prosperous at this time - doubtless due to the combined effects of Scottish raids and fatalities caused by the recent Black Death - and many tenements were lying waste due to lack of tenants.

Subsequently, Sir Henry Heton (a son of the illegitimate individual referred to above)

29. The north front of Chillingham Castle (Shaun Dodds: courtesy of Sir Humphry Wakefield)

resorted to violence in order to gain control of Chillingham. Together with several companions, he managed to gain entry to the castle where he seized Sir Alan and incarcerated him in one of its towers. Consequently, in February 1387, Peter Tyliol, a royal official in Northumberland, was ordered to make his way to Chillingham and secure Sir Alan's release. But upon arriving, Tyliol was prevented from entering the castle. In May, his hand was strengthened when Henry Percy, the first Earl of Northumberland and another magnate, John Neville of Raby, were instructed to accompany him to Chillingham to enter the castle in the name of Richard II, to free and restore Sir Alan and bring those guilty of his capture and imprisonment to the king. But by this date Sir Alan was no longer in the realms of the living. He had died - perhaps violently - on 21 March and Sir Henry Heton thus became Chillingham's new owner.

During the 15th century Chillingham Castle passed into the hands of the Grey family, lords of Heton to the north, several of whom had served the Bishops of Durham as Constables of Norham Castle, a mighty fortress beside the River Tweed. Of the Greys' connection with Chillingham, Cadwallader Bates commented: 'It does not appear to be known when or how the Greys of Heton first became possessed of Chillingham.' Bates thought it likely that Sir Ralph Grey, who died in 1443, (and whose splendid tomb with alabaster figures of Sir Ralph in full armour beside his wife in court dress, can be seen in Chillingham church), was the first of the line to own Chillingham. More recently, however, Constance Fraser and

Kenneth Emsley have commented as follows: 'The tomb is a blatant piece of family publicity, because the Ralph Grey commemorated was not an owner of Chillingham. It was his son who acquired the property about 1455 from the heirs of the Heton family, ploughing the profits of war into a compact estate, complete with massive castle. The tomb was the final decorative touch, supplying "instant ancestors"'.

In 1514 or thereabouts, early in the reign of Henry VIII, it was reported that Chillingham was capable of billeting 100 horsemen, while in 1533 there was a muster at Chillingham for a raid into Scotland. In late 1536 Chillingham was subjected to a siege during the unsuccessful rising known as the Pilgrimage of Grace. At this time the head of the Grey family was a minor and his guardian, Sir Robert Ellerker, defended the castle when it was attacked by the Percies, key figures in the revolt, who are sometimes said, and likely correctly so, to have employed cannon against its walls. Following the revolt, Ellerker carried out repair work and in 1541 the castle was described as 'in measurably good reparations.'

Subsequently, major alterations occurred: the north range, for instance, was remodelled to serve as the entrance front and provided with a grander appearance. This work is usually attributed to Sir William Grey, who was granted a baronetcy in 1619 and was elevated to the peerage in 1624 as Lord Grey of Wark. But at least some of the work was doubtless done by his father, Sir Ralph, who negotiated with James VI of Scotland on the subject of the succession to the English throne (the king became James I of England in 1603 upon the death of Queen Elizabeth) and some of whose correspondence with Lord Burghley, one of Elizabeth's senior ministers, has recently been discovered hidden in the masonry of the castle.

In 1674 Ralph, the second Lord Grey, acquired an estate in Sussex when Uppark passed into his hands by marriage. He died the following year and was succeeded by his son, Forde, a remarkable figure of some ill-repute. Among other things, he was found guilty of eloping with his wife's 18-year-old sister. Moreover, he was arrested and imprisoned in the Tower for complicity in the Rye House Plot, a conspiracy intended to result in the assassination of Charles II and his brother, James, Duke of York. Grey managed to escape and fled to Holland. There, he joined forces with the Duke of Monmouth - an illegitimate son of Charles II - and accompanied him on his invasion of England in 1685. Monmouth hoped to supplant his recently enthroned uncle, James II, and Grey led the cavalry of the ill-fated force. Like Monmouth, he was captured and condemned for high treason. Monmouth died bravely at the hands of an executioner wielding an axe with singular incompetence. Grey, whom *The Complete Peerage* describes as a 'cowardly and incestuous traitor', gave evidence against his former colleagues in arms and was pardoned: according to some, he only gave evidence on the understanding that the lives of those against whom he testified would be spared. During the reign of William III, Grey received various honours. Most notably, he was created Earl of Tankerville in 1695, by which time he had just built a splendid mansion at Uppark, now one of the National Trust's most celebrated properties. In making him Earl of Tankerville, William III revived an ancient title bestowed in the early 15th century on a member of the Grey family who had distinguished himself by capturing the castle of Tanqueville in Normandy during the Hundred Years War.

Forde died in 1701 and was succeeded by his brother, who became fourth Baron Grey of Wark (the earldom became extinct). In 1706 he likewise died, whereupon the barony also ceased to exist.

Chillingham, and other property, then passed to Charles Bennet, second Lord Ossulston, Forde's son-in-law, who was made Earl of Tankerville in 1714. His successor, (who died in 1753), sold Uppark in 1747 but retained Chillingham Castle, whose south range he remodelled and the quality of whose grounds he enhanced. Furthermore, an arched tunnel was erected in 1752 over the old moat outside the south range and above which earth was placed to form part of a level lawn that adjoined the building at first floor level.

Work undertaken at Chillingham in the 19th century included the enhancement of the castle's setting by Sir Jeffrey Wyatville (1766-1840), who arrived at Chillingham in 1828, and who created avenues and a formal Italian garden. Changes were also made to the castle and included the construction of a large service wing against the east face in 1872-3.

An eminent Victorian visitor to Chillingham was the painter Sir Edwin Henry Landseer, who spent some of his time here instructing the ladies in the art of drawing and painting. In 1872, moreover, the Prince of Wales (the future Edward VII) visited the castle.

Following the death of the seventh earl in 1931 the castle was abandoned, and two years later its contents were sold by auction. During the Second World War Chillingham was used as a barracks, but following the war the castle once again lay empty and wet and dry rot destroyed much of the interior decoration, some of which had already been destroyed by soldiers.

In 1980 the ninth Earl of Tankerville decided to give the decaying castle to a baronet, Sir Humphry Wakefield, who bought the surrounding lands. The earl died soon after this and his plans were carried out by his Trustees. Sir Humphry, born in 1936 and educated at Gordonstoun and Trinity College, Cambridge, served as a captain in the 10th Royal Hussars, participated in an Antarctic expedition in 1993, and is among other things President of the Northumberland National Park Search and Rescue team. His wife, Lady Katherine, whom he married in 1974, is a granddaughter of the fifth Earl Grey - whose seat was Howick in Northumberland. She traces descent from Sir Edward Grey, (a younger son of Sir Ralph Grey of Chillingham) who acquired Howick - where Greys had held land since 1319 - in the late 16th century.

The Wakefields have overseen an admirable programme of restoration at Chillingham, which they have opened to the public. Among other things, Chillingham now serves as a venue for events such as weddings, and medieval-style banquets. Moreover, holidaymakers can stay in the castle which contains a number of self-catering apartments.

Description

Chillingham Castle stands on a spur of high ground, and a short distance to the east a stream flows through a wooded valley. The castle is quadrangular, measures approximately 102 by 115ft (31 by 35m), and has angle towers rising between 52ft and 62ft (16m and 19m): their ground floors are vaulted.

The castle is entered from the north and the principal feature of the facade is a frontispiece dating from about 1620. It rises three storeys, has coupled Tuscan columns, and an entrance archway reached via a flight of steps.

Upon progressing through the north range, one enters the courtyard, which is paved with stone flagging. The courtyard is bounded to the south by a two-storeyed addition, likely erected in the 17th century, and comprising an open arcade and a closed upper storey surmounted by a terrace. The upper storey is approached via an open stair erected in the mid 18th century, but with 17th century stone balusters that were removed from bordering the southern moat prior to the construction of the arched tunnel mentioned above. The stair ascends to a doorway flanked by attached Ionic columns. Moreover, at a slightly lower level, corbels running along the façade either side of the stairway carry small statues, while above the doorway the balustrade of the terrace forms a gable with a seventh statue placed centrally: the statues are the remaining seven of the Nine Worthies that had previously lined the southern moat.

The Great Hall occupies the first floor of the south range and is reached from the courtyard via the stairs just mentioned. The hall is 21 ft (6.4m) wide and 60ft (18.3m) from east to west. On the whole, given its stone flagged floor, tapestries, armour and arrow slits, it has a strongly medieval atmosphere. Two early Georgian white marble fireplaces were installed here by Wyatville. Brought from Wanstead House in Essex, a house designed by Colen Campbell that was demolished in 1822, they are no longer visible for they were recently covered by mock fireplaces put in place by the makers of the award-winning film, *Elizabeth*, (a portrayal of Queen Elizabeth I, played by Cate Blanchett), part of which was filmed at Chillingham.

A doorway at the north-west end of the Great Hall opens to stairs that as-

30. The south side of the courtyard, showing the stairs leading to the Great Hall (Shaun Dodds: courtesy of Sir Humphry Wakefield)

cend to what is known as the Edward I room, located high in the south-west tower, and which has been restored in a manner said to accord with his period. On its west side is a small two-light Decorated window whose tracery, to quote Pevsner, 'points to 1344 rather than to an earlier date', that is, several decades after Edward I stayed at Chillingham. Of it, the late Herbert Honeyman has stated that it is 'the only visible untouched fourteenth century detail remaining on the exterior' of the castle.

At a lower level, the stairs give access to the James I Drawing Room, named after a monarch who visited Chillingham in 1617. Located above the west end of the Great Hall, the room's most notable feature is a good Jacobean ceiling with patterned ribs and pendants that was restored in 1988. To the east, and likewise in the south range, are the Library and Dining Room; both with 17th century chimneypieces.

From the Dining Room one heads northward into the Museum, in the east range, which houses a large assortment of material associated with the castle's history. After perusing its varied collection, one descends a spiral stair and arrives back in the Great Hall - this time in its north-east corner - en route to the former chapel located in the south-east corner tower.

Upon leaving the former place of worship, one heads northward into the Minstrels' Hall, located in the east range. This has a gallery at its south end from which one looks down into the body of the room. The Minstrels' Hall has two fireplaces and the overmantel of the principal fireplace has a relief of Susannah and the Elders. After descending from the gallery to the main part of the room, the Minstrels' Gallery is exited by walking into the courtyard.

From the courtyard the visitor enters a tunnel-vaulted cellar beneath the Great Hall. This has been transformed into a 'torture chamber', with a gruesome and illuminating display comprising an iron maiden and various other fiendish instruments designed to inflict suffering.

The castle grounds include long avenues of trees and terraces, as well as a formal Italian garden with clipped hedges of box and yew. The latter lies immediately to the west of the castle and dates from the days when Wyatville was employed at Chillingham. It has been lovingly restored on Sir Humphry Wakefield's behalf by Isobel Murray, a native of Northumberland who worked as a secretary in Edinburgh for some years before deciding to return to Northumberland to devote herself to landscape

31. The south-west tower from the Italian Garden
(Shaun Dodds: courtesy of Sir Humphry Wakefield)

gardening. In an article on Chillingham in the 26 July 1986 issue of *The Guardian* newspaper - in which the garden is described as 'a masterpiece of restoration' - Murray is quoted as saying: 'It was like going into a secret garden at first. You could see the actual outline of the garden under the growth, the original hedges were there. For the first couple of years it wasn't a gardening job at all, it was jungle clearance. I gave up all my other work to concentrate on it until the opening.'

Finally, a pleasant woodland walk leads south-eastward from the castle to an ornamental lake, before heading back towards the castle on the far side of the ravine mentioned above. En route, visitors may catch sight of deer and red squirrels, while snowdrops, bluebells and rhododendrons add colour to the walk in due season.

CORBRIDGE ROMAN SITE

Corbridge Roman Site is one of the best known Roman sites in the north of England and lies less than a mile (1.6km) north-west of the town of Corbridge. It is often thought to have been called *Corstopitum* in Roman times, though *Coriosopitum* is probably more accurate, and occupied a strategic position at the point where Dere Street, the main route north into Scotland, crossed the Tyne. Moreover, Corbridge lay at the junction of Dere Street and another Roman road, the Stanegate, which headed west towards Carlisle.

The area's association with the Romans began in the last quarter of the 1st century A.D. when Governor Agricola advanced into the region as part of his programme of extending Roman rule over the whole of Britain. In A.D. 79 members of Agricola's army established a fort and a bath house about half a mile (0.8km) north-west of the present site. The fort's ramparts were of earth or turf and its internal buildings of timber, whereas the baths were built of stone. The fort was a large installation erected to hold supplies for the army as it pushed on further into hostile country.

It was however replaced within a decade or so by one constructed on today's site, a terrace just above the River Tyne where the new fort could provide protection for Dere Street and control the point where the road crossed the river. Although remains of this turf and timber fort have been uncovered during excavation, none of it is visible. The fort, the first of a series of forts on the site, was larger than its successors and may have enclosed up to 16 acres (6.5 hectares) within its defences. In the centre of the fort were the headquarters, the commanding officer's house, accommodation

32. An aerial view of Corbridge from the east, showing the visible remains and the cropmarks of Roman roads beyond (Professor Norman McCord, University of Newcastle upon Tyne)

for administrative staff, a workshop and two granaries, while to the north and south were barracks.

At Hexham Abbey, not far from Corbridge, one can see the tombstone of a Roman soldier named Flavinus, a standard-bearer belonging to an approximately 500-strong unit of cavalry, the *Ala Petriana*, that is believed to have formed Corbridge's garrison in the late 1st century. The tombstone, one of the most impressive military tombstones from the region, depicts Flavinus in full uniform riding down a hapless barbarian. Its inscription states that Flavinus was 25 years old when he died and that he had completed seven years of service.

In the early years of the 2nd century, by which time the Roman frontier lay along the Tyne-Solway isthmus following the gradual abandonment of Scotland, the fort was dismantled and burnt, having evidently previously been reduced significantly in size. The fort's destruction is sometimes attributed to hostile forces, but some believe that it was deliberately destroyed by the Romans themselves. In about 105, a replacement rose from the ashes. It faced south towards the river crossing, as perhaps had its predecessor, and its internal buildings were wholly of timber.

Subsequently, in around 122, this fort was largely rebuilt and altered to some extent during a programme of restructuring the frontier: instead of having a line of isolated forts and signal stations linked by a road - the Stanegate - it had been decided to erect Hadrian's Wall, a continuous solid frontier which was thus constructed on an east-west axis about 2½ miles (4km) north of Corbridge, which is thought to have been garrisoned by infantry following its rebuilding. Forts were soon provided along the line of the Wall itself to accommodate troops and it was once thought that the rebuilt fort at Corbridge was therefore abandoned in favour of Halton Chesters (a fort on Hadrian's Wall) and perhaps provided with a 'caretaker garrison.' But according to M.C. Bishop and J.N. Dore, there is no archaeological evidence to support this view and so 'there is no reason to doubt continuity' at Corbridge.

In AD 139 Roman policy changed yet again. Emperor Antoninus Pius decided to occupy lowland Scotland. Consequently, the frontier moved to the narrow isthmus of land between the Clyde and the Firth of Forth, where the turf Antonine Wall was erected. The change of frontier did not mean that Corbridge was rendered redundant. Indeed, additional buildings were provided (inscriptions record construction work in 139-40) and the fort received a new garrison. For the first time in the series of forts at Corbridge, stone buildings were erected, although some structures were of timber (until large-scale restructuring of the site occurred around 158), or may have had timber superstructures as was the case with some buildings following the restructuring referred to. Turf and timber defences were however retained throughout the life of the fort.

The Antonine Wall was abandoned in about 163 and the frontier once again became Hadrian's Wall. Corbridge's military role now evidently largely ended - the ramparts were levelled at about this date and most of the internal buildings demolished - and the fort gave way instead to a new function for the site, that of a small town occupying about 27 acres, (11 hectares) although a small legionary depot lay in the nucleus of the settlement that was centred on the site of the previous fort. The development of the town, whose houses and other buildings lay along roads and lanes arranged in a roughly rectangular manner, was a gradual one and was evidently retarded by unrest that erupted in the region in around 182 when hostile tribes managed to make their way past Hadrian's Wall and wrought havoc, until their depredations were ended by an able and ruthless governor named Ulpius

Marcellus. Extensive burnt deposits have been uncovered at Corbridge and may well date from this period of turmoil.

Little is known about the history of Corbridge in the 3rd and 4th centuries. It appears to have survived until at least the close of the 4th century, and perhaps remained occupied well into the 5th following the Roman abandonment of Britain in the early years of that century.

Civilian inscriptions found at Corbridge indicate that its population was cosmopolitan. For instance, a high priestess dedicated an altar to Herakles in Greek, and there is another in Greek to Astarte, while a further inscription testifies to the presence of a Palmyrene merchant who seems to have supplied flags to the army.

Extensive excavations were conducted at Corbridge in the years 1906-14 and uncovered most of the plan of the Roman town plus a substantial amount of objects. Further excavation ensued, shedding additional light on the history of the site, while aerial photography has likewise contributed to our knowledge of Roman Corbridge.

Description

The first port of call is the site museum. This contains a wealth of information on the history of Roman Corbridge and many objects uncovered by excavation such as military equipment, inscriptions and sculpture. Here, too, one can see Samian ware, fine red tableware that was imported to Britain in enormous quantities from a number of potteries in Gaul from the beginning of the Roman occupation until the late 2nd century when large-scale importation ceased.

The museum is located in the north-west corner of the area open to the public, which is bisected by the Stanegate, the former main road of the Roman town, located on an east-west axis. But before reaching the road, one first sees the remains of a pair of granaries located immediately off the north side of the Stanegate. Construction work evidently commenced in about 180, but was likely only completed in the early 3rd century following an interruption, probably caused by the barbarian incursion quelled by Marcellus. That construction work did not progress smoothly can be deduced by, among other things, the different styles of work visible in the masonry.

The granaries were built to store large amounts of grain for lengthy periods and were filled from the street. Each had a loading platform - only that of the east granary survives - sheltered by a portico whose columns still stand beside the road, albeit in greatly truncated form. The granaries had stone-flagged floors (that of the west granary is the best preserved),

33. The granaries

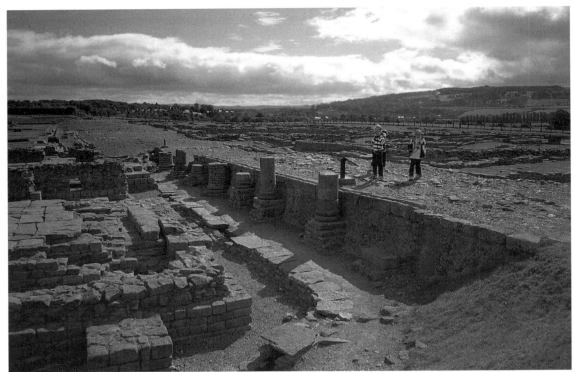

34. The Stanegate: note how the road level rose over the years until it was significantly higher than the bases of the columns of the porticoes which sheltered the loading bays of the granaries

and were well ventilated so that the grain could be kept cool and dry. The floors, for instance, were raised above ground level and supported by low walls with air reaching the underfloor area through vents in the main walls: one of the vents in the east granary contains a mullion, the only surviving mullion in a granary ventilator slot in Britain.

The level of the Stanegate is higher than it was originally (it was probably first laid down c. AD 90), for the road was resurfaced a number of times during the Roman period, the last such occurring some time after 364. In the vicinity of the granaries (and at the east end of the site) the surface is thus 4th century, but in the middle sections of the road much of the surface is earlier, for during early excavations material was removed as it contained pieces of re-used sculpture. The road surface is only exposed in the area open to visitors. Beyond this it lies under fields.

Upon progressing eastward down the Stanegate from the granaries one immediately comes to the remains of a fountain house, believed to have been erected at about the same time as work commenced on the granaries. It was an ornate structure whose pediment bore the inscription 'LEG XX VV FECIT' i.e., 'the Twentieth Legion, called Valeria Victrix, built this.' The fountain house was the principal distribution point for the public water supply. Here, a large aeration tank contained water that flowed into it from the north along an enclosed aqueduct located parallel to the granaries. From the aeration tank (where the water's freshness was restored by contact with air after its journey along the aqueduct) the water was discharged through spouts into a large stone trough beside the main road. Just set back from the trough, and flanking the aeration tank, were two statues, the pedestals of which can still be seen.

East of the former fountain house, and again on the north side of the main road, lies what is known as Site 11, consisting of the remains of a courtyard building likely started c.180. It occupies nearly an acre, (0.4 hectare) that is, over a quarter of the entire present site. Little other than the foundations have survived of the large square building, which was ranged around a central courtyard, and different interpretations have been offered as to its function. Initially it was thought to have been a forum, the main administrative building of a Roman town. Subsequently, it was suggested that it was a storehouse forming part of a military depot, while more recently still it has been proposed that it could have been a market. Evidently, construction work was never completed: work on the north range for instance appears not to have proceeded beyond foundation level. On this point, J.N. Dore comments: 'The reason the building was never finished was probably the serious unrest in the province, which occurred towards the end of the second century AD. There is evidence of fire at about this time in a number of places at Corbridge, though whether this was the result of direct enemy action or organised Roman withdrawal is uncertain.'

Within the courtyard lie the partial remains of two earlier stone buildings, ones belonging to the final phases of the series of forts erected at Corbridge. The western remains are those of offices and a shrine room belonging to a headquarters building. Those to the east are the remains of a commanding officer's house.

In 1964, during excavations of the early forts at Corbridge, the remains of a wooden chest were uncovered under the south-east corner of the courtyard of Site 11 near what was probably a workshop or storebuilding. It contained a mixture of weapons and other objects, either bundled up in cloth or tied with string, and buried in the first half of the 2nd century, perhaps around 120 or shortly thereafter.

Its contents included parts of at least six folded up sets of segmental breastplates, as well as a scabbard, catapult bolts, spearheads, saws, chisels, a crowbar and gaming counters and other objects. Many of the items were damaged and it has thus been suggested that they likely formed the scrap-metal contents of the supposed workshop which were assembled together and then buried for subsequent use when the fort was evacuated by its unit.

Of the hoard, Stephen Johnson comments: 'It is ironic that the modern study of this scrap metal, painstakingly carried out over several years, should have led to a significant advance in our knowledge of how the segmental breastplates functioned, and, for those with an interest in Roman armour at least, form one of the most significant groups of material found anywhere within the Roman world.'

In places the ground south of the Stanegate undulates significantly, the result of subsidence over ditches that are believed to have been part of the southern defences of the fort following its reduction in size at about the beginning of the 2nd century. The area south of the road mostly contains the low remains of various buildings that were located in two legionary compounds built c.200 or shortly thereafter, enclosures walled off from the surrounding town: several buildings fronting the main road pre-date the construction of the compound walls and lie outside them. The compounds are divided by a side street branching off the Stanegate and the main entrances to them are located towards the south end of this street. In the 3rd or 4th century the compounds were linked by building a wall across the north end of the side street.

35. The undulating nature of the ground in the compounds

The nature of the remains in the east compound is mostly very fragmentary. One of the buildings appears to have been a workshop - it had several hearths and furnaces - while a further structure was perhaps a barrack block. The most substantial remains within the compound are of residential accommodation, likely that of officers in command of the legionaries who formed the garrison of the compounds, legionaries who perhaps performed administrative, financial and policing duties in the frontier area.

Immediately to the right of the main entrance of the west compound are the low remains of a small building that pre-dated the compound. It is thought to have been a temple. It had a portico at its east end, an apse at the west end, and was a well built structure, the inner faces of whose walls were plastered. To the north and south of this structure were buildings that evidently functioned as workshops for part of their existence. At the west end of the compound are the remains of what was evidently a headquarters building. It experienced significant alteration during its history and had an underground strongroom, much of which has survived.

To the north of the headquarters building, and opposite the granaries mentioned above, lie the remains of what are thought to have been temples, as well as one building known as the 'Pottery Shop' on account of the quantity of pottery found here. These buildings lay outside the west compound.

Of Corbridge, Stephen Johnson comments: 'Many highly crafted sculptured stones have

36. The temple

been found at the site. One of the best known, the Corbridge lion - in origin probably a tombstone, with a favourite motif of the lion devouring its prey - was found re-used as a fountain in one of the substantial houses on the terrace overlooking the river. Other sculptured stones, mainly of religious character, are of startling quality.' The reference to houses on the terrace overlooking the Tyne (houses whose remains are not visible) is a reminder that visitors to Roman Corbridge only see a fraction of what once existed.

Corbridge Roman Site is in the care of English Heritage.

37. The strongroom of the headquarters in the west compound

CRAGSIDE

C ragside is arguably one of the most enchanting places in Britain. Located in the heart of Northumberland on high ground above Rothbury, it comprises a fascinating house and a well-wooded picturesque estate of over 1,700 acres (688 hectares) largely surrounded by bleak moorland. The house and estate are the creation of a remarkable man, the first Lord Armstrong, one of the greatest of all Victorians, who transformed Cragside into a veritable paradise.

The creator of Cragside, William George Armstrong, was of middle class birth. He came into the world on 26 November 1810 in Newcastle, the second child and only son of a local corn merchant, while his mother was the daughter of a man who owned a colliery in the village of Walbottle.

As a child, Armstrong did not enjoy robust health for he had a bad chest. He attended schools in and near Newcastle before attending a grammar school at Bishop Auckland in County Durham. His father wished him to become a lawyer and hoped that he would join the firm of a prominent Newcastle solicitor, Armorer Donkin, the family's closest friend. Although interested in mechanics, in 1828 Armstrong did indeed take articles under Donkin before travelling to London to receive a legal training at the hands of his own brother-in-law, William Watson, a Special Pleader at Lincoln's Inn.

In 1833 he returned to Newcastle and became a partner in Donkin's law firm. Yet he still retained his interest in mechanics and experimentation. Years later he recalled: 'All the time, although I had no idea of abandoning the law and regularly attended to my professional duties, I was an amateur scientist, constantly experimenting and studying in my leisure time.'

During his days in Bishop Auckland, he had met the Ramshaws, a family of builders and engineers and in 1835 he married Margaret Ramshaw, three years his senior, and they moved to Jesmond, a village that became part of Newcastle that year and soon became the residential suburb for Newcastle's wealthiest inhabitants.

It was in 1835, moreover, that Armstrong became keenly interested in the subject of hydraulics, that is of harnessing water power as effectively as possible. He subsequently became particularly fascinated by the idea of using water power to produce electricity, a subject on which he corresponded with no less a figure than Michael Faraday.

At the beginning of 1847, shortly after being elected a Fellow of the Royal Society, (Britain's oldest and most prestigious scientific society), Armstrong abandoned his legal career. Together with several partners, one of whom was Donkin, he established W.G. Armstrong & Company, which soon had works at Elswick on the western outskirts of Newcastle. A wide variety of equipment and machinery was manufactured by the company in the early years of its existence, including dock gates, steam engines and most important of all, hydraulic cranes.

In the 1850s Armstrong became involved in a new field of endeavour - designing and producing artillery that was superior to the ponderous, inaccurate and outmoded heavy ordnance whose limitations had been revealed during the Crimean War. Armstrong's first gun appeared in 1855. It was a breech-loading weapon with a rifled barrel made of wrought

38. A view of the house from the south-west

iron and fired an elongated cylindrical projectile rather than cannonballs: not for nothing has it been said that modern artillery dates from 1855. However, acceptance of Armstrong's gun was not forthcoming by the British military until late 1858 and the following year - in which he was knighted - Armstrong established the Elswick Ordnance Company to manufacture his gun for the British government: in 1863 the ordnance and engineering works at Elswick merged. The gun was also made for export and among foreign orders that followed were ones from both the Confederates and Unionists during the American Civil War.

In 1863 the 52-year-old Sir William Armstrong began buying land above Rothbury, the nucleus of the future Cragside estate which then merely consisted of a vast expanse of bare moorland overlooking the upper reaches of the River Coquet.

He was no stranger to the area. As a child he had regularly visited Rothbury where his family had stayed at a house owned by Donkin. In 1888, Armstrong recalled, 'my earliest recollections consist of paddling in the Coquet, gathering pebbles on its gravel beds, and climbing amongst the rocks on the Crag.' Such visits had benefited his precarious health. 'More than once', he recollected, 'an apparently incurable cough was quickly removed by coming to Rothbury, and had it not been for its curative effect there would have been no Cragside at this day.'

His love for Rothbury and Upper Coquetdale in general was deep and abiding, but such was the pressure of work following the establishment of W.G. Armstrong & Company in 1847 that he was not able to visit the area frequently. Indeed, in 1863 when he visited Rothbury with business partners, it was the first time that he had been to the picturesque town for fifteen years.

Now, acting on impulse, he set about buying up as much land as possible in the Debdon valley, just east of Rothbury, beginning with a piece of land 20 acres (8.1 hectares) in extent. Moreover he soon built a modest residence, a lodge suitable for shooting or fishing parties, on a hillside overlooking the ravine of the Debdon burn that flows through the site. Subsequently, moreover, he transformed the nature of the ground by for example providing lakes, planting a wealth of shrubs and predominantly coniferous trees, and having hundreds of large round boulders manhandled into position to form a rock garden between the house and the Debdon burn. In connection with this process Armstrong recalled that 'it had been a pleasure to me to add to the locality's natural beauty by operations which have given healthy employment to a large section of the population.' Lady Armstrong was heavily involved in the landscaping scheme for she was a keen and able gardener with whom her husband had already engaged in landscaping and planting at Jesmond.

Of Cragside, William Weaver Tomlinson wrote in 1888:

'Words are inadequate to describe the wonderful transformation which Lord Armstrong has made on the barren hill-side as it existed previous to 1863. Every natural advantage has been utilized by the great magician. Shrubs and trees that grow best in exposed situations have been planted among the boulders of Cragside with admirable results. Rhododendrons, azaleas, and other plants of rich coloured bloom, with native heather, bracken and ling, soften and brighten the hard features of the landscape till it smiles again.'

Meanwhile, in 1869 Armstrong had engaged the services of Norman Shaw to enlarge the house. Born in Edinburgh in 1831, Shaw was the most gifted of all later Victorian architects, although in 1869 he was little known despite having already designed Leyswood in West Sussex, (built in 1868-9) a house for which he achieved celebrity not long after turning his attention to Cragside, which resembles Leyswood in some respects.

After enlarging Cragside, by extending the north front, Shaw was called upon to make further additions. In all, three campaigns of building occurred, ending in 1884, about ten years after Armstrong had begun residing at Cragside for most of the year. It was in 1884, moreover, that the Prince and Princess of Wales visited Cragside while engaged on a tour of the North East.

At Cragside Armstrong used his technological genius to the full. As Andrew Saint comments, 'he created the most extensive and ingenious hydraulic system ever found on a country estate, one that pumped water, turned spits, powered a saw-mill, farm machinery and a dairy, made silage and, eventually, ran a dynamo providing electric light.' Indeed, in the late 1870s Cragside was the first house in the world to be lit by water-generated electricity.

In 1887, in Queen Victoria's Golden Jubilee Honours List, Armstrong was elevated to the peerage as the first Baron Armstrong of Cragside. Some years later, in 1894, he purchased Bamburgh Castle on the coast of Northumberland. By this date he was a widower (his wife had died the previous year) and he acquired Bamburgh with the aim of converting it into a convalescent home to honour her memory.

Lord Armstrong died at Cragside on 27 December 1900, leaving a fortune of £1,400,682 gross and over 10,000 acres (4,047 hectares) in Northumberland. In character he was a self-possessed, well-adjusted man with a calm, modest, kindly disposition. Moreover, although it must be conceded that he played his hand badly during an engineers' strike in 1871, on the whole he was noted for his loyalty, good judgement of men and generosity.

His marriage had proved childless and so his title died with him. Cragside and other property passed to his great-nephew, William Henry Watson-Armstrong, who had lived at Cragside since the 1880s and had been formally adopted as Armstrong's heir in 1889. In 1903 he was ennobled as the first Baron Armstrong of Bamburgh and Cragside. Together with his wife, he divided his time between Cragside, Bamburgh and the south of France. But their lavish lifestyle suffered a reverse in 1908. Risky business ventures turned sour, leaving Lord Armstrong facing debts of over half a million pounds. He thus sold off some of Cragside's finest assets such as paintings by Constable, Turner and Millais collected by his great-uncle.

The first Lord Armstrong of the second creation died in 1941 and was succeeded by a son who died in 1972. Following this, Cragside remained the home of the Armstrong family until 1977 when the third Lord Armstrong forsook it in favour of Bamburgh Castle and the house and 911 acres (369 hectares) of the estate were transferred to the National Trust. In 1987 (eight years after the house was first opened to the public) the third Lord Armstrong of Bamburgh and Cragside died, whereupon the title became extinct.

39. The entrance front

Description

Cragside has been aptly described as the most dramatic Victorian mansion in the north of England. It stands in a commanding position on a shelf of high ground expressly quarried out of the hillside and is overlooked by woodland, while immediately to the west the ground falls steeply away towards the picturesque Debdon burn that flows through the estate and, within sight of the house, the ravine is crossed by a steel footbridge just over 150ft (46m) long dating from the early 1870s and presumably manufactured at Armstrong's Elswick Works.

The core of the house dates from 1864 and is by an unknown architect. But of course what makes Cragside impressive is the work of the talented Norman Shaw who transformed the house into a remarkable structure with a marked Tudor accent. 'The site is Wagnerian', wrote the late Sir Nikolaus Pevsner, 'and so is here Shaw's architecture . . . . What he was concerned with was high picturesqueness for his design, and he has without doubt achieved it.'

The house is approached from the north - after passing Tumbleton Lake located at the entrance to the estate - but is entered from the south after heading through a service court-yard partly enclosed by the house.

The arched entrance lies towards the west end of the south front and opens to the modest Entrance Hall, from whose north side one progresses to the service rooms. The most notable of these is the Kitchen, in the centre of the east side of the ground floor and reached from the Entrance Hall via a back corridor. Among other things, it has a massive 'Eagle' range by H. Walker & Son and a hydraulically turned spit and roasting fire. Stairs in a corner of the large room lead down to the scullery and game larder. At this level, moreover, in a short passage off the scullery one can see the Scotch turbine that worked the Kitchen spit above. From here one can also see into the Jigger Room (accessible via steps in the service courtyard), which houses a hydraulic ram that powered a lift mainly used by servants engaged in such tasks as carrying coal from the basement to fireplaces in rooms on other floors.

From the Kitchen, the back corridor heads north passed the Butler's Room to the Dining Room, at the north end of the ground floor. The Dining Room, which can also be reached via the main corridor that runs directly to it from the Entrance Hall, is one of the finest rooms at Cragside and terminates with a broad bay window. Its decoration includes oak panelling and at dado level, panels are carved with intricate reliefs of fauna and flora. The wallpaper, in two shades of green, is not original but was especially made to resemble the initial wallpaper supplied to Cragside in 1872. The focal point of the room is the recessed fireplace on the east side, set back behind a large broad stone Gothic arch and flanked by small stained-glass windows with figures representing the Four Seasons. Among paintings adorning the room is one of Lord Armstrong by Henry Hetherington Emmerson, a Newcastle artist much patronised by the founder of Cragside. Painted in the early 1880s, it portrays the yet to be ennobled Armstrong sitting in the inglenook reading a newspaper, wearing slippers and accompanied by two dogs.

A doorway in the south-west corner of the room opens to the Inner Hall - located at the north end of the main corridor - and this gives access to the Library, a large room that adjoins the west side of the Dining Room and enjoys splendid views of the Debdon ravine, in particular ones provided by a bay window at the north-west end. The top lights of the bay window have some excellent stained-glass by the firm of Morris & Company: the panels depict figures such as Dante, Chaucer, Spenser and Milton as well as episodes from the life of St George. The walls are partly panelled in light oak and small panels are ornamented with reliefs of plants and animals. Furthermore, there is an ornate beamed and coffered ceiling. Some of the finest paintings of Lord Armstrong's collection used to hang in this room. Pictures by minor members of the Pre-Raphaelite school now do so. They are all on loan with the exception of a painting by Rafael Sorbi that Armstrong acquired in 1869. From 1880, the Library was the first room in the world provided with a permanent system of incandescent electric lighting powered by a hydroelectric generator that Armstrong had installed in the grounds. Below the Library, and reached via stairs from off the Inner Hall, is a Turkish bath-suite at basement level.

When heading south along the main corridor, whose walls are covered with orna-mented glazed earthenware tiles, one sees three rooms ranged along the west side of the passage. The southernmost is the Study, an attractive room with a moulded plaster ceiling, a partly gilt cornice, red wallpaper and an unimposing chimneypiece of marbled slate. Hanging in the room is a portrait of Armstrong by James Ramsay, painted in 1831 when Armstrong was a law student.

A modest staircase off the Entrance Hall and located in the south-west corner of the house, leads up to rooms on the first floor such as the Boudoir and Morning Room. The former, located at the top of the stairs, contains watercolours and drawings that rank among the finest in the house and include several views of Cragside, whereas the Morning Room, above the Library and reached via a long corridor, contains part of Armstrong's collection of exotic butterflies.

At the south end of the corridor just mentioned are stairs that ascend to the Gallery, which runs eastward along the top of most of the entrance front. Originally Armstrong's personal museum, it was transformed into a picture gallery by 1879 and most of the paintings are portraits of the family. However, many will probably find a painting of an attractive local girl selling oranges the most appealing work. It its a charming piece by Edward Patry and dates from 1885. Marble busts are also on display.

Stairs at the inner end of the Gallery ascend to the 'Guest Chambers' or 'Owl Suite', rooms located directly under the gables of the south-west corner of the house and used as their suite by the Prince and Princess of Wales when visiting Cragside in 1884.

At the far end of the Gallery is Cragside's most impressive room, the magnificent Drawing Room, added to the south-east end of the house in 1883-4 and jutting boldly south of the entrance front. Its most eye-catching feature is a massive, indeed breathtaking,

40. The magnificent Drawing Room (Andreas von Einsiedel, © The National Trust)

41. One of Cragside's lakes

elaborately carved Italian marble chimneypiece with neo-Renaissance detailing. It was designed by William Lethaby, a former pupil of Shaw, and is said to weigh ten tons. The cream of Armstrong's collection of paintings hung in this room, such as Millais' superb *Chill October,* purchased by Armstrong in 1875 and described by him as 'the finest landscape that has been produced in the present generation.' Sadly, in common with many of the finest pieces belonging to the Armstrong collection, it was sold by his successor in 1910.

The Drawing Room is adjoined to the east by the Billiard Room (which dates from 1895 and was designed by Frederick Waller) and to the north of which is the Gun Room, a contemporaneous room by the same architect: it contains the first Lord Armstrong's collection of stuffed birds.

In addition to the house, the estate contains several lesser buildings of historic and technical interest. One such is the Tumbleton Ram House, 400 yds (366m) to the north-west of the house and located just beneath Tumbleton Lake. The building dates from around 1866 - the year Armstrong dammed the Debdon burn at this point to create the lake - and housed a hydraulic engine that drove a pair of pumps which pumped water up to a reservoir 200ft (61m) above the house. The water then flowed down into the house where it was used for domestic purposes such as powering labour-saving equipment including the spit in the Kitchen and the hydraulic lift. The Cragside estate also has a number of fine walks, drives, lakes and a wealth of rhododendron bushes which delight many visitors when in bloom from late May until mid June.

Cragside is in the care of the National Trust.

DUNSTANBURGH CASTLE

The windswept ruins of Dunstanburgh Castle, which occupy a larger area than any other castle in Northumberland, stand on the coast and present a majestic spectacle when approached from the south by walking along a grass track from the village of Craster.

Dunstanburgh Castle was part of the barony of Embleton and was built during the reign of Edward II, which witnessed bitter Anglo-Scottish conflict that included raids into Northumberland by forces from north of the border. Construction work commenced in 1313 and the castle was evidently in use by 1319 at the latest. It was built by Thomas Plantagenet, Earl of Lancaster, whose father had been granted the barony of Embleton by Henry III. At Dunstanburgh, Lancaster employed the services of a master mason named Elias, who had been trained in the school of Master James of St George, the celebrated architect of Edward I's great castles in Wales such as Harlech, a castle with which Dunstanburgh has close similarities.

Thomas of Lancaster was no ordinary earl. He was a grandson of Henry III and therefore a cousin of Edward II, while his mother had been Queen of Navarre. In short, he was the richest earl in England, enjoying vast estates and the power that went with such wealth. His annual income has been estimated at over £11,000, surpassed only by that of the king.

In 1311 Lancaster was the principal figure involved in compelling Edward, a weak, foolish monarch, to accept measures known as the Ordinances, regulations ordained by a committee of magnates and intended to safeguard the interests of the realm. The following

42. Dunstanburgh Castle, as seen when approaching from the south

year Lancaster was the ringleader in events which culminated in the seizure and judicial murder of the king's favourite, the much-hated Piers Gaveston, something that inevitably increased the level of animosity Edward felt for his cousin.

It was in such circumstances, with Thomas of Lancaster embroiled in political discord with Edward II, and with his northern lands subjected to Scottish incursions, that Lancaster began building Dunstanburgh Castle in 1313: stone commenced being quarried for the task on 7 May. One of the cart horses used to carry building material to Dunstanburgh was seized by Scottish raiders and Henry Summerson suggests that perhaps one of Lancaster's motives for building Dunstanburgh was to remind Edward II that 'the defence of his realm against invasion, was what he should be attending to, instead of engaging in bitter quarrels with most of the English nobility.'

In 1314 Edward was soundly defeated by the Scots at Bannockburn when engaged in an invasion of Scotland. As a result, his reputation sank even lower, rendering him at the mercy of his political enemies in England, chief of whom was his powerful and ambitious cousin who had played no part in the campaign. Hence Thomas and his faction of baronial friends and supporters were very much in the ascendant. The king had to sit back and watch as positions of importance were filled by friends and supporters of his cousin.

Fortunately for Edward, Lancaster's dominance soon waned. He proved an inept, supine character and other men came to the fore. His personal life also proved a failure. In 1317 his wife, Alice, (from whom he had derived much of his wealth), left him to live with a lame squire of no great birth, whom she was to marry in 1322.

Lancaster's end was violent. Together with other discontented nobles he rose in revolt in 1322, only to be defeated at Boroughbridge in Yorkshire when falling back towards Dunstanburgh. Taken to nearby Pontefract Castle, one of his own fortresses, he was sentenced to death as a traitor. On the morning of 22 March he was led out of the castle, wearing penitential garb, and beheaded in front of a jeering crowd, some of whom had pelted him with snowballs.

Another famous individual associated with Dunstanburgh Castle is John of Gaunt, who was created Duke of Lancaster in 1362 and was a leading figure in the history of England in the late 14th century. Born in Ghent in 1340, he was a younger son of Edward III and in 1359 married Blanche, a daughter of Henry Plantagenet (the nephew of Dunstanburgh's founder) who had been created Duke of Lancaster in 1351 and died ten years later. Interestingly, Blanche died of plague in September 1369 when still young and within months of her death Geoffrey Chaucer composed one of his earliest masterpieces, an elegiac poem known as the *Book of the Duchess*.

In the early 1380s, John of Gaunt made radical alterations to the castle, employing firstly the services of the distinguished northern architect John Lewyn, and secondly those of Henry Holme. The former, whom Gaunt took into his employ in 1380, had completed his task by 17 July 1381 and was evidently responsible for constructing a mantlet wall that created an inner courtyard or ward immediately to the north of the gatehouse. Subsequently, on 1 December of the same year, Gaunt commissioned Holme to work at Dunstanburgh on his behalf, work that was evidently completed by 20 July 1383 when Gaunt authorised the payment of £20 to Holme for making, among other things, a secondary gatehouse and 'six houses with six vaults, six chimneys, and windows pertaining to the said houses.' The gatehouse, located at the north-east corner of the inner ward, was evidently a replacement for one that had led from that courtyard to the main ward, while the houses may have been built within the inner ward to accommodate members of Gaunt's retinue.

But this was not all. On that very day - 20 July 1383 - Holme was engaged by Gaunt to undertake more work at Dunstanburgh. His task? - to construct a vaulted gatehouse that would serve as a new entrance to the castle, one located along the west curtain wall at a point immediately to the north of the inner ward and therefore opening directly into the main enclosure or outer ward. The resulting gatehouse was approached from the south via a barbican erected parallel to the west side of the original gatehouse and the inner ward. This led to a forebuilding (or inner barbican as it is sometimes called) in front of the new gatehouse where one had to turn 90 degrees to enter the outer ward. From here, to reach Thomas of Lancaster's former imposing gatehouse - which was transformed into a keep and its entrance passage blocked up - one had to head eastward, turn right, and then right again, in order to enter the inner ward en route to the main apartments. Hence, as a result of Gaunt's reorganization of the castle, the apartments in the former gatehouse were rendered more remote and as Malcolm Hislop comments, 'access to them could not only be subject- ed to a sustained defence, but, in addition, it echoed the staged and drawn out approaches to the chambers of the lord that are to be found in other fourteenth century castles.'

In February 1399 John of Gaunt died, shortly after his heir, Henry, had been banished from England by Richard II. Henry soon returned from exile however, rallied support, and overthrew Richard later in the year, becoming King Henry IV in the process. Although thus in Crown hands, Dunstanburgh subsequently suffered neglect. In 1427 it was described by its newly appointed constable as being in a 'ruinous condition'. Extensive repairs were undertaken as a result.

Dunstanburgh played a part in the subsequent Wars of the Roses. In the autumn of 1461 it submitted to Yorkist forces, but its Lancastrian constable Sir Ralph Percy, (a younger son of the second Earl of Northumberland), was allowed to remain in command in the belief that he would prove loyal to new masters. It proved a vain hope. Late 1462 found Percy throwing in his lot again with the Lancastrian party following the arrival of Margaret of Anjou from France (see page 35) and so Yorkist troops moved north and besieged Dunstan- burgh, whose garrison surrendered conditionally on Christmas Eve.

After swearing allegiance to the Yorkist king, Edward IV, Percy was allowed to retain command of Dunstanburgh. But in March 1463 he allowed a Franco-Scottish force to occupy both Dunstanburgh and Bamburgh Castle, of which he was likewise now in command. Subsequently, after the defeat of a Lancastrian army at Hexham in May of the following year, (by which time Percy had been killed in a previous encounter), Dunstanburgh was surrendered to the Yorkist Earl of Warwick, none other than the 'Kingmaker', who spent the feast of the Nativity of St John the Baptist (24 June) in the castle.

In subsequent years Dunstanburgh was neglected again. In fact in about 1524 materials were removed and used to repair the castle of Wark on Tweed. In 1538 Leland wrote that 'Dunstunburght' was 'a very ruinous house and of small strength', with the only accommo- dation being afforded by the keep and the Lilburn Tower, both of which were in need of repair. In 1550 Sir Robert Bowes described the castle as being 'in wonderfull great decaye.' Limited repairs were subsequently undertaken, but further deterioration then followed for the castle was no longer deemed of use.

In 1929 Sir Arthur Sutherland, the last in a long and diverse line of private owners of Dunstanburgh dating from the early 17th century when James I had sold the castle, gave it into the hands of the Ministry of Works.

43. The stark remains of Thomas of Lancaster's great gatehouse

Description

Dunstanburgh Castle stands on a dolerite headland, which terminates on its north side in a 100ft (30m) cliff that plunges towards the North Sea. Although the ground falls away less steeply to the east, natural protection was provided here by a rocky foreshore. To the west the gradient is sufficient to have been a serious obstacle to would-be assailants, (for good measure a ditch was nevertheless dug along the west side of the castle), and it was only from the south that an attack could be launched without difficulty.

It is here, in the south-west corner of the defences, which enclose an area of 11 acres (nearly 4.5 hectares), that one finds the impressive gatehouse, a majestic spectacle and the chief glory of the castle: a forebuilding erected in front of the gatehouse no longer exists.

The gatehouse comprised a tunnel-vaulted entrance passage flanked by two great towers. The towers had semicircular projections to the fore that were five storeys high and thus two storeys higher than the main part of the gatehouse. Furthermore, high up on their inner sides each of the projections had a square stair turret attached that rose even higher. The gatehouse also possessed tall turrets further back, at the north-east and north-west corners, where spiral staircases rose from ground level.

The entrance passage was protected by strong wooden gates and a portcullis. At ground floor level, each of the towers has a porter's lodge (that to the west has a cell beneath its floor that likely served as a prison), and one large semicircular chamber that

44. The first floor of the gatehouse
(Andrew Stephenson)

would have been a guardroom. The function of the rooms on the first floor is unclear. Two of the rooms were in the towers and perhaps accommodated leading members of the garrison whilst the third, located above the gate passage, appears to have been entirely devoted to defensive purposes. It was here that the portcullis was raised and lowered. Openings in the south wall enabled missiles to be discharged against assailants below, or water to be dropped to quench flames if the wooden gates had been set alight. The second floor is known to have contained the Great Hall, with the kitchen to the west and the great chamber to the east. The Great Hall was separated from the adjoining rooms by timber-framed partitions and was a stately chamber with windows to north and south.

The gatehouse passage leads to a small enclosure, John of Gaunt's inner ward. It contained, among other things, a well, oven and lodgings. In the north-east corner is a much-ruined tower which protected a gateway opening into the inner ward from the main enclosure.

The south curtain wall, running east from the original gatehouse, still stands to a good height and roughly midway along its length is the Constable's Tower, the residence of the castle's commanding officer. It is a well-built three-storey structure with a spiral stair in its north-east corner and a fireplace on each floor. Adjacent to this are the foundations of a number of small buildings formerly used by the constable and his staff. The foundations of other buildings are known to lie buried on either side of the visible remains.

Continuing along the curtain wall, one comes to a projecting square turret that provided flanking fire along the south curtain, and beyond which lies the Egyncleugh Tower in the south-east angle of the defences. This had a gateway which gave access (via a drawbridge over a moat) to the coastline and a small port that developed to the south of the castle. Above the gateway, the Egyncleugh Tower had two upper floors reached by a spiral staircase. Each had a single room with a fireplace, a latrine and at least one window.

Running north from the Egyncleugh Tower is the east curtain wall, overlooking the rocky foreshore. This is lower than the south curtain and the quality of the masonry is poorer and it has been suggested that this section of the defences was erected by the peasantry of local villages performing labour service for their lord. The wall has two posterns and three garderobes: the latter were probably used by local people who sought shelter in the outer ward during times of trouble. Approximately halfway along the east wall's length, the outline of a large rectangular enclosure can be seen just to the west. This may have enclosed a vegetable garden. Running along its west side are the foundations of a building that was presumably used for storing produce, either from the supposed garden or from the barony of Embleton.

Given the strong natural defences on the north side of the castle in the form of the sheer cliff, strong defences were never required at this point. A now vanished wall is known to have existed here - it is mentioned in a 16th century source and was only 7½ft (2.3m) high - and was no doubt intended to prevent livestock or people from falling over the clifftop.

And what of the west curtain wall? This is in a fragmentary condition but the most notable feature along its length - the Lilburn Tower - still stands to an impressive height. It is a projecting rectangular three-storey structure, with taller angle turrets formally

45. Lilburn Tower, as viewed from near the north-east corner of the defences, a view showing the strong protection afforded to the north side of the castle by the steep cliff

connected by stepped parapets. It was built, or more probably completed, by John Lilburn who was appointed keeper of Dunstanburgh in 1323. Its ground floor likely held provisions, while some of the garrison were doubtless accommodated on the upper floors, where each storey appears to have consisted of a single large chamber with a fireplace, well executed two-light windows, and a latrine: two garderobe-shutes resting on corbels are against the exterior face of the west wall. At first floor level, moreover, the east wall was punctured by a passage forming part of the wall-walk of the curtain wall, enabling members of the garrison in the tower to rapidly man the curtain if thought necessary.

Upon progressing southward from this point, the remains of Gaunt's gatehouse are visible. Only vestiges of the building and its associated structures remain, but in their day they would have proved a formidable obstacle to anyone trying to assault the castle at this point.

Dunstanburgh Castle is in the care of English Heritage.

46. Lilburn Tower

ETAL CASTLE

E tal Castle stands beside the River Till in northern Northumberland and guarded a bridge over the Till on what was then the main road north to Cornhill or Wark, thereby witnessing a great deal of coming and going.

The castle was once the residence of the Manners family, which is known to have been connected with Etal by the mid 13th century. In 1250, for instance, a Robert Manners is said to have held the manor of Etal from Robert Muschamp, whose barony was centred on Wooler.

In 1341 another Robert Manners applied to Edward III for permission to fortify his residence here, a decision perhaps partly inspired by rivalry with the neighbouring Heron family of Ford who had received permission to fortify their residence in 1338.

In 1355, the year after Robert Manners' death, Etal was described as a 'fortalice', leading to the suggestion that at this date the tower-house that forms the heart of the castle stood alone. If so, the fortifications were soon extended by the creation of a curtain wall enclosing a substantial area and complete with at least one tower and a gatehouse. In 1368, Etal was described as a castle.

The head of the family at this time was Robert's son, John, who by 1402 had in turn been succeeded by his own son called Robert, a popular family name. During his lifetime, a feud between the Manners family and the Herons reached boiling point. Of the dispute, I.S. Nelson comments: 'Nothing is known of the origins of the feud but, judging by the number of sympathetic supporters each side could count upon, it is possible that at the heart of the feud lay a tangled web of boundary disputes and feudal rights.'

In 1427 it was alleged that Robert Manners' son and heir had killed William Heron of Ford and one of his companions. A commission was established to investigate the grievances between the two parties, with Heron's widow maintaining that her husband had been 'maliciously slayne' by John Manners. Not so, argued Manners. Heron had brought his death upon himself. He had come to Etal at the head of an armed following and had led a 'gret assaut made in shotyng of arrowes and stryking with swerdes' and had been killed as a result, though not by Manners, who maintained that he was over a spear's length away when the fatal blow was struck. Judgement was nevertheless given against John Manners, whom the commission reported 'repented' of Heron's death. He had to pay Heron's widow 250 marks and undertook to find a chantry priest to say 500 masses for her late husband's soul. Acrimony between the two families persisted for another decade or so, nonetheless.

John Manners predeceased his father. Hence upon the latter's death in 1438, Etal passed to John's younger brother, Robert, who inherited a denuded patrimony. Doubtless due to a combination of Scottish raids and the feud, Etal Castle was in a dilapidated state and the estate likewise in a poor condition. Robert, a vigorous character, turned the situation around. He also served alongside Sir Henry Percy and received a knighthood for the part he played in assisting him with Border affairs. He died in 1461.

In 1513, during the Flodden campaign, James IV of Scotland captured Etal Castle. Shortly thereafter, James and his army were defeated not far away by an English force at Flodden Field and the captured Scottish artillery was brought to Etal following the battle and stored for a while.

47. Etal Castle, with the gatehouse in the foreground and the tower-house to the rear

It was in 1513 that the then head of the Manners family, George Manners, (who held the title, Lord Roos), died. He appears to have ceased residing at Etal during his headship of the family and subsequent heads of the line likewise lived elsewhere, but Etal Castle remained the possession of the family.

By 1541 its condition was poor. Commissioners responsible for surveying Northumberland's fortifications observed: 'The castle of Etal . . . is for lacke of reparacons in very great decaye and many necessary houses within the same become ruynous and fallen to the ground.' A few years later, in 1547, Thomas Manners, who had been created Earl of Rutland, exchanged the property for lands elsewhere and Etal became the property of the Crown.

In 1564 the Marquis of Winchester visited Etal and observed, 'the Queen's house at Etal is greatly decayed, scant able to lodge the captain.' In 1584 royal commissioners again commented likewise, Etal was 'decaied for want of reparacion of longe contynciance.'

Since 1908, when the first Lord Joicey purchased the estate, Etal has belonged to the Joicey family.

Description

In its final form, Etal Castle was roughly 164ft (50m) square, with a curtain wall linking a substantial gatehouse in the south-east angle of the defences with a tower-house located diametrically opposite.

Some believe that the four-storey tower-house dates from the 13th or early 14th century (and so pre-dates the licence to crenellate granted to Robert de Manners in the reign of Edward III), and that the fourth storey was an addition: it is of yellowish sandstone in contrast to the reddish hue of the masonry in general.

Now a roofless shell, the tower is a building of modest proportions, measuring 46 by 32ft (14.1 by 9.8m). On its east side it had a projecting forebuilding, again of yellowish sandstone, which contained the entrance complete with a portcullis, a spiral stair leading to the upper floors, and an upper chamber from which the portcullis was operated. A short passage from the forebuilding led into the tower's ground floor, a tunnel-vaulted chamber with seven chamfered transverse arches. It was used for storage and lit by a small window in the 8ft (2.4m) thick west wall. Evidently the first floor contained the Great Hall, a well appointed chamber with a large fireplace and windows furnished with window seats. Moreover, doorways gave access to small mural chambers to the north and south as well as a latrine in the north-east angle. The floor above no doubt served as the private suite of the family. Off the main chamber here were further little rooms in the thickness of the walls, including another garderobe located above the one on the first floor. In contrast to the well appointed first and second floors, the uppermost storey was much simpler, lacking a fireplace and mural chambers other than one housing a latrine, and it has been suggested that it served as a barrack room for a garrison in times of danger from which the battlements could be rapidly manned if needed.

Near the south-west corner of the tower are the low remains of a section of the curtain wall, most of which has vanished. The wall ran south to a small tower, of which only the basement still stands: it is incorporated into a house. From this tower, which occupied the south-west corner of the defences, the curtain wall ran east to the gatehouse. This section of walling still stands. It is just over 3ft (1m) thick and its wall-walk had to be corbelled out on its inner side to increase its width. Ancillary buildings were evidently erected against its interior face. The wall also possessed two posterns that were later blocked.

The gatehouse stands to an impressive height. A barbican was evidently intended to project from its east or front face but whether this scheme was brought to fruition is doubtful. The gatehouse is approximately 36ft (11m) square and on its eastern side the deeply recessed entrance was flanked by two square projecting towers rising higher than the rest of the building. That to the north has a doorway in its east wall that opened, or was planned to open, to the battlements of the barbican. Further protection for the entrance was provided by a portcullis, behind which was a massive pair of gates.

At ground floor level on either side of the gateway is a vaulted guardroom, while a straight staircase at the rear of the gatehouse rose in the thickness of the north wall to a landing at first floor level, from which the first floor's substantial main chamber was entered. The room had a fireplace and was lit by Decorated two-light windows with window seats. A doorway in the south-east corner opened to a small chamber in the tower flanking the south side of the gatehouse's entrance. At this level moreover, a spiral stair located in the opposite tower rose to another chamber and the roof.

It has been suggested that the curtain wall ran from the north side of the gatehouse to a small tower in the north-east angle of the castle perimeter. An excavation in 1978 failed to find any trace of such a building. Moreover, the former existence of the stretch of curtain wall in question is uncertain: there is no sign that one adjoined the north side of the gatehouse and it has been suggested that there was perhaps merely a stockade instead.

Etal Castle is in the care of English Heritage.

HEXHAM ABBEY

Hexham Abbey, or priory as it should really be called, was founded in the second decade of the 12th century by the Archbishop of York as a house for canons belonging to the Augustinian Order, then coming into vogue in England (for a brief discussion of Augustinian canons see page 49) and was situated in an outlying part of the archdiocese of York known as Hexhamshire. The priory is sometimes said to have been founded in 1113 by Archbishop Thomas II, but was more probably established shortly thereafter by his successor, Thurstan, who became archbishop in 1114.

But the archbishop's foundation was not the first monastic presence at Hexham. Centuries earlier, in the days when Hexham lay within the Anglo-Saxon kingdom of Northumbria, another monastic community had been founded here. Its founder was Wilfrid, a notable figure in the English Church in the late 7th and early 8th centuries. Wilfrid established several monasteries whose monks had to live in accordance with the Rule of the celebrated 6th century Italian abbot, St Benedict, which enjoined on those who vowed to obey it a self-sacrificing lifestyle devoted to the service of God.

Hexham was one such monastery. It was established in about 674 on ground overlooking the Tyne and was built by craftsmen brought from Rome, and according to Wilfrid's biographer Eddius Stephanus - who knew him well - Wilfrid provided the monastic community with such a fine church that none elsewhere north of the Alps could compare with it.

48. Hexham Abbey from the south

Wilfrid's church was dedicated to St Andrew and lay where the church of the subsequent Augustinian priory was built. Excavations have uncovered traces of it beneath and near the nave of the medieval place of worship, which greatly exceeded it in size. It was formerly thought that Wilfrid's church had transepts, but this was evidently not the case and it was of more modest scale than previously imagined with its core comprising a small rectangular chancel, above a subterranean crypt, and a long narrow rectangular nave.

In 678 or 681 Hexham became the seat of a bishopric as part of a programme of diocesan reform in England undertaken by the Archbishop of Canterbury. The diocese of Hexham stretched from the River Aln south to the Tees and lasted until 821, by which time Viking raids on England had begun, and in 875 Hexham was severely sacked by a Danish army. The church was subsequently repaired and served as the parish church but was not thoroughly restored.

At some point during the Saxon period a small chapel with an apsidal east end was built a short distance to the east of Wilfrid's church and on the same alignment. Analogy with sites elsewhere suggests that it was a high status mausoleum that contained either episcopal or royal burials. Eric Cambridge has for example suggested that it may have served as a mausoleum for Aelfwold, a Northumbrian king murdered near Hexham in 788.

As noted above, in 1113 or shortly thereafter, a community of Augustinian canons was established at Hexham. The sequence of events seems to have been as follows: Archbishop Thomas II introduced secular canons - individuals whose lifestyle was not monastic - to serve the old Saxon church, only for his successor Thurstan, a keen promoter of the Augustinian Order, to rapidly replace them with regular Augustinian canons, thereby founding Hexham Priory.

It appears that for some years after the priory's foundation, an individual named Eilaf, the descendant of hereditary priests at Hexham, retained his interest in the church and did so until shortly before his death in 1138, by which time a cloister and stone monastic buildings had been erected immediately to the south of the place of worship.

The replacement of the Saxon church with a larger, Romanesque structure with transepts and an apsidal east end, followed, offset slightly to the north of Wilfrid's church. By the mid 1150s the east end had evidently been completed, but work on the rest of the building may have continued until well into the second half of the century. Indeed, it is possible that the church had not been completed when the decision was taken, around 1180, to begin all over again and build a new church on a far grander scale. As usual, work on the new church progressed from east to west, and continued into the 13th century.

On occasion during its history the priory was caught up in Anglo-Scottish conflict. In 1138 for example a Scottish army carried out depredations in the neighbourhood, including the murder of women and children, thereby causing much suffering and fear. Richard of Hexham, a canon who witnessed such brutal deeds from the walls of the monastery, referred to the invading force as 'more barbarous than any race of pagans.'

Moreover, on 28 June 1296, during another Scottish incursion, the priory was set alight and gutted thereby destroying shrines, books and relics of saints. The following year, when most of the canons were resident elsewhere, the Scots returned, led by William Wallace who granted the canons a letter of protection on 7 November, doubtless after they had agreed to pay protection money. Wallace returned to Hexham shortly thereafter - having devastated much of Cumbria in the interim - and found only three canons still remaining. He demanded to hear Mass and then left the church to discard his weapons before returning for the service. In his absence, some of his men (likely lawless individuals from Galloway) stole the chalice and other sacred altar vessels. Angered and embarrassed by this, Wallace vainly demanded to know which of his men had committed the sacrilege, whereupon he told the canons that the perpetrators of the crime were rough, uncivilised men, devoid of a sense of shame. The Scottish warlord remained at Hexham Priory for two days, using it as a base from which the neighbouring countryside could be raided, and then left, heading down the valley of the Tyne.

From this period until some point between 1320 and 1336, the priory was often deserted owing to destruction wrought during Scottish raids or through fear that history would repeat itself: the canons were dispersed to other Augustinian houses in Yorkshire and Nottinghamshire.

On the other hand, Hexham Priory also witnessed positive developments during the 14th century. For instance, the church was enlarged by the provision of five small chapels against the east end of the chancel, while a sacristy or chapel was erected against the chancel's south wall. The chapels were most likely added in the late 1340s. The sacristy or chapel was probably either exactly contemporaneous or nearly so and was possibly destroyed following the Dissolution of the Monasteries in the 16th century, whereas the eastern chapels lasted until 1858 when they were demolished.

From time to time the canons were visited by the Archbishop of York, who came to inspect the manner in which the house was run. On this point, Richard Lomas comments: 'From Henry Murdac in 1152 to William Lee in 1535 no archbishop seems to have been happy with what he found: discipline was lax; the rule was ignored; and some [canons] consorted with women.'

Tempers were raised following a visit in 1307 by Archbishop William Greenfield. Led by one of their number, Robert of Whelpington, the canons reacted to his visitation in an insubordinate manner. As a result, Whelpington was subsequently sent to a canonry in Gloucester on the archbishop's instructions. Later, in 1311 when Hexham's prior requested permission to resign, Greenfield attempted to impose an outsider from Nostell as his replacement, anxious to have the house run by a firm hand. But rather than accept this violation of their rights, the canons responded by electing Robert of Whelpington to the priorate, whereupon the angry archbishop resorted to excommunicating the canons and sequestrating their property. Stung by this, they indignantly petitioned parliament for assistance and Greenfield subsequently backed down, annulled the excommunication, restored what he had seized, and accepted Whelpington as the new prior, conceding that the canons had the right to choose their own head.

On 28 September 1536, royal commissioners arrived at Hexham with the intention of dissolving the priory, part of a nationwide programme of monastic closures authorized by the government of Henry VIII. But resistance was encountered from both the canons and townsfolk who had rallied to their side and the commissioners had to withdraw. The priory thus remained in being, albeit briefly, for in 1537, by which time opposition had ceased, Hexham Priory was dissolved and the priory's land and conventual buildings were granted to Sir Reynold Carnaby, the king's representative in Hexhamshire. On the other hand, the church survived and became the parish church.

It is interesting to note that throughout its existence, the Augustinian priory lay within the liberty of Hexhamshire; a compact block of territory belonging to the Archbishop of York and comprising land on both sides of the Tyne. Among other things, within the liberty

- which dated from the late 11th century - the archbishop could deal with all legal matters and retain the profits of justice, including the lands of felons and traitors. Indeed, the only rights reserved by the Crown were the right to impose taxation and to licence fairs and markets.

Inevitably, repairs and alterations have been made to the church over the centuries. In 1858, for example, the celebrated northern architect John Dobson rebuilt the east end of the chancel after it had collapsed.

Description

Hexham Abbey stands in a commanding position in the heart of the town of Hexham. Internally, the church, essentially a fine example of the Early English style, is 225ft (68.7m) long and is entered from the east via the slype, a rib-vaulted passage. Here, a doorway in the north wall opens to the south transept.

The transept is three bays long, save for the ground floor where the slype occupies what would have been the third bay, and has a rib-vaulted east aisle whose arcade has piers with four major shafts and slender tripartite secondary ones in the diagonals, and the piers support triple-chamfered arches. Above the arcade arches, the triforium has in each bay, a large arch that contains two pointed arches and the spandrels are ornamented by being pierced with various shapes. At clerestory level on the east and west sides of the transept is

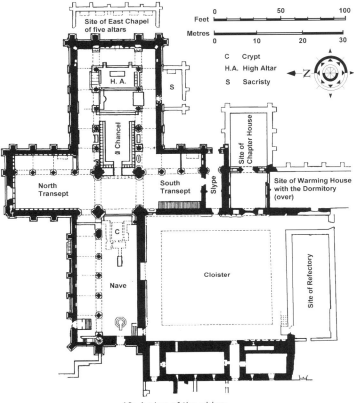

49. A plan of the abbey

tripartite arcading: each bay has a window within an arch flanked by smaller blank arches. The timber roof dates from the 15th century.

The most notable feature of the west side of the transept - indeed one of the most notable features of the church - is the wide night stair, a straight flight of well-worn steps that lead to a balcony located above the slype where one doorway opened into the dormitory in the former east claustral range and another into the treasury over the east end of the slype.

At the foot of the night stair is the late 1st century tombstone of a Roman soldier named Flavinus. Depicted in full-dress uniform, Flavinus was a standard-bearer belonging to a cavalry regiment that was evidently based at Corbridge a short distance to the east. The tombstone was found beneath the floor of the slype in 1881.

The crossing has tall arches on substantial piers and is surmounted by a low tower. Between the east pair of piers is a wooden rood screen erected by Thomas Smithson, prior in the years 1491 to 1524. It is ornamented with intricate blank tracery and paintings depict-

50. An interior view of the church, looking north from the south transept (Shaun Dodds, courtesy of Hexham Abbey)

ing, among other things Bishops of Hexham, while 21 little niches on the west side once carried statues or images. The rood screen is a prominent part of the church's interesting collection of late medieval and early Tudor woodwork.

The nave, to the west of the crossing, is six bays long, almost entirely dates from the years 1905-08, and is in the Decorated style. The lower courses of the west and south walls are however survivals from the 15th century. Earlier still, is the base of the west respond of the north (and only) aisle which dates from the days of the 12th century Romanesque church, as well as some courses of the north wall which may be 12th or 13th century work.

The crypt of Wilfrid's church lies below the east end of the nave and was discovered by accident in 1725. Of it, Colin Dallison has aptly commented: 'With its primitive simplicity and associations with early Christian Northumbria, it is the most moving part of the church.' In the nave of the present church, visitors can descend stairs which lead to a small vestibule from which pilgrims may have peered through a grille at relics in the main chamber of the crypt. The principal chamber lies east of the vestibule and, in common with the rest of the crypt, is built of Roman stones evidently brought from Corbridge. It measures about 14 by 8ft (4.3 by 2.4m), is 9ft (2.7m) high, and its tunnel vault still has much of its original plaster.

A little chamber lies directly to the north of the vestibule. In addition to being entered from the vestibule, this could also be reached from the east by descending steps that led to a passage running to the north of the crypt's main chamber. Further steps and another passage lay to the south of the main chamber, and in this case led directly to it. The presence of the three approaches to the crypt has led Eric Cambridge to comment that they raise 'the possibility that the two eastern entrances to the crypt were intended to permit visitors to enter by one of the passages, venerate whatever relics the main chamber contained, and then exit by the other, without entering the church proper at all', in which case the western approach, located within the church, would no doubt have been used by the clergy.

And what of the north transept? This appears to date from slightly later than the south transept and is more elaborate. It has blank trefoil arcading running along the lowest level of the walls with sunk quatrefoils in the spandrels, save for in the east aisle where instead of quatrefoils one finds various compositions using stiff-leaf. The aisle was divided into three chapels by walls that no longer exist. It is moreover rib-vaulted and the vaulting is ornamented with foliage bosses. The piers of the aisle arcade each have four major shafts and tripartite secondary ones in the diagonals, and the subordinate shafts are more slender than their counterparts in the south transept. The piers carry richly moulded arches. The triforium is identical to that of the south transept save for the presence of some dogtooth, and the clerestory on both the east and west sides likewise corresponds with that of the south transept. The main windows in the west wall are

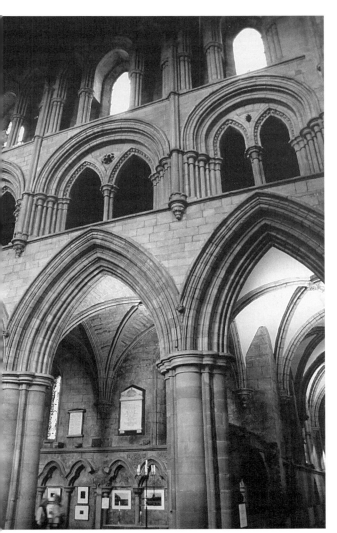

51. The junction between the north transept and the north aisle of the chancel (Shaun Dodds, courtesy of Hexham Abbey)

tall lancets interspersed by blank arcading, while the north wall has two tiers of lancets, the uppermost stepped. Again, the timber roof dates from the 15th century.

The chancel, (which of course lies east of the crossing), is aisled, six bays long and mostly dates from the period of rebuilding that commenced in around 1180 and lasted into the early 13th century: the easternmost bay and east wall were rebuilt by John Dobson in 1858.

Before dealing with architectural details, it is interesting to note that at the west end of the chancel lies what is known as the Frith Stool or Wilfrid's Chair. It is a stone chair, carved from a single block, and believed to date from c.675-700 and is thus a relic of the first monastery. It stands in the first bay of the chancel from the west, a bay that occupies most of the site where the small apsidal Saxon chapel mentioned above once stood. It will moreover be recalled that the Romanesque church had an apsidal east end and this is known to have lain in the third bay from the west of the present chancel.

The chancel arcades have piers of four major and four minor keeled shafts and some piers of the north arcade have capitals with stiff-leaf foliage, making them more ornate than the plainer capitals of the south arcade. The piers carry finely mould-

52. The chancel (Shaun Dodds, courtesy of Hexham Abbey)

ed arches and those of the south arcade have hoodmoulds with nutmeg decoration. In form, the triforium corresponds with those of the transepts. On the south side, dogtooth appears in the bay and a half closest to the crossing, whereas dogtooth was used in all the bays on the north side suggesting that the triforium on the south side of the chancel was erected first. On both sides, as elsewhere in the church, the clerestory has a wall passage and tripartite arcading with a window in the middle of each group of three arches. Finally, although vaulting shafts were provided, rising from corbels just below triforium level, no vault was actually built: timber was used instead and again the present roof dates from the 15th century.

The chancel aisles are elegantly rib-vaulted and have bosses with stiff-leaf foliage. The north aisle contains a number of Saxon grave covers. Here, too, one can see 15th century paintings on wooden panels depicting the Passion: other medieval paintings can also be seen in the church. In the south aisle of the chancel are badly defaced monuments, the one being of a cross-legged knight, Gilbert d'Umfraville of Prudhoe, a senior Northumberland baron who died in 1307, and the other that of his wife.

As far as the monastic quarters are concerned, much has gone. South of the nave lay the cloister. An arcade runs along the exterior face of the west wall of the south transept and incorporates a now blocked doorway from the cloister into the transept and another doorway to the slype. To the south, the slype is adjoined by a chamber (now a gift shop) that served as a vestibule to the chapter house that projected eastward from the east claustral range and is no longer extant. South of the vestibule lay the warming house, while the canons' dormitory lay on the first floor of the range. Presumably, to the south or east lay the infirmary and reredorter.

The south range no longer exists, save for fragments, but contained the refectory over an undercroft. In contrast, much of the west range has survived, although its upper floor was rebuilt in the late 18th century and then altered again in 1819 following a fire. The most notable medieval feature is the lavatorium, against the exterior face of the east wall, and close to the former entrance to the refectory. Believed to date from around 1300, it has seven gabled blank arches, (of which the largest is the centremost) and geometrical tracery. Of the lavatorium, Charles Clement Hodges commented that 'there is not its equal in the country.'

53. The lavatorium

HOUSESTEADS ROMAN FORT

Housesteads, on Hadrian's Wall, is the most famous Roman fort in Britain and attracts over a hundred thousand visitors annually. It occupies a commanding position on the Great Whin Sill, a fold of rock of volcanic origin that runs across Northumberland, stands amid wild, windswept countryside, and is the most complete example of a Roman fort to be seen in Britain. It was founded in the AD 120s as part of the programme of creating Hadrian's Wall to serve as the northern frontier of Roman rule in Britain.

Initially, a turret (36b) was erected at the site, together with the foundations of a section of Hadrian's Wall. Work then began on the fort itself, with the north wall being located beyond the foundations mentioned, and it was only after the fort had been constructed that work resumed on the Wall, now built on the same alignment as that of the fort's north wall and to a narrower gauge than first planned.

Factors that presumably led to the decision to build a fort at this point include its accessibility to water (a stream known as the Knag Burn flows through a gap in the Whin Sill escarpment a short distance to the east); its relatively sheltered position; the fertility of ground in the vicinity of the site and its proximity to suitable building stone.

The Roman name for Housesteads is sometimes said to have been *Borcovicus*, a name gleaned from a document dating from the early 5th century. However, the fort was most probably known as *Vercovicium*, a name of Celtic origin that perhaps meant 'hilly place' though a more favoured translation is 'place of the effective fighters.'

Evidently, when first built, Housesteads had ten barracks capable of housing approximately 800 men. The identity of the first garrison is not certain. But by AD 200 inscriptions show that *cohors I Tungrorum milliaria* ('the first cohort of Tungrians a thousand strong') was stationed at the site. The unit was of Germanic origin and had served in Britain since the 1st century AD, though its strength had been reduced to 500 men for a while during the 2nd century.

In about AD 129, if not later, members of the unit are known to have undertaken construction work at Carrawburgh, a fort a few miles east of Housesteads and also on Hadrian's Wall. It may have been the case that at this date the regiment was already based at Housesteads, having perhaps moved up to the fort from Vindolanda on the Stanegate a few miles to the south, where the unit appears to have been based at about the time work on the Wall commenced, Vindolanda being the closest of the Stanegate forts to Housesteads.

Germanic names found at Housesteads suggest that the regiment was still recruiting some of its manpower from the Tungrians' homeland in what is now southern Belgium and Holland, (and was perhaps doing so as late as the 3rd century), but other members of the unit were evidently native British recruits.

In about 142 the First Tungrians were part of the garrison of the Antonine Wall in Scotland, (which temporarily superseded Hadrian's Wall as the Roman frontier during the mid 2nd century) but Housesteads may nonetheless have still had a garrison of sorts during this period. On this point James Crow comments, 'Housesteads shows no obvious signs of abandonment during the occupation of the Antonine Wall and an inscription of

54. An aerial view of Housesteads. The fort and Hadrian's Wall are in the foreground: buildings belonging to the civil settlement lie towards the top of the picture, outside the fort's south gate
(Professor Norman McCord, University of Newcastle upon Tyne)

soldiers from the Second Legion "on garrison duty" may be evidence of a caretaker garrison at this time.' There may also have been a detachment of the Sixth Legion, too.

As noted above, the First Tungrians were at Housesteads at the beginning of the 3rd century, if not earlier, and are recorded as still being so in the early years of the 5th century. By the 230s, however, they had been supplemented by Germanic irregulars, a *Cuneus Frisiorum*, possibly a cavalry unit recruited from the coastlands of what are now northern Holland and Germany which lay outside the frontiers of the Roman Empire. The Frisians erected a temple dedicated to the Germanic god of war, Mars Thincsus, and the Alaisiagae (the god's female attendants) on Chapel Hill, an outcrop of limestone on lower ground to the south-east of the fort that became the focus of religious life in the 3rd century. Some of the dedicants identified themselves as coming from the district of Twente in north-eastern Holland.

Another altar dedicated to Mars Thincsus raises the possibility that there was a further unit of German irregulars, *numerus Hnaudifridi*, identified by the name of its commander or tribal chief, Hnaudifridus or Notfried. But it has been plausibly suggested that this was perhaps the same unit as the *Cuneus Frisiorum*, in the one instance identified as a *cuneus* in its official title and in the other as a *numerus* by the name of its leader.

In common with most other Roman forts, Housesteads was associated with a civil settlement that developed outside its walls. It is generally thought that the settlement was initially located on lower ground south of the *Vallum* (see page 9) at the foot of Chapel Hill and that during the course of the 2nd century civilian buildings of timber were erected just outside the fort, although occupation continued on and around Chapel Hill. James Crow has however recently questioned this sequence of events and has suggested that civil settlement north of the *Vallum* may have begun more or less contemporaneously with that in the vicinity of Chapel Hill.

In the early 3rd century, stone buildings were constructed outside the fort's south and east gates, (in some instances on the site of former timber structures) with the area of densest occupation apparently being outside the south gate. There is reason to believe that perhaps some of the garrison in the 3rd century resided in a number of the buildings outside the fort, for the bulk of a distinctive type of pottery associated with the Frisian troops mentioned above has been found in the extramural settlement.

Building inscriptions record phases of construction work during the fort's history, such as during the reign of Septimus Severus (193-211) and the days of Diocletian and Maximian who reigned jointly in the years 286-305. For instance, during the latter phase, the fort's long barrack blocks were done away with and replaced by rows of separate dwellings, referred to as 'chalets'. It has often been said that these soon probably not only housed members of a smaller garrison, but also their families who moved into the fort following the general abandonment of the civil settlement around 320, but the archaeological evidence does not support this. No evidence has moreover been found at Housesteads that rebuilding work was ever required as a result of destruction wrought by barbarians.

Housesteads doubtless remained garrisoned until the early years of the 5th century when Roman rule in Britain ceased. At some date late in its history, the fort's decaying defences were either wholly or partly encased in earth banks into which timber towers were set. Some archaeologists are of the opinion that this happened towards the end of the Roman period; others suggest that it perhaps occurred after Roman rule had ceased.

Housesteads became a place of no consequence. There is no reference to it dating from the Middle Ages, though there is reason to believe that there was nonetheless a limited human presence. Later, during the Tudor and Stuart eras, Housesteads was the haunt of Border reivers and other lawless individuals, most notably the Armstrongs of nearby Grandy's Knowe late in the 17th century. Subsequently, interest in its Roman past brought antiquaries and archaeologists to explore the remote site and begin the process of describing and uncovering its remains and history. The first archaeological excavations occurred in 1822 and were conducted by a distinguished figure in Romano-British studies, the Reverend John Hodgson.

Description

Housesteads is approached from the south by most visitors and conforms to the standard plan of a Roman fort, though owing to the lie of the land it is more elongated than normal and unlike most forts along the Wall, is aligned east-west rather than north-south. The fort was shaped like a playing card, had a gate in each of the straight sides, internal angle towers in each corner, and a central range of official buildings across the centre flanked to the east and west by rows of buildings that were mostly barracks. The north-east angle tower was however soon replaced by one a short distance to the west, at the point where Hadrian's Wall joins the north wall of the fort, to give a view of either side of the Wall down to the

Knag Burn. Moreover, internally the fort's perimeter wall was backed by a bank of turf and clay, though this was removed during the fort's history, only to be at least partially reinstated during late Roman times when the defences were rebuilt and strengthened around 300.

The south gate was conventional in plan: two arched entranceways were separated by masonry and, on its outer side, each entrance had a guard-chamber with a tower above, while between the towers and above the entranceways was an upper room. By the early 3rd century, however, the east portal had been blocked up. Projecting southward from the east guard-chamber is post-medieval fabric, the remains of a bastle house typical of the 16th century. From the south gate a road, the *via principalis*, bisected the fort, heading directly towards the north gate.

Doubtless for many visitors, the most fascinating structure at Housesteads is that of the latrines, located near the south-east corner of the fort and built against the south curtain. Members of the garrison who used the latrines (there were others elsewhere in the fort) walked on to a central flagged platform located along the middle of the structure, and to the north and south of which were the lavatory seats, likely consisting of a continuous bench with keyhole-shaped slots. Hence in line with communal latrines elsewhere, no provision was made for individual cubicles. The latrines discharged into a deep sewer flowing in an anti-clockwise direction to an outflow beneath the fort wall immediately west of the neighbouring angle tower.

The flagged platform has a shallow channel along which water flowed for the benefit of those using the latrines. It is often said that the channel enabled them to rinse sponges used in lieu of toilet paper, and it has been suggested that the keyhole-shaped slots would have allowed these sponges, attached to a stick, to have been used by someone seated on the latrine without the individual having to rise to perform the task. But it has recently been questioned whether sponges would have been imported into Britain in sufficient quantity

55. The latrines

to satisfy the lavatorial requirements of the Roman army and it has thus been suggested that other material, such as bracken grown in the vicinity of Housesteads, was probably used instead.

The latrines were erected here so that advantage could be made of the lie of the land. Surface water and drains were channelled down to cleanse the sewer and carry the effluent into the outflow through a large stone conduit underneath the wall of the fort. Spells of dry weather would inevitably cause problems. As a result, cisterns were provided. One, consisting of sandstone slabs sealed with lead caulking, was erected against the angle tower to collect water from the tower roof. It could hold as much as 2,800 gallons (12,729 litres) that could be used to flush the latrines.

Progressing around the curtain wall from the latrines and the south-east angle tower, one comes to the remains of the east gate, overlooking ground that falls away towards the Knag Burn. This gate was the fort's principal entrance and was approached via the Military Way, a road running along the south side of Hadrian's Wall. Nonetheless, the gate's south passageway was blocked and the portal converted into a coalshed. In contrast, the deeply worn threshold of the other portal bears testimony to the passage of many vehicles.

Beyond the east gate, lie the remains of a bakehouse in the north-east corner of the fort and located within a subsequent 4th century interval tower. The bakehouse (which had two ovens) was one of several at Housesteads.

Many of the low remains of the buildings at Housesteads are overlain by grass and so are not visible. This is true, for instance, of three barracks located east of the north-south road. But beyond these, and located north of the road running from the east gate towards the centre of the site, one can see three buildings.

The first of these dates from around 300, but occupies the site of earlier structures. It was an impressive building, evidently two storeys high, whose surviving masonry comprises smartly dressed large blocks. Its function is unclear. James Crow suggests that it was likely 'an imperial storehouse for the collection and distribution of taxation in kind (*annona militaris*) the late Roman government's response to the rampant inflation of the third century.' Its east end was demolished in the late 4th century so that a small bath suite, with a suspended floor heated from a stoke-hole at its north end, could be erected. Despite its small size, it is possible that the bath house replaced low lying external baths located near the Knag Burn. The latter baths, nearly 656ft (200m) from the fort and hidden from its view, were perhaps deemed too dangerous to use in the worsening conditions of late Roman Britain.

The other structures began life as long barrack blocks in the days of Hadrian. Initially they each had ten compartments sub-divided into a front room and a sleeping area, and each compartment housed about eight men. Furthermore, at the east end of each building was a larger apartment for a centurion accompanied by a few household slaves and perhaps his family. The number of compartments in the southern of the two barracks was subsequently reduced from ten to eight. Then, in around 300, both barracks were radically altered (entailing large-scale demolition) and transformed into rows of individual 'chalets', small dwellings fewer in number than the compartments of the former barracks and divided by narrow alleys. This process also occurred with the fort's other barrack blocks.

Nearby lie the remains of the north gate, which was similar in plan to the other main gates but has massive foundations as a result of the terracing that was required at this point to make the best use of the restricted nature of the site. Apparently the east portal was

never used, whereas the other entrance witnessed significant use until at least the late 2nd century. Thereafter, it is thought that traffic passed through a 3rd century gate added to Hadrian's Wall at the Knag Burn, from where the ascent to the fort's east gate was less steep than the external approach to the north gate.

West of the north gate, lie the exposed foundations of Turret 36b mentioned above, on either side of which are fragments of the foundation of the Broad Wall, as the first phase of the construction of Hadrian's Wall is known.

56. Hadrian's Wall approaching the north-east corner of the fort, crossing the Knag Burn en route

To the south-east of Turret 36b lie two granaries, located immediately west of the north-south road. These were initially a single building. In both granaries rows of square stone pillars can be seen (some of these have been removed in the south granary) and these carried raised timber floors to keep

57. One of the granaries

foodstuffs dry, while splayed vents in the walls enabled air to circulate below floor level. The south granary was subsequently divided by a cross-wall: the west part seems to have been used for accommodation in the late 4th century. Much later, in the 18th century, a corn-drying kiln was inserted into the granary.

To the south of the granaries lie the remains of the headquarters building, which faced eastwards towards the fort's principal gate. From east to west, the headquarters consisted of a colonnaded courtyard (the colonnades were blocked off in the 3rd century, probably to create offices), a lofty cross-hall with an east aisle, and five rooms located along the hall's west wall. The hall was a place of assembly and housed a tribunal - whose remains can be seen in the north-west corner - from which the commandant issued instructions and dispensed justice. The centremost of the five rooms off the hall was the shrine, the most sacred place in the fort where regimental standards would have been kept and venerated. Here, too, were statues of the emperor, the imperial family, and altars to deities such as the goddess of Discipline. The northernmost room likely contained the pay and savings of members of the garrison, but later became an armourer's workshop and weapons store. Evidently, in the late Roman period an upper floor was erected above the two rooms north of the shrine.

Immediately to the south of the headquarters building, and entered off the *via principalis,* is the commanding officer's house, the largest building in the fort. This is on sloping ground and was therefore constructed on several levels. It consists of rooms ranged

58. The commanding officer's residence, as viewed from the south-east

around a still partly paved central courtyard and is rectangular in plan. Only the north and west ranges, plus part of the east side, are original. Initially the house was thus not rectangular, unless timber buildings formed the south range and part of the east range before being replaced with stone. The north and west ranges were doubtless the main living area for the commandant and his family and included a kitchen in the north-east corner and, in the centre of the north range, a dining room that had underfloor heating and heated flues in the walls. The house experienced much alteration during its existence - the heated dining room for instance is a late addition dating from about 300.

Behind the headquarters building, are the remains of what was evidently a hospital. Ranged around a courtyard in which medicinal herbs may have been grown, it consists of small rooms on three sides and a larger room, perhaps a surgical ward, to the north. The courtyard was paved over during the building's existence, and the north room was apparently converted to domestic use in the 4th century.

Six buildings are known to lie buried in the western third of the fort. However, one can see the remains of the south-west angle tower and, more importantly, those of the west gate which stands up to 6½ft (2m) high and is one of the best preserved gates at any fort on Hadrian's Wall. Both its carriageways were blocked in late Roman times and two parallel banks and ditches were provided across the Military Way a short distance in front of the blocked gate, to impede any approach from that direction.

And what of the civil settlement? Twenty-six buildings have been excavated or traced. These range from substantial stone-built structures that are much larger than the soldiers' apartments in the fort's barrack blocks, to crudely constructed smaller buildings of comparable size to the 'chalets' mentioned above. Judging by finds of pottery, the latter were associated with the Frisian troops that formed part of Housesteads' garrison in the 3rd century.

Only six buildings of the civil settlement are on display and mostly lie just outside the south gate. Here one can see the low remains of structures, some of which evidently served as shops and taverns. Further to the south, and thus on lower ground, are the remains of a building where an intriguing find was made during excavation: beneath the clay floor of one of its rooms, two skeletons were uncovered. The most complete skeleton was that of a middle-aged man, while the other remains are thought to be those of a female. The former had a fragment of a knife in his ribs. Burials within Roman settlements, other than those of infants, were forbidden by law (Housesteads had cemeteries on low ground to the south-east and south-west of the fort such as in the vicinity of Chapel Hill) and the skeletons were undoubtedly those of murder victims, killed and concealed in the 3rd century.

Finally, on the sloping ground south of 'the Murder House' and elsewhere, is terracing that dates from around A.D 200; an extensive system of terraces that will have substantially increased the amount of agricultural land in the fort's vicinity.

Housesteads Roman Fort is owned by the National Trust and is in the care of English Heritage.

LINDISFARNE CASTLE

L indisfarne Castle is located on a small tidal island, known as Holy Island, lying over a mile (1.6km) off the coast of Northumberland, and at high tide is thus cut off from the mainland by the North Sea. In the Middle Ages, oyster beds existed in the shallow tidal water, which serves as a feeding ground for visiting flocks of wildfowl and waders in the autumn and winter.

When the water retreats, access to the island is gained via a causeway completed in 1954, and it is sometimes possible to see the odd seal sunning itself on the mud flats. Prior to the modern causeway, the usual route across the sands lay to the south. It is known as the Pilgrims' Way and is marked by a line of tall posts and refuge boxes which were last renewed in 1987 to commemorate the 1300th anniversary of the death of the principal figure in the island's history, St Cuthbert.

Upon reaching the island, the road from the causeway is flanked to the north by an extensive system of sand dunes that probably only began developing during the 15th century owing to a change in climate which resulted in an increase in stormy, windy weather. Furthermore, the island is not well wooded. Again, the situation differs from previous times. The pollen record indicates that trees were more prevalent during the medieval period, though much woodland had already been cleared for farming, a process which continued during the Middle Ages.

Lindisfarne Castle is however post-medieval. It was evidently founded by the Crown in about 1549 during the reign of Edward VI to defend the harbour of Holy Island from raids by the Scots, a small harbour which had been used to land English soldiers and supplies during campaigns waged against the Scots in the previous reign, that of Henry VIII, and was still deemed of strategic importance given its proximity to the border. On this point a contemporary, Sir Robert Bowes, commented, 'The Holy Island is . . . a place much necessarye to be defended and preserved for there is a harborough sufficient for a great range of shippes to rest safely in and very aptly for the warrs towards Scotland.' He also noted that the castle, which he referred to as 'the fort of Beblowe', lay 'very well for the defence of the Haven', though he believed that it could be strengthened by the provision of a moat, a suggestion that was not put into practice.

In 1559 the garrison consisted of a non-resident captain, two master gunners, a master's mate and twenty soldiers, a state of affairs that continued into the first half of the 17th century. In the meantime, further construction work had occurred and by 1571, states Robert Young, 'it seems that the basic shape of the castle as we now know it was completed.'

In 1635 a much-travelled Cheshire gentleman, Sir William Brereton, described Lindisfarne Castle as follows: 'This is a daintie little fort built towre-wise upon the toppe of a little round hill, which is a rocke.' He then notes the presence of ordnance before commenting that the castle possessed 'neate, warme and convenient roomes.'

Subsequently, in 1648, Captain Batton, who was in command of Lindisfarne Castle, received an offer from a diehard Royalist officer named Sir Marmaduke Langdale, who had just taken Berwick for Charles I. If Batton agreed to swap sides and hold the castle for the

59. Lindisfarne Castle from the west

king, Langdale would endeavour to ensure that arrears of pay owed to Batton and his men would be duly paid. However, Batton refused to comply and an unsuccessful siege lasting six weeks ensued.

The castle was however captured during the Jacobite rising of 1715, when adherents of the exiled House of Stuart rose on their behalf in Northumberland (and elsewhere) against the Hanoverian dynasty. The castle was seized by two Stuart supporters, Launcelot Errington, the captain of a merchant vessel that had arrived in the island's harbour, and his nephew, Mark, the ship's mate. They achieved their end by stealth.

According to one version of events, several members of the small garrison were invited to board their ship, where they were rendered incapable of action by being plied with drink, whereupon Errington and his nephew made their way to the castle, knocked down a sentinel, surprised and ejected remaining members of the garrison, shut the gates and hoisted the Jacobite colours.

In reality, Launcelot Errington visited the castle to have his beard shaved by the master gunner - one Samuel Phillipson - who worked as a barber in his spare time. He then left the castle, only to promptly return with his nephew, maintaining that he had mislaid his watch key. Once inside, they turned on Phillipson, pistols in hand, before ejecting him and a colleague from the castle - other members of the garrison were not present at the time. Then they unfurled the standard of the Old Pretender, as the Stuart claimant to the throne is known to history, and fired off cannon shots, likely as a signal to expected reinforcements.

Shots were also exchanged with members of the garrison who attempted to retake the castle. While the Erringtons were not joined by a force of fellow Jacobites, their opponents duly received support from a garrison based at Berwick and Lindisfarne Castle was soon in government hands again. Launcelot Errington (who had been wounded during the retaking of the castle) and his kinsman were hauled off to gaol in Berwick, from which they nonetheless succeeded in escaping.

The castle continued to be garrisoned until 1819, but suffered from neglect. In 1841 a naval detachment began using the site as a coastguard station and from 1851 the personnel involved were civilians. In around 1860 the castle was used by the local militia, a role it retained until about 1885, after which the condition of the fabric declined significantly.

But salvation was at hand. In 1902 the castle was bought by Edward Hudson, the owner of *Country Life* magazine (founded in 1897) who had visited the castle for the first time the previous year while touring Northumberland. The outside walls were still complete. Internally, it was a different story. Hudson thus employed Edwin Lutyens, a close friend, to restore and remodel the derelict castle on his behalf, with the aim of using it as a retreat.

Born in London in 1869, Lutyens was to prove the greatest English architect of his generation. He had been introduced to Hudson by Gertrude Jekyll and a number of houses that he had designed had been featured in *Country Life*, thereby furthering his career. Moreover, in 1901, Lutyens had built Hudson a house at Sonning, Berkshire, one of the finest of all Lutyens' houses.

Lutyens' work at Lindisfarne began in 1903 and was completed in 1912. Of it, Colin Amery comments: 'Throughout the castle there is evidence of [his] eye for detail and of his ability to create a style that suits the elemental qualities of the castle.' Roderick Gradidge describes the castle as 'very romantic and impractical. There are very few places in which anyone can live, but that did not matter much for Hudson lived most his life in London . . . . None the less it is a wonderful thing: as one moves round the castle shapes continually change, new forms emerge and others disappear, and everywhere the balance is maintained.'

In 1908 the castle was visited by the Prince and Princess of Wales, and the royal party numbered twenty people. Among other visitors were Lord Baden-Powell and the historian and critic Lytton Strachey. The latter, who spent a week at the castle in 1918, thought its setting magnificent, despite the fact that it was 'surrounded by cormorants and quicksands', and referred to the 'amazing prospects' that could be enjoyed from the battlements. On the whole however, he was not impressed. With characteristic acerbity he described Hudson as 'a pathetically dreary figure', and wrote that the castle was 'all timid Lutyens - very dark, with nowhere to sit, and nothing but stone under, over and round you, which produces a distressing effect - especially when hurrying downstairs late for dinner - to slip would be instant death. No, not a comfortable place, by any means.' But Strachey did thoroughly enjoy the companionship of one of the other guests, a celebrated cellist, Guilhermina Suggia, (who frequently stayed at the castle over the years) and to whom he was attracted. 'Her music was of course marvellous - and I got such masses of it! I used to go with her, her mother . . . and the accompanist, to her bedroom; she would then lock the door (to prevent the ingress of Hudson, I fancy), and practice - for hours - playing Bach suites one after the other, and every kind of miracle.'

In 1921, Hudson sold the castle to a banker named Oswald Falk. In 1944 its then owner, another banker named Sir Edward de Stein, gave the property to the National Trust.

Description

Lindisfarne Castle lies in the south-east corner of the island and occupies a commanding position on the top of an outcrop of the Great Whin Sill, and from a distance seems to grow out of the rock. As Peter Anderson Graham comments in an article published in *Country Life* in June 1913, 'The rock and dwelling do not stand apart like hostile neighbours, but cling to one another like twin brethren. The outline and composition of the group of buildings and the choice of right materials and their appropriate treatment make the work of man look like a continuation and completement of that of Nature.'

The castle has a roughly east-west orientation, is approximately oval in shape and measures some 220ft (68m) in length. The area within the perimeter contains both a central and west range of buildings as well as east and west wards, also known as the lower and upper batteries, both of which had gun platforms. Lutyens made use of the fact that the castle had wards on two levels for gun emplacements by constructing a sequence of rooms linked by stairs and passages that give the impression of having been hewn into the rock.

The castle is entered from the south-east via a cobbled ramp cut into the side of the rock face and now devoid of its protective parapet which was removed by Lutyens. The ramp, whose cobbles are laid in a herring-bone pattern, a favourite Lutyen's motif, ascends westward to a gate formerly defended by a portcullis which is now seldom lowered. Upon entering a small vestibule, a straight flight of steps located beneath the central range leads up to the lower battery, comprising the east side of the castle, from where one can enjoy panoramic views of the island and coastline. There are, moreover, two fine gun emplacements built into the perimeter wall.

To the west, the lower battery is enclosed by the central range. Here a doorway opens to the robust Entrance Hall, which has a markedly Romanesque character with round chamfered arches supported by sturdy columns and responds.

Off the south side of the Entrance Hall lies the Kitchen, which has a brighter, less cold feel. Within a wide stone fireplace designed by Lutyens, is a coal-burning range that was used for cooking and heating the room. Lutyens also designed some of the room's furniture although the curved settle - a long wooden bench with arms and a high back - dates from the 18th century. Among other items on display, are copper utensils such as moulds and kettles, as well as blue and white china. A tiny scullery lies off the Kitchen and contains a sink and wooden draining racks, as well as the machinery for raising and lowering the portcullis.

Upon returning to the Entrance Hall, one heads through a doorway on the west side of the room that opens to a narrow descending passage. Off this, to the right, lies the Dining Room. This rather dark, cave-like room, has a steeply pointed tunnel-vault cut away on one side to form an opening for the only window. The floor consists of red bricks laid in a herring-bone pattern. The oval dining table is likewise by Lutyens, but the chairs date from the 18th century.

Continuing down the passageway, one enters the Ship Room: the Dining Room and the Ship Room are believed to have originally been the ammunition storerooms of the castle. The Ship Room is a larger, more welcoming chamber than the Dining Room, and has a less steeply pitched pointed tunnel-vault from which hang two 17th century Dutch brass chandeliers and a wooden model of a three-masted ship, an early 19th century merchantman, the *Henrietta* of Amsterdam. The presence of this model gives the room its name.

Openings on one side of the room contain windows which, like that in the Dining Room, have a stone window seat and look medieval but were in fact inserted by Lutyens. The windows face north and provide views of a small walled garden (designed on Hudson's behalf by Gertrude Jekyll) lying a short distance from the castle. In terms of its furnishings, the Ship Room has a strong 17th century feel. An outstanding piece of furniture is a Dutch china cupboard of that date, ornamented with finely painted rural scenes.

From the Ship Room, one heads back up the passage, passing the Dining Room en route. To the right, near the Entrance Hall, steps ascend in a rather tortuous manner to the Long Gallery - the sunniest place in the castle and where guests assembled before meals. It is mostly by Lutyens, has a partly Romanesque character, and provides access to a row of bedrooms, of which the East and West Bedrooms are the most important.

The former contains furniture designed by Lutyens and a bed bearing the date 1753 and, in common with the

60. The Ship Room (Andreas von Einsiedel, © The National Trust)

other bedrooms, has a simple, utilitarian character with whitewashed walls. The West Bedroom, which lies off the far end of the Long Gallery, has a beamed ceiling and is dominated by a large Flemish bed of essentially 17th century date, with panelled and carved oak.

Stairs at the west end of the Long Gallery ascend to the Upper Gallery, a long narrow room which looks like an interior scene in a painting by Vermeer.

Upon returning to the Long Gallery, a door near the West Bedroom opens to the upper battery, a more confined space than the larger lower battery and a place from which one can again enjoy splendid views of the island and the Northumberland coast.

LINDISFARNE PRIORY

Lindisfarne Priory was founded in Norman times by Benedictine monks from Durham Cathedral Priory and lies in the south-west corner of Holy Island, on the outskirts of the only village.

Centuries earlier, however, another religious house had existed on the island, (which is also known as Lindisfarne) and evidently occupied the same site as the subsequent Benedictine priory. It was founded in 635 by a celebrated figure in the history of northern Christianity, Aidan, a monk from Iona - an island off the west coast of Scotland - who settled here with the blessing of the King of Northumbria, Oswald. The king was eager to have Christianity established among his pagan people and Aidan and his companions, fellow Celtic monks, soon gained a reputation for sanctity. They engaged in evangelical work, travelling extensively across Northumbria, preaching and baptizing, and spent the rest of the year living an ascetic life in humble dwellings associated with a simple timber church. Aidan and his successors, the most notable of whom was St Cuthbert (who died on nearby Farne Island in 687) not only served as the abbots but were also the Bishops of Bernicia - northern Northumbria.

In 793 tragedy struck. Viking raiders sacked the monastery - the first such raid on an English monastic house. During the 9th century Danish raids against England increased and in 875, following another assault, the monks decided that Lindisfarne was too vulnerable. They abandoned the site, never to return, taking with them their most treasured possessions, chief of which was the uncorrupt body of St Cuthbert. In time, they settled at Chester-le-Street and about a century later, in 995, with Vikings once again at large, their successors moved to Durham.

In the Norman period, as noted, Lindisfarne evidently became a cell of Durham Cathedral Priory and it was at about this time that the island became generally known as Holy Island. Just when Lindisfarne Priory was established is uncertain. It is sometimes said that monks from Durham founded a community here in the late 11th century. For example, it has been said that building began at almost the same time as it did on Durham Cathedral, where work commenced in 1093. According to Eric Cambridge however, the earliest evidence records events later than this and mentions the activities of a Durham monk named Edward, who organized the building of a church on Lindisfarne dedicated to St Cuthbert in or prior to 1122.

It is normally assumed that the present priory church is the structure in question. But Edward's church may have been a short-lived affair which was then replaced by a grander one, for this is known to have occurred at other monastic sites in the 12th century. If this were the case, Edward's church must have been rapidly replaced. The style of the existing ruins indicates that c.1150 at the latest was the date of their completion.

As Lindisfarne Priory occupied a site connected with the north's premier saint it was of great significance to the mother-house, whose members wished to emphasize their links with St Cuthbert. And what of pilgrims? Did the priory act as a magnet for them? It would be natural to assume that this was the case. Records reveal otherwise. It is evident that nearby Farne Island (where Cuthbert had once lived as a hermit and had of course died) attracted more devotees of his cult.

The priory was staffed by monks from Durham who did not usually stay long before being recalled to the mother-house or sent to one of Durham's other cells, and the community was never large. There is reason to believe that the initial complement was very small and that it was not until the late 12th century that the size of the community was such that regular conventual buildings began to be erected. Double figures were seldom if ever reached. Indeed, by the early 15th century the community had dropped to three monks.

The decline was principally due to the uncertainty and economic dislocation caused in the area during the 14th century by the Scottish wars that had begun in 1296. Much of the priory's income, for instance, was provided by the corn-tithes of the parish of Lindisfarne, which not only comprised Holy Island but a sizeable extent of the adjacent mainland, one of the parts of Northumberland most exposed to enemy activity. Revenue from tithes declined substantially owing to the destabilization of the area caused by conflict with Scotland. In 1327, for instance, a monastic accountant lamented the fact that the tithes which had been worth £107 before the commencement of hostilities had dropped to £21 that year. Renewed warfare in subsequent years, combined with deaths caused by plague - most notably the Black Death - led to a decline in population and the amount of land under cultivation, with obvious repercussions on the priory's income.

During the 14th century, Holy Island was frequently used as a venue by royal purveyors for goods in transit to English armies campaigning in Scotland. Fear that this might lead to Scottish aggression against the island may well have been one of the factors which caused the monks to decide to fortify the priory. Just when this work was undertaken is unknown, but it appears to have occurred by the mid 14th century. Among other things, a new perimeter wall with a wall-walk was constructed; strong defences were provided for the

61. The ruins of the priory church, looking east

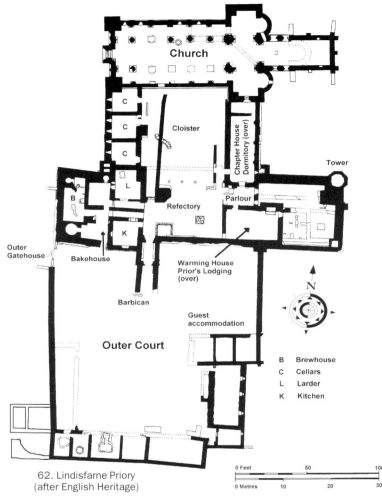

62. Lindisfarne Priory
(after English Heritage)

B   Brewhouse
C   Cellars
L   Larder
K   Kitchen

prior's lodging at the southeast corner of the claustral buildings; and the church was provided with low-pitched roofs with embattled parapets, and arrow slits in the upper part of the west gable and perhaps elsewhere. Further measures were taken to safeguard the priory. We hear, for instance, that in 1346 during the campaign which culminated in the Battle of Neville's Cross, the monks paid 6d. for the services of a watchman who had to give warning of any threat by invaders. Moreover, according to Barrie Dobson 'the Holy Island account rolls never give an impression of more hectic military activity on the island than they do between 1380 and 1388.'

In November 1462, during the Wars of the Roses, a party of French troops that had arrived in the North East to fight on behalf of the Lancastrian branch of the English royal family came to grief on Holy Island. Having been shipwrecked in the vicinity, they sheltered in the priory, only to be attacked and overwhelmed by Yorkist soldiers. According to some accounts, men were actually killed in the very church itself.

Lindisfarne Priory was dissolved in 1537, during the Dissolution of the Monasteries.

Description

The ruins are very interesting. This is especially true of the church, much of which stands to a good height. Although its scale is modest, it was an elaborate structure and similarities to Durham Cathedral suggest that it was designed and built by masons sent from Durham. As Cambridge comments, 'the possibility that the appearance of the church which housed Cuthbert's shrine was . . . deliberately emulated in this outpost of his cult cannot be ignored.' Chevron ornament was used throughout the church, unlike at Durham where it was introduced well into the building programme, and this supports the view, derived from records, that work on Lindisfarne began some years after it did so at Durham.

The church was built of dark red stone which, owing to weathering, has lost much of its hue. The visitor comes first to the west front, carefully rebuilt by the Crown following the collapse of much of the fabric in the 1850s. Here, there is a slightly projecting porch with a typically Norman doorway. There are three orders of columns with cushion capitals supporting round arches with chevron moulding, and between the columns are geometrical motifs. Above the doorway are two round-headed openings, of which the lower one would initially have been concealed behind a steeply pitched gable that doubtless housed a minute chamber above the entrance.

The doorway is flanked by four blank arches, two on either side. At each corner of the west front was a projecting turret: that to the north has virtually disappeared whereas its southern counterpart survives to nearly full height. Both contained a spiral staircase leading to the upper parts of the church, including two cross-shaped arrow loops in the parapet high above the entrance porch.

Inside the church, the west doorway has two orders of columns with cushion capitals and finely moulded arches. Above, is a narrow wall passage which gave access to the chamber over the entrance. The passage has an arcade open to the nave comprising five arches on short columns, and with the middle arch slightly larger than the others.

The nave is of six bays and is reminiscent of that of Durham Cathedral. The piers are, or were, alternately compound and cylindrical (only the two eastern bays of the north aisle arcade survive), and again, like Durham, the cylindrical piers were incised with chevron, diaper and fluting ornament. Drawings executed in the 18th and 19th centuries indicate that

63. An engraving of the nave, looking west (J. R. Billing)

above each aisle was a triforium with paired arches opening to the nave in each bay, and that above each pair was a small window. Hence the nave had a three-storeyed elevation: those of the transepts and chancel were of two storeys.

The nave was vaulted, as was the rest of the church, a further sign that although modest in scale Lindisfarne was intended to be a building of note, for it was highly unusual for vaults to be provided throughout monastic churches at this date in England, one of the few other examples being, not surprisingly, Durham Cathedral. Lindisfarne's nave was covered with groin vaults. On this point, J.P. McAleer comments: 'That the nave of Lindisfarne was covered by rectangular groin vaults, after ribbed vaults had been used everywhere else in the building, is both unexpected and seemingly perverse.'

The church had a crossing tower, but this collapsed in the late 18th century. On the other hand, this part of the church contains a fortunate survival, a rib (popularly known as the 'rainbow arch') extending diagonally from the north-west to the south-east crossing pier. It has elaborate chevron moulding and is a striking feature that has a unifying effect. Just above the level of the springing of the arch, can be seen openings that gave access to small arcaded passages which ran around each side of the tower.

And what of the transepts? These are small and have a shallow semicircular apse on their east side: each apse would have housed an altar. The north transept, moreover, has a large north window. Furthermore, a spiral stair in the west corner of each transept ascended to the upper parts of the church.

Turning to the chancel, this was originally two bays long and terminated in an apse, the lower courses of whose wall are visible within the present chancel. But no sooner was the church finished than it was decided to lengthen the chancel, which was extended by about 16½ft (5m) and given a straight end, making the church approximately 161ft (49m) long. Evidently, the high altar was placed right at the east end of the extension. The three large windows of the extension date from the 14th century and are now devoid of tracery.

In contrast to the church, the monastic buildings are of grey stone and date from the late 12th century or later. Little remains of the east range, the last of the claustral ranges to be built, which dates from the 13th century. A door in the south transept gave access to a sacristy, beyond which was the chapter house. Unusually, this had its longer axis parallel to the east cloister walk instead of at right angles to it. The monks' dormitory was above the chapter house. Beyond the chapter house was a parlour and then the warming house. The latter occupied the ground floor of a two-storey building on an east-west axis whose upper floor served as the prior's principal chamber (his study and chapel were probably located above the parlour). The fireplace on each floor is preserved, as is the large chimneystack that served both, and were built in the 14th century during a reconstruction of the prior's apartments.

To the east of the parlour and the building just referred to, is an area enclosed by 14th century defensive walls, and in the north-east angle are the remains of a much ruined tower. In the enclosed space, are the remains of what was probably an infirmary built in the 13th century.

West of the warming house and prior's lodging, lie the scanty remains of the refectory in the south range. The range was originally built slightly to the north but was rebuilt in its present location in the 13th century, a transformation which led to the cloister becoming oblong instead of square.

At the west end of the refectory (or as it became in the course of time, the prior's hall),

64. A view of the site from the south-east. On the left is St Mary's Church, essentially a 13th century structure, but containing possible Anglo-Saxon fabric. It was not part of the priory.

was a passage on a north-south axis with doorways opening westward to the kitchen and larder, with the former being the southernmost of the two. In the 14th century, a block containing a bakehouse and a brewhouse was built against the west end of both rooms. To the north, the larder is adjoined by the rest of the west range, fabric likely dating from the late 12th century. In the 14th century, the ground floor here was divided into three vaulted rooms which served as cellars. Initially, the first floor may have functioned as the prior's lodging, but in due course it probably housed important guests.

Finally, mention must be made of the outer court. This is located to the south of the claustral ranges and was entered via the passage referred to above, one of whose functions was thus to connect the inner parts of the monastery with the more public space of the outer court. During the troubled years of the 14th century, a barbican was provided to defend the entrance to the passage from the latter. Fortunately, the perimeter wall of the court still stands to a good height - an unusual feature - and the remains of a gatehouse near the north-west corner of the perimeter can be seen. This controlled entry into the court from the outer world. The low walls of a number of buildings in the enclosed area are also visible. The structures situated along the south wall of the court may have been used for the storage or preparation of food, while it is apparent that the large building in the south-east corner served as a guest-house. The court would have contained more buildings than the remains suggest, and among such would have been accommodation for livestock such as cows and pigs.

Lindisfarne Priory is in the hands of English Heritage and is one of its most popular sites.

NEWCASTLE UPON TYNE CASTLE

In 1080, following a campaign in which he had penetrated far into Scotland, William the Conqueror's eldest son, Robert Curthose, founded a castle overlooking the lowest bridging point of the River Tyne at the site of a former Roman fort.

The castle, built of earth and timber and surrounded by a ditch, strengthened the Norman presence in the region and was situated in a strong position about 100ft (30m) above the Tyne, to which the ground fell away steeply on the south side. To the north, moreover, was a deep ravine through which a tributary stream flowed east towards the Lort burn, which in turn flowed through low ground just to the east of the castle en route to the Tyne. Only to the west of the castle was there relatively level ground.

William the Conqueror's relationship with his eldest son proved difficult. Hence, upon his death in 1087, William left England to another son, William II, whereas Robert inherited the ancestral duchy of Normandy.

In 1095, William II was faced with a rebellion by Robert de Mowbray, the Earl of Northumberland, who enjoyed possession of the castle founded on Tyneside by Robert Curthose. William thus marched north to crush the revolt, and during the campaign the castle was captured by royal forces.

In 1100 he was succeeded by another brother, Henry I who, like him, was on poor terms with Robert Curthose. Henry subsequently defeated Robert in battle in Normandy in 1106 and had him brought across the Channel where he ended his days in captivity at Cardiff in 1134, by which time a town had begun to develop outside the 'New Castle' Robert had founded beside the Tyne over fifty years earlier, a castle from which the town derived its name.

Shortly thereafter, in 1139, the earldom of Northumberland was granted to the eldest son of the King of Scotland by King Stephen. It is sometimes said that the castle at Newcastle was excluded from the grant but this appears to be incorrect: evidence shows that both David and his son spent time at Newcastle and various charters and grants were made here.

In 1157 Northumberland returned to the hands of the English Crown in the person of Henry II - a monarch doubtless best known for his quarrel with the Archbishop of Canterbury, Thomas Becket. In 1168 Henry began rebuilding the castle of Newcastle in stone, a massive programme that lasted ten years, cost £1,144, and included the erection of an impressive keep. A pause then ensued during the reign of Richard the Lionheart before construction work resumed in the early years of the 13th century when Henry's youngest son, John, was on the throne. John was perhaps also responsible for constructing a no longer extant aisled hall against the east curtain hall: the earliest reference to the hall dates from May 1237 during the reign of his son, Henry III.

A decade later, the latter monarch added the Black Gate and an inner barbican at the northern apex of the roughly triangular-shaped defences, with the new work adjoining the north-west end of an earlier structure, the North Gate. Indirectly, additional protection was subsequently provided when the castle was enclosed by the construction of formidable town walls in the late 13th and 14th centuries.

In late 1297, following the severe defeat of an English army at Stirling Bridge in Scotland, Northumberland's inhabitants expected the Scots to conduct cross border incursions - as had happened the previous year - and thus, states the chronicler Walter of Guisborough, 'were petrified with fear.' Newcastle prepared for the worst. Wallace gave Newcastle a wide berth, however, and after plundering parts of Northumberland, devastated much of Cumbria before returning to Northumberland later in the year. He then advanced in bitterly cold weather down the Tyne valley towards the partially fortified town of Newcastle whose castle garrison had comprised 6 men-at-arms, 60 crossbowmen and 40 other archers since 6 November. In the event, Wallace again failed to press home an attack and headed north, homeward bound.

At the time of the Battle of Bannockburn in 1314, the castle was said to be in a good state of repair. In 1334, things were different. The fortress was said to be suffering from neglect. Repair work ensued in the years 1336-38 and in the 1350s. However, the provision of the town defences appears to have rendered the castle obsolescent: few repairs of the fabric are mentioned after the middle of the 14th century.

65. The keep and forebuilding

On a number of occasions over the years, the heads or quartered remains of executed individuals were displayed on the keep, as was the case for instance in 1323 when a quarter of the body of Andrew Harclay, the Earl of Carlisle, was treated in this manner after he had been executed for treason for endeavouring to end Anglo-Scottish conflict during the dark days of Edward II's troubled reign.

In 1589, during the days of Queen Elizabeth, the castle was described as being ruinous. From the early 17th century onward this state of affairs was exacerbated by the construction of shops and houses on much of the site, a process that resulted in the piecemeal destruction of much of the castle.

In 1643, during the Civil War, the Royalist Mayor of Newcastle, Sir John Marley, is known to have repaired the keep and he was no doubt also responsible for a general refortification of the castle, something that among other things entailed the removal of houses.

Scottish armies that entered England in 1644 to aid parliament's war effort, besieged Newcastle twice that year. The main siege began during the summer and bitter fighting ensued in which the castle managed to hold out until 22 October, three days longer than had the town.

The keep served as a prison from the 16th to the 18th century, but nonetheless continued to slowly decay. In 1777, it was observed 'that during the assizes at Newcastle, the county prisoners are, men and women, confined together seven or eight nights, in a dirty damp dungeon . . . in the old castle, which, having no roof, in wet seasons the water is some inches deep. The felons are chained to rings in the wall.' It was in the late 18th century, moreover, that a garden is said to have existed on the battlements of the keep. Furthermore, by the latter part of the 18th century much of the keep's ground floor was being used as beer cellars for a nearby public house.

In around 1790 an anonymous writer commented as follows: 'The immediate environs of the keep . . . especially on the south side, are in a very nasty state, there being many pigstyes, dunghills, and receptacles of filth all thereabouts.'

'By 1800', states John Nolan, 'the population and buildings . . . had reached their peak of growth . . . . There were now more than fifty houses within the castle boundary into which several hundred persons . . . were packed.'

This state of affairs was not destined to continue: the 19th century witnessed a change of fortune. In 1809 Newcastle Corporation bought the keep and provided it with a roof and new battlements. Moreover, the private dwellings occupying the area of the castle were subsequently demolished partly, it has to be said, to make way in the middle years of the century for the construction of a railway viaduct that lies immediately north of the keep and thus bisects the site of the castle.

In addition, guns were placed on the keep's battlements to be fired during festive periods. In 1812, however, during the festivities of Ascension Day, a cartridge exploded and an unfortunate gunner was blown over the parapet to his death.

The following year witnessed the inauguration of the Society of Antiquaries of Newcastle upon Tyne in the keep, and the society's connection with the castle has continued to this day: the Black Gate, which houses the society's library, was restored from a state of dereliction in 1883.

Description

The castle was divided by a cross wall into north and south baileys and the keep, which as mentioned above dates from 1168-78, stood in the south-west corner of the former, on the most elevated part of the site. The keep was accessible from the south bailey, and stood near a gatehouse (demolished in 1810) located just to the south-west in the castle's perimeter wall.

Most of this wall has gone. However, a substantial extent of the south curtain survives. It was excavated and restored between 1960 and 1971 and, among other things, part of a flight of stairs that led to the wall-walk can be seen, as can the south postern, through which one can approach the keep.

The keep, one of the finest examples of its type in the country, is roughly square in plan, measures 62 by 56ft (19 by 17m), and rises 81ft (24.7m) to the flat roof, while corner turrets rise approximately 6½ft (2m) further. Some of the masonry on the south and west faces dates from restoration work undertaken in the 1970s. In its heyday, the keep served as the main strongpoint of the castle and as the residence of the garrison's commander. Each floor contains one large room. The keep also has additional chambers located within the walls - which are about 15ft (4.6m) thick - as are stairs, latrines, galleries and a well room. The main spiral stair, which ascends to the battlements, is located in the south-east turret.

The keep is entered from the south via a forebuilding against its east side. The forebuilding contains a straight staircase that leads up to the second of the keep's upper floors - normally such stairs would only lead to the first floor - and this feature is also found at Dover where a splendid keep was erected by Henry II, evidently employing the services of the same architect or master mason, named Maurice, who worked on his behalf at Newcastle. To one's left, when standing at the head of the stairs, is a very ornate doorway with lozenge and nailhead decoration. Restored by Dobson in 1847, it opens to a tunnel-vaulted passage that leads to the Great Hall, the largest room in the keep.

66. The keep's ornate doorway reached via steps in the forebuilding

However, nowadays visitors enter the keep from the forebuilding stairs at first floor level via a doorway that only dates from the 19th century. This opens to a ticket office, occupying a small chamber formerly used to observe the movement of people on the stairs in the forebuilding. The room was originally only reached from the main spiral stair in the south-east turret.

To the west, lies the first floor's principal room, which serves as a museum dealing with the history of the site and is entered directly from the ticket office, although originally there was no direct access between the rooms. It is a hall, divided into two sections by a 19th century circular pier with a plain octagonal capital from which spring two single-chamfered arches. Off the north-west corner of the room, lies the Queen's Chamber, which had access to a latrine in the west wall.

The ground floor is reached by descending the main spiral stair. At this level, the forebuilding contains a small chapel (which originally could only be entered from outside the building), and consists of a nave with a chancel set at right-angles to it on an east-west axis. The nave, measuring about 17 by 12ft (5.2 by 3.66m), is two bays long, vaulted - the ribs of the northernmost bay are the most richly ornamented - and lit by two round-headed windows that are larger than was originally the case. Along the west and east walls, moreover, are arches enriched with chevron. At the north end of the nave is a semicircular arch, again bearing chevron ornament, that opens to the chancel, which measures approximately 20 by 12ft (6.1 by 3.66m) from east to west and is lit by two round-headed windows. It is 21ft high (6.4m) and, like the nave, has quadripartite vaulting, save for the west end which is lower and covered by a tunnel-vault.

The largest chamber on the ground floor is the Garrison Room, which probably housed storage before later accommodating prisoners. During the Second World War it served as an air raid shelter. In the centre, is a cylindrical pier from which spring chamfered ribs that divide the vault into eight cells, and the ribs are also carried by chamfered corbels set at different levels around the walls. Two loops admit light.

From here, one heads back up the spiral stairway, en route to the second floor and the Great Hall. This measures 30ft (9.1m) from north to south by just under 24ft (7.3m), and is lit by two-light windows, two of which are placed high in the south wall, and one each at a lower level in the east and north walls. The roof dates from the 19th century and is higher than was originally the case. From the north-west corner of the Great Hall a passage led to a latrine in the west wall of the keep, whereas an opening in the west jamb of the north window gave access to a small chamber.

Off the hall's south-west corner is a former private room known as the King's Chamber. This had a fire-place, four windows, and access to a latrine located in the keep's west wall. On the other hand, off the north-east side of the hall lies the well room. In the early 20th century the well was cleaned out and was found to descend to a depth of 99ft (30.2m).

Also at second floor level, a straight stair leads off the spiral stair in the south-east corner of the keep and heads

67. The Black Gate, viewed from the south

68. The Black Gate, originally approached
across a drawbridge

through the east wall to another spiral stair in the north-east angle. The spirals ascend to a high wall-passage running right around the four walls of the keep. This gallery has openings that provide views of the Great Hall below. Originally, however, they overlooked its roof and when within the hall, one can see, just below the gallery openings, the beam slots that held the timbers. Furthermore, a gallery also runs along the south side of the keep at a lower level, connecting the windows on the south side of the Great Hall and terminating at an unfinished staircase in the keep's west wall. Finally, as far as the keep is concerned, the northern spiral, like its counterpart in the south-east turret, ascends to the battlements.

Apart from the keep, the most notable part of the castle to have survived is the Black Gate, which lies to the north. Described by William Henry Knowles as 'an excellent example of a military structure skilfully planned', it was built in the years 1247-50 and was first referred to as the Black Gate in 1649. How high the gatehouse was originally is uncertain, but there were doubtless three floors. Its appearance was transformed when a brick house with mullioned and transomed windows was erected above original fabric in the early 17th century.

The Black Gate was approached via a drawbridge across a moat. On the outer side of the moat was a bridge abutment consisting of a mound of brown clay and stones, and revetted on three sides by walls of ashlar. Below the outer half of the gate passage itself, and visible beneath a modern fixed bridge, are slots in which the counter-weights of the drawbridge swung.

The gatehouse is roughly oval in shape and consists of a gate passage flanked by towers and covered by a pointed tunnel vault. At the outer end of the passage was a portcullis, beyond which, in the middle of the entranceway, was a gate. Moreover, on either side of the passage was a rib-vaulted guardroom with three arrow slits with widely splayed jambs. Upon progressing through the gatehouse one entered a small enclosed space, turned southeastward and apparently crossed another drawbridge before passing through the North Gate, whose remains are fragmentary.

NORHAM CASTLE

Norham Castle occupies a strong position beside the River Tweed on the border between England and Scotland, and commanded one of the fords crossing the river.

For much of its history, Norham was situated in an outlying part of the palatinate of Durham (see pages 11-12) and was thus administered by officials answerable to the Bishop of Durham, the most important of the officers being the Sheriff of Norham who was more often than not also the constable of Norham Castle.

The honour of founding the castle belongs to Bishop Ranulf Flambard (1099-1128), who gave orders for its construction in or about 1121 in order to protect his property in the area. Flambard was a colourful figure. Prior to becoming Bishop of Durham he had gained notoriety by raising revenue for his master, William II, in an exacting and unscrupulous manner. As bishop, he likewise gave cause for comment. William of Malmesbury, for instance, tells us that Flambard used to dine on meals served by young ladies wearing figure-hugging dresses.

Norham Castle had an eventful existence. The first recorded incident occurred in 1136 when it was captured during an invasion of Northumberland by David I of Scotland, an ambitious monarch eager to extend his authority southward. It was soon handed back to its rightful owner, only to be recaptured again in 1138 during another invasion, at which time its fortifications were subjected to substantial destruction.

The castle remained derelict until the episcopate of Hugh du Puiset (who held the bishopric of Durham between 1153 and 1195), a man of whom the historian William of Newburgh wrote acidly, 'the more Hugh was anxious to build on earth, the more remiss he was in building in heaven.' Puiset certainly had a fondness for grandeur and left behind him an important architectural legacy that includes much of the fabric at Norham. He is usually credited with transforming the derelict castle into a stone fortress, though as will be seen the widely held assumption that timber had been entirely used in lieu of stone by Flambard is evidently incorrect. The work was probably undertaken under the direction of Richard of Wolviston, the bishop's architect, and was apparently completed by 1174 when Hugh was forced to surrender the castle into royal hands after favouring the losing side in a rebellion.

Consequently, Norham was placed under constables appointed by the Crown and garrisoned by the king's men, a situation that continued until 1197 (two years after Hugh du Puiset had 'gone the way of all flesh') when it was restored to his successor, Bishop Philip of Poitou, who in subsequent years was to prove a loyal adherent of King John.

In 1209 the king came to Norham. The castle was in royal hands again, following Philip's death the previous year. Scotland's monarch, William the Lion, was likewise present and did homage to John and agreed to pay his more powerful neighbour tribute. For his part, in the years 1208-11 John lavished money on Norham, which was thus maintained in good condition and provided with a strong garrison. It was just as well. In 1215 Alexander II of Scotland besieged the castle, but was forced to abandon the attempt after a siege lasting forty days. Two years later, the castle was once again restored to the bishopric of Durham.

John was not the only English monarch to visit Norham. His formidable grandson,

69. Norham Castle as seen from the west, showing the main entrance,
with the imposing keep in the background (Andrew Stephenson)

Edward I, did so more than once. For example, he was present in late 1292 when Scotland's monarch, John Balliol, swore fealty (loyalty) to him. Four years later, however, war broke out between the two countries for many Scots resented the fact that Edward viewed himself as overlord of Scotland. The Bishop of Durham at this date was Antony Bek, who had strengthened Norham's defences, and during part of the subsequent campaigning Edward's second queen, a young woman by the name of Margaret, resided in the castle.

Hostilities continued intermittently in the early decades of the 14th century and witnessed a number of Scottish incursions. On some such, attempts were not made to take Norham, but in 1318 King Robert the Bruce laid siege to the castle at the head of a powerful force. It proved too strong a nut to crack. True, the Scots managed to occupy part of the castle - the outer ward - but were driven back after holding it for three days. The siege dragged on for nearly a year before the Scots finally had enough. The following year, they were back. But once again they were thwarted, this time after a siege lasting seven months. In 1322 yet another unsuccessful siege occurred.

The second siege is associated with the name of an English knight, Sir William Marmion. He journeyed to Norham from Lincolnshire in obedience to the command of his lady love that he should make his way to the most dangerous part of England, and there, by deeds of gallantry, make famous a helmet with a gilt crest that she had sent to him. Four days after his arrival, the 'most spirited chivalry of the Scottish Marches' appeared before the main gate. Aware of the reason for Marmion's presence, the constable of Norham told him to charge into the midst of the enemy, promising that he would render support. Hence Marmion, 'all glittering with gold and silver, marvellously finely attired with the helmet on his head', sallied forth alone. He was unhorsed, wounded, and in dire danger. But just in time, reinforcements under the constable appeared and routed the enemy. During this, and the other two sieges mentioned, Norham's constable was Sir Thomas Grey of Heton, a local knight who had been captured by the Scots at Bannockburn in 1314.

In early 1327 a retreating Scottish army that had ravaged much of the border region, stormed Norham while returning home. Its stay in Scottish hands proved brief. Peace was soon agreed between the countries and Norham was restored to the Bishop of Durham.

In 1355, Norham's constable was another member of the Grey family of Heton, Sir Thomas Grey II, the son of the constable who had steered the castle through its most turbulent period. In August of this year, Grey sallied forth from the castle against a party of Scottish spearmen who were raiding in the vicinity. It proved a mistake. He was ambushed and taken north to Edinburgh where he was to remain in confinement for two years. But Grey's loss of freedom was our gain. During his captivity he put quill to parchment and wrote a book called *Scalacronica*, that includes an account of his times that contains much of interest.

The 15th century proved more peaceful for Norham than the 14th. The castle was nonetheless kept in good repair and improvements made to make it conform to the more civilized standards of the age. Moreover, it did witness further conflict. It did so during the Wars of the Roses in the latter half of the century. In 1462, Norham was held for the Yorkist, Edward IV. In the summer of the following year a large Lancastrian army under his adversaries, Henry VI and Queen Margaret, partly comprised of French and Scottish soldiers, laid siege to the castle and did so for eighteen days until Yorkist forces arrived on the scene and relieved the defenders. The Wars of the Roses witnessed many twists and turns of fortune, and the Yorkist stance of Norham's garrison did not prove constant. In early 1464 Norham changed sides, only to surrender to the Yorkists later that year following significant reverses for the Lancastrian party in Northumberland.

Norham's defences were strengthened early in the episcopate of Bishop Fox (1494-1501). The prelate was present at Norham when the castle was besieged in August 1497 by Scotland's king, James IV, a highly able and extremely popular monarch, an adventurous, high-spirited character who loved hunting, hawking and womanizing and was described by Spain's Ambassador to Scotland as 'of noble stature, neither tall nor short, and as handsome in complexion as a man can be.' He put Norham's defences to the test for two weeks, employing artillery, (an arm of war in which he was deeply interested), until Norham was relieved by the approach of an English army. Repair work ensued. Furthermore, new buildings were added at this time and in the early 16th century.

In 1513 James IV laid siege to Norham once again shortly after invading England at the head of what was probably the most powerful Scottish force ever to do so, complete with an impressive artillery train drawn by 400 oxen. James crossed the Tweed at or near Coldstream on or about 23 August and moved downstream, determined to take Norham, whose capture was a major objective of the campaign. For several days his guns pounded its defences and much of the walling was destroyed. The outer ward was stormed and, on 28 or 29 August, the castle surrendered. Within weeks, however, Norham was back in English hands for on 9 September James was defeated and killed in battle at Flodden Field a few miles to the south-west after engaging an English army under the Earl of Surrey.

Immediately after hearing of Flodden's outcome, Bishop Ruthall of Durham made his way to see Norham, of which only the keep and a section of the west wall were standing, and restoration work rapidly began. By August, 1515, the bulk of this had been undertaken. But further construction work ensued until 1521 when Lord Dacre reported that the inner

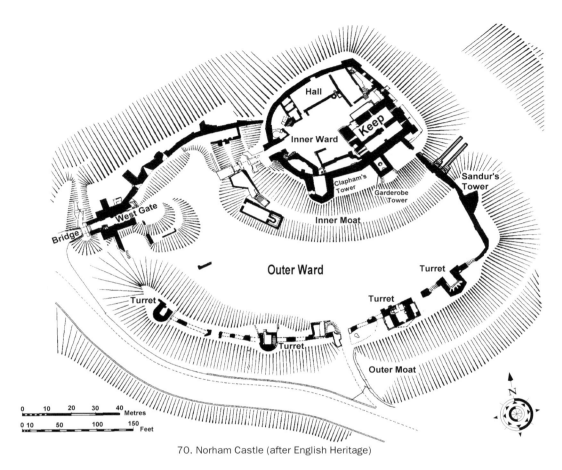

70. Norham Castle (after English Heritage)

ward had been completed and was of such strength that 'with the help of God and the prayer of St Cuthbert it is unprignable.' However, Dacre also commented that more artillery and gunpowder were needed for the gatehouses and the outer ward. Two years later the Earl of Surrey, in his capacity as Lord Warden of the Marches, added to Norham's defences and had expert gunners brought up from Portsmouth to serve as members of the garrison. In 1542, Sir Robert Bowes reported that the castle was in a good condition and 'well furnyshed and stuffed with artillery, munitions, and other necessaries.'

Norham remained well cared for throughout the 1540s, a period of conflict between England and Scotland, but thereafter it suffered neglect and the garrison was reduced. In 1571 the castle was described as being in such a state of decay that unless repair work was undertaken no one could live in it - Norham's great days were well and truly over.

Description

Norham Castle stands in a commanding position on the south bank of the Tweed, towards which the ground falls away sharply to the north. Additional natural protection was afforded by a deep ravine to the east. An artificial ditch was however required to help protect the west and southern sides of the fortress.

Norham consists of an inner ward located on a mound surrounded by a deep ditch, which formed the core of the castle, and a larger outer ward to the south and west, (to which it was connected by a drawbridge), which housed ancillary buildings.

One enters the outer ward via one or other of two gateways in the curtain wall: the West Gate and the Sheep Gate, both formerly strongly fortified gate towers. The former was Norham's principal entrance, but most visitors will enter the castle through the Sheep Gate, located on the south side of the outer ward, as it is closest to the visitors' car park. The Sheep Gate dates from the late 12th or early 13th century and is approached over a causeway occupying the former site of a drawbridge across what was a wide and deep moat. Little of the gate tower (whose upper storeys served as the constable's accommodation) has survived.

More survives of the West Gate and it is advisable to enter the castle by wandering around to where it stands at the north-west corner of the outer ward, looking towards the village of Norham on lower ground a short distance to the west. Previously known as Marmion's Gate, it was built in the 12th century. A period of disuse followed when it was closed in the 14th century. It was then reopened and greatly altered early the following century. The gate tower was demolished, save for some of the lower masonry - substantial remains of which still survive - and a new gate built and provided with a barbican. A draw-

bridge formed part of the ensemble and was pivoted at the centre, so that when its outer half was raised the remainder descended into a pit that can be seen below the present bridge.

Much of the curtain wall running eastward from the West Gate, along the top of a steep wooded bank that falls sharply away towards the Tweed, dates from a period of rebuilding in the early 16th century. Upon walking alongside the wall, one comes to the site of the castle chapel. This stood against the curtain wall, at the north end of the moat of the inner ward, and was above a cellar, only part of which has survived.

A modern wooden bridge, occupying the site of a former drawbridge, leads across the moat of the inner ward to the most extensive remains at Norham, those of the keep and associated buildings in the inner ward, buildings formerly approached through a gateway on the inner side of the moat.

Immediately to one's left, upon passing the vestiges of the inner ward gate-

71. The keep, with the inner moat in the foreground

way, are the low remains of a kitchen, including its huge oven. The kitchen was built against the inner face of the north curtain wall and was adjoined to the east by a buttery, pantry and service passage. Beyond these, occupying much of the north side of the inner ward, and again against the curtain wall, lies what has survived of the bishop's hall. The fabric is believed to date from the early 16th century, but the hall, measuring 60 by 30ft (18.3 by 9.1m), no doubt stands on the site of earlier great halls. A well lies outside the south-east corner of the bishop's hall, while at the east end of the hall, and at right angles to it, is the site of the Great Chamber, 23 by 49ft (7 by 14.9m). A range of chambers above cellarage was moreover built against the east curtain wall of the inner ward.

Externally, the keep, which stands in the south-east corner of the inner ward, measures 84 by 60ft (25.6 by 18.3m) and rises to a height of 88ft (26.8m). It is usually dated to the days of Bishop Puiset, save for subsequent alterations and rebuilding. Philip Dixon and Pamela Marshall disagree. They maintain, and evidently correctly so, that the keep's earliest fabric was erected by Flambard and belonged to a rectangular two-storeyed building whose upper floor likely comprised a grand ceremonial chamber, around 59ft (18m) long and nearly 23ft (7m) wide, entered from the north via an external flight of steps located near its west end.

Subsequently, no doubt during the episcopate of Puiset, extra chambers were built against the south side of the original structure, with the eastern end of the new work rising higher than any of the other fabric and containing an upper room at third-storey level. Later, still, in around 1422-25, further alterations and additions were made which included heightening the keep to provide additional accommodation, and the construction of a newel staircase in the centre of the west wall that provided access to each floor and rose to a look-out turret above roof level. To quote Dixon and Marshall, this work 'converted the jumbled elevation of the early works into a regularly shaped rectangular tower (but with a new function as a lodging block without any particularly grand or lofty rooms), and thus provided students of the castle with another apparent example of the conventional Romanesque rectangular donjon.' Moreover, in 1429-33 a garderobe tower was erected at the west end of the south front. Then, in the 16th century, the topmost storey was subdivided to form two very low floors, with the result that the keep comprised five storeys.

At ground floor level, a spine wall divides the keep into two unequal portions. That to the north, lit by splayed loop windows, is partly covered by an early Norman vault that comprised four groin-vaulted bays divided by three transverse ribs: the two eastern vaults are still intact. The southern part of the ground floor is narrower and covered by a tunnel-vault, except at its west end where it is groin-vaulted. Here, the

72. The north portion of the keep's ground floor, covered by an early Norman vault

73. The narrower, southern section of the keep's ground floor

74. The east end of the first floor chamber attributed to Flambard by Dixon and Marshall, with a stone bench below a window. In the far right of the picture is fabric dating from the days of Hugh du Puiset

west wall contains a 15th century doorway and window. Only one original loop survives - in the centre of the east wall.

Dixon and Marshall attribute the northern portion of the ground floor to Flambard, and the narrower southern section to Puiset. Above the former are the remains of what, as mentioned above, was likely Flambard's grand ceremonial hall with, at the east or 'high' end, a stone bench below a blocked window. At this end of the room was an opening in the north wall. This gave access to a

75. The keep as viewed from the outer ward. The low remains of Clapham's Tower lie to the left (west) of the keep

mural passage that perhaps led to a latrine with an outlet through the east wall. Evidently, in the 15th century, the passage was blocked off when the wall was refaced during the heightening of the keep to provide additional storeys.

The first floor of Puiset's addition, formerly entered towards the east end from Flambard's hall through a doorway in the intervening spine wall, but now reached via the 15th century newel stair in the west wall of the keep, either contained a single bipartite chamber (the eastern end of which was groin-vaulted, while the remainder was beneath a wooden roof), or was divided into two rooms by a timber partition. Windows in wide embrasures provided light, and there was a fireplace towards the west end of the south wall. At the extreme west end of this wall is a blocked opening that presumably gave access to a latrine with a chute corbelled out from the wall: later, as mentioned above, a garderobe tower was added at this point, serving chambers in newly built upper storeys.

Above the groin-vaulted east end of Puiset's first floor, lay the 12th century upper chamber mentioned previously. How access to this third storey room was achieved is unknown. Probably it was via an internal timber stair rising from the west part of the first floor and located against the spine wall. The chamber was lit by a recessed window in the east wall, by two windows in the south wall, and perhaps by others in the walls that have gone, one of which may also have had a fireplace. The outline of the chamber's steeply pitched timber roof is visible in the east wall. Following the alterations to the keep made in the 16th century, it is believed that the whole keep was surmounted by a flat roof.

A short distance to the west of the keep lie the remains of Clapham's Tower, boldly projecting from the curtain wall of the inner ward. Built c.1513, this had portholes for artillery on two levels intended to command the outer ward.

Upon leaving the inner ward and following the inner moat around to the left, one passes Clapham's Tower and the remains of the garderobe tower, en route to the east curtain wall. Here, the fabric dates from the 12th century. It is bonded to the keep but not flush with the east face, for the keep projects somewhat beyond the curtain wall. Where it crosses the inner moat, the east curtain contains a low round-headed opening, beyond which lie the remains of an aqueduct built by Bishop Fox in 1495 to lead a stream into the moat which could therefore be flooded if thought desirable: at the same time, to provide an outlet for the water, a chamber with openings and gates was erected beneath the chapel at the north end of the moat. Just to the south of the aqueduct, and projecting eastward from the curtain wall, stands what is left of Sandur's Tower, probably erected in the 13th century but rebuilt with a triangular end in the 16th.

It is thought that the defences running from the south-east corner of the outer ward to the West Gate originally consisted of a moat, low bank and palisade. Sooner or later a curtain wall was provided, probably in the 13th century. An unusual feature of the vestigial curtain wall is an arcade of semicircular arches. Originally these were not visible. They were buried beneath an artificial bank - which has been largely denuded - and formed the sub-structure of a solid curtain wall running along the top of the bank. A number of projecting turrets exist along the line of the curtain wall and owe their present form to rebuilding work undertaken in the 16th century.

Finally, to the south of the Sheep Gate, and on the opposite side of the road running past the site (the road has obliterated much of the outer moat), are earthworks that may have formed a substantial outer enclosure of the fortress.

Norham Castle is in the care of English Heritage.

PRUDHOE CASTLE

Prudhoe Castle stands on a ridge about 150ft (46m) above the River Tyne, a short distance to the north, and was first mentioned in 1173 when it was besieged by the Scots. It lies amid lovely grounds in a fertile stretch of the Tyne valley and commanded the crossing of the river at Ovingham, as well as the east-west road from Newcastle to Carlisle.

Archaeological excavations have indicated that the site was occupied from around the mid 11th century and initially consisted of at least two timber buildings within an enclosure formed by a timber palisade. Following the Norman Conquest, the Umfraville family arrived on the scene. Evidently, the first member of the line associated with Prudhoe was Robert d'Umfraville. He was formally granted the barony of Prudhoe by Henry I (1100-35) for the service of two and a half knights' fees, but as Laurence Keen states, had probably already been granted Prudhoe (and Redesdale) in the closing years of the 11th century. Robert was no doubt responsible for the next phase of Prudhoe's development when it was strengthened, chiefly by replacing the palisade with a massive rampart of clay and stones, with, it seems, an entrance tower set into the rampart. Subsequently, perhaps in the second quarter of the 12th century, substantial changes were made again, largely entailing the construction of a stone curtain wall and the lower part of the present gatehouse.

76. Prudhoe Castle from the south (Gavin Dodds)

130

In 1173 William the Lion of Scotland invaded the North East. The head of the Umfraville family at this date was Odinel II, Robert's grandson. He had been brought up in the household of the Scottish king's father. In view of this, William had expected Odinel to support his claim to the earldom of Northumberland, an earldom that had formerly belonged to William's father but had since been taken over by England's king, Henry II. Angered by Odinel's refusal to do so, William attempted to capture Prudhoe. He failed. The Scottish lords did not relish the prospect of a lengthy siege and encouraged him to abandon the attempt.

But the following year, William invested the castle again. Jordan Fantosme, a contemporary chronicler, tells us that on this occasion William found that Prudhoe had been 'newly provisioned . . . Odinel had settled some excellent men in the castle, making it such a fortress that I never saw better ones anywhere.' The siege only lasted three days but some damage was done to the defences. Having devastated the surrounding countryside, the Scots then headed off in the direction of Alnwick. Fantosme comments that 'outside [Prudhoe] they have lost their fields and their standing crops of wheat and their gardens were stripped by their evil adversaries; and anyone who could think of nothing worse to do barked the fruit trees, thus working off his spite.' Odinel had abandoned the castle as the Scots had drawn near, having been persuaded by the garrison to leave Prudhoe in the knowledge that if the castle fell he could expect little mercy from William.

Following the siege, Odinel rebuilt and remodelled the fortress. He died in 1182 and was succeeded by a son named Richard, who was to rank among the opponents of King John. As a result, his property, including Prudhoe, was forfeited and remained such until 1217, the year after John had breathed his last at Newark and had been succeeded by his young son, Henry III.

During Henry's reign the royal administration reduced the number of baronial castles in the country. Richard d'Umfraville was affected by this policy. He was ordered to demolish Harbottle Castle - an Umfraville stronghold in the upper Coquet valley since the mid 12th century - but successfully argued that it served a useful defensive role against the Scots.

Richard died in 1226 and was succeeded by a son, Gilbert, who was in turn followed in 1245 by an infant son of the same name. Through his mother, a Scottish heiress, Gilbert II inherited the title of Earl of Angus and vast estates in Scotland. Nevertheless, he continued spending some of his time at Prudhoe. Andrew Saunders comments, 'It would seem that the period after the sieges and through the thirteenth century was a period of considerable rebuilding and improvement at Prudhoe,' work partly attributable to Gilbert.

Gilbert II died in 1307, having sided with Edward I in warfare against the Scots. Robert d'Umfraville IV became the new head of the line and likewise participated in the Scottish wars. In 1314, for instance, he was captured at Bannockburn. Two years later, with the North subjected to repeated Scottish incursions, Edward II granted Robert 700 marks to maintain a garrison of 40 men-at-arms and 80 hobelars (light horsemen) at Prudhoe.

On 5 January 1381 the last of the line, Gilbert III, died without surviving issue and his widow proceeded to marry Henry Percy, the first Earl of Northumberland. In the early years of the 15th century the Percies revolted against Henry IV. The rebellion failed and Prudhoe was taken into royal hands. In June 1405 it was granted to the future Duke of Bedford, (a son of Henry IV) and stayed in his hands until his death in 1435, whereupon it reverted to the Crown.

The Percies regained ownership of Prudhoe in 1440 following a prolonged legal battle.

Subsequently, however, following the death of the third Earl of Northumberland on the losing side at Towton, it was granted by Edward IV to his younger brother, George, Duke of Clarence, on 10 August 1462. Clarence, who was executed in 1478, likely by being drowned in a butt of malmsey wine, only possessed Prudhoe briefly for it was soon granted by the king to Lord Montague, only for it to become Percy property once again in 1470 when it was restored to the family. Prudhoe remained in their possession until 1536 when the castle again passed to the Crown following Percy involvement in the rebellion known as the Pilgrimage of Grace. The following year, it was described as 'a verey stronge fortresse . . . being more strong than comodyous.' Percy control of Prudhoe resumed in 1557.

During the 17th century the castle suffered neglect and slowly fell into a ruinous state. But in the early 19th century restoration work was undertaken by the second Duke of Northumberland between 1808 and 1818. Moreover, he removed a number of ruinous buildings enclosed within its walls and constructed a modest manor house to accommodate one of his employees.

Description

Prudhoe Castle, as noted above, stands in a commanding position on the south side of the Tyne. It is partly enclosed by a deep moat. To the north, the ground simply falls steeply away and is covered in woodland, whereas a deep ravine lies just to the east. The castle is entered from the south and the approach is flanked to the left by a millpond (in existence by the 16th century), and to the right by the remains of a post-medieval water mill on lower ground.

As mentioned, Prudhoe has experienced changes and additions over the centuries. This is certainly true of the entrance. For one thing, the castle is entered via a barbican that was evidently added in the first half of the 14th century. This is 49ft (15m) long and has walls rising up to 20ft (6m) and on either side flights of steps led to the wall-walks. At its north end, (which is higher than the rest of the barbican, for the ground level rises), it evidently terminated at a point where a drawbridge gave access over the moat to a forebuilding - again a later feature - immediately in front of the gatehouse.

The gatehouse dates from the early 12th century. It is a simple structure with single-chamfered round-headed arches and a tunnel-vaulted passageway with a transverse arch supported by a pair of corbels in the form of grotesque heads. Instead of possessing guard-rooms, the walling either side of the passage is solid, further testifying to the gatehouse's early date. The gatehouse possesses two upper rooms, reached via an external flight of steps within the enclosure. The first room is a 13th century chapel, whose altar was located within a bay projecting slightly from the east face and lit by lancets. Subsequently, and most probably in the late 14th century, an additional storey was erected above the chapel to store archives and valuables and its construction entailed lowering the height of the chapel.

Upon progressing through the gatehouse, one enters the outer ward, formerly the public area for business and ceremony. It contains the low remains of a number of buildings. On the north side of the ward was the Great Hall, built against the curtain wall. The present remains are those of a substantial structure, a single storey building open to the roof and measuring some 60 by 46ft (18 by 14m), erected in the late 14th or early 15th century. Windows with seats in the north wall afforded splendid views across the Tyne.

A two-storey cross range lay against the east end of the hall, and on the first floor, above what was doubtless a service room, was a residential chamber with a latrine in the curtain wall. Further east, in the north-east corner of the ward, lay a kitchen.

As the 15th century drew to a close, the Great Hall was replaced by a smaller one located to the west. Apparently at first floor level, the new building had one or more chambers at its west end.

Among the low remains visible in the outer ward are those of a 16th century brewhouse located at the east end of the ward, immediately in front of an east tower known as the Watch Tower. A water trough and the fire-reddened base for the brewing vat survive. As can clearly be seen, much of the masonry of the neighbouring tower itself is post-medieval. It dates from restoration work undertaken in the 19th century.

The west side of the outer ward is bounded by the Georgian manor house. Built around 1808, it is a plain structure, with windows in its bow-fronted northern end that provide fine views across the Tyne. The ground floor contains a visitors' shop and exhibition rooms: the upper floor is the residence of the custodian. Prior to the manor house, most of the ground upon which it stands was occupied by a residential range erected in the late 13th century and subsequently altered.

At the south end of the manor house is an arched carriageway that leads to the inner ward, and it is worth noting that just beyond the carriageway the south curtain wall contains a fine example of an embrasure with a cross loop for a crossbowman.

The main feature of the inner ward is the keep, a ruinous structure which is adjoined to the east by a building generally referred to as a forebuilding. The latter is often said to date from the 12th century, but according to Andrew Saunders it was erected in the early 13th century as 'a narrow masonry domestic range' and is thus misleadingly referred to as a forebuilding. A newel-stair rises the full height of the structure, whose principal chamber, which had a fine fireplace, is at first floor level.

77. The gatehouse and barbican, viewed from within the outer ward (Gavin Dodds)

78. The castle as seen from the pele yard (Gavin Dodds)

The keep's history and development have been interpreted differently by various authorities. It has been suggested that it dates from the first half of the 12th century (Pevsner thought that it was 'probably older than any other Northumbrian keep'), whereas some favour a later date, just before or after the siege of 1174. The keep, which has walls 10ft (3m) thick, is of modest proportions: internally, it measures 24 by 20ft (7.3 by 6.1m). Initially, it consisted of two storeys beneath a double-pitched roof, the lines of which can be seen on the internal face of the west wall, and was perhaps supplemented by a hall, possibly of timber, built against the north wall. In the late 14th or early 15th century, though, the pitched roof was removed and a third storey and new battlements were added, of which only the south-west turret remains. A tall round-headed window at first floor level has survived in the north wall. A mural passage in the north wall at this level led to stairs that can be seen rising through the thickness of the west wall.

Running along the west side of the inner ward and concealing what remains of two 13th century corner towers, are a former conservatory, stables and carriage house dating from the 19th century and now used as maintenance workshops.

Opposite the keep, and within the 13th century north curtain wall (owing to instability, the curtain was built and rebuilt during the castle's history), is a garderobe reached via stairs within the masonry. Likely, the latrine served the proposed residential building mentioned above, built against the north side of the keep and thus lying between the keep and the north curtain wall.

A stroll around the castle's exterior will provide a fuller appreciation of its setting and defensive features. Moving clockwise from the entrance, one first enters the pele yard (an extensive lawned area located to the west of the barbican and millpond); a bailey that once housed the chantry chapel of St Mary, founded in 1300, and doubtless other buildings such as barns and stables. From the pele yard fine views of the curtain wall can be gained, including a line of large beam holes running along the south curtain just below parapet level; holes that held the timbers of wooden fighting platforms. Loops for crossbowmen are also evident. Between the south-west and north-west tower are two levels of such cross loops.

Only the base of the south-west tower remains. In contrast, the north-west tower stands to almost full height. The tower has three tiers of cross loops, staggered at each level, and fire from here could of course have been supplemented by that of archers manning the battlements above. Upon walking along the north face of the castle, under the shade of the trees growing on the precipitous slope, other features such as projecting turrets for latrines and windows in the curtain wall can be seen.

79. The north-west tower (Gavin Dodds)

When nearing the gatehouse, after almost completing the circuit, another latrine projection is visible. This served a late medieval two-storey building (perhaps used as lodgings) erected against the interior of the south curtain wall and adjacent to the gatehouse. Just beyond, and bonded with the gatehouse, is a section of curtain wall dating from the 12th century: a more substantial extent of 12th century curtain wall can be seen on the west side of the gatehouse.

Prudhoe Castle is owned by the Duke of Northumberland, but is managed by English Heritage.

SEATON DELAVAL HALL

S eaton Delaval Hall, one of the great architectural masterpieces of early 18th century England, lies close to the coast in south-east Northumberland and was designed by Sir John Vanbrugh for Admiral George Delaval.

The first member of the line connected with Northumberland was Hubert de la Val, one of the first Normans to settle in the county: he may have been granted his estate in the late 11th century by Robert de Mowbray, the Earl of Northumberland. De la Val held a barony comprising two small blocks of territory, one in the parish of Newburn in the middle Tyne valley; and the other, including Seaton, in the parish of Earsdon on the Northumberland coast. He granted the tithes of his manors of Callerton, Dissington and Seaton to the monks of Tynemouth Priory, a monastery founded by Mowbray.

Hubert was succeeded by a son named Robert. In 1161 the barony was in the hands of a certain Hugh FitzRoger who had evidently married a Delaval heiress, for his son and successor Gilbert, claimed descent from the Delavals whose surname he himself bore.

In the early 13th century - a century during which the family residence became established at Seaton Delaval - Gilbert was an opponent of King John and a participant in the events that led to the signing of Magna Carta. He died in about 1229.

The next head of the line, Gilbert's son Eustace, met his death while campaigning against the Scots in 1258. He died childless and was followed by a brother who expired in or about 1270 and was in turn followed by a grandson, a minor, Robert Delaval II, born at Seaton Delaval in June 1263. His life ended violently. It was cut short on 11 September 1297 at the Battle of Stirling Bridge in Scotland when an English army was humiliatingly routed by Scottish nationalists, one of whose leaders was William Wallace.

In 1311, upon the death of Delaval's sister and heiress, Margery de Smytheton, the family estates passed to a cousin, Sir Robert Delaval III, who subsequently defended Tynemouth Priory in 1317 during an insurrection led by a Northumberland knight, Sir Gilbert de Middleton.

Among subsequent heads of the family worthy of note is Sir John Delaval. In about 1522, he was said to be able to spend £100 a year and to serve the king with 50 horsemen. He took part in several border forays during the reign of Henry VIII and was Sheriff of Northumberland on five occasions. He died in 1562, and left behind a reputation for being a fine, honourable gentleman.

His great-grandson, Sir Ralph Delaval, was likewise a prominent figure in the county, in this case during the reign of James I. He was three times Sheriff of Northumberland, and of him one of his sons wrote: 'He kept an open, great, and plentifull house for entertainment . . . . His life was religious . . . . He governed his people in excellent order, and stocked and managed his whole estate himselfe . . . . He never rid to any publike assembly without five or six men in liveries and two or three of his sons to attend him . . . . He understood the Latine and Greek tongues, and in his younger dayes did write much of severall subjects.'

Sir Ralph's grandson and successor, also named Ralph, was made a baronet in 1660 following the Restoration. He built a sluice at Seaton Sluice, on the coast a short distance from Seaton Delaval, to ship coal and salt from his property and thereby enhanced his wealth.

80. Seaton Delaval Hall from the north

In early 1718 Sir John Delaval, the third baronet, (whose only child was a daughter), sold Seaton Delaval and other property to a kinsman, Captain George Delaval, who belonged to a junior branch of the family that had settled at Dissington a century earlier. Born in 1660, the purchaser of Seaton Delaval had amassed a fortune through a diplomatic and naval career - he had for example served as an envoy to the Emperor of Morocco in 1700 and 1707. Moreover, he represented the Cornish town of West Looe in parliament in 1715 and was to do so again in 1722, the year in which he became a vice-admiral. It was this individual, best known as Admiral George Delaval, who engaged Vanbrugh to design Seaton Delaval Hall.

Vanbrugh, who was born in London in 1664, began his career as a regular soldier. In 1688 he was arrested as a spy in France and remained captive for four years. Following his return to England, he became a dramatist, producing comedies such as *The Relapse* and *The Provok'd Wife*, both dating from the late 1690s. It was at this time that he became interested in architecture and in 1699 he was commissioned by the third Earl of Carlisle to design Castle Howard in North Yorkshire. In the opening years of the 18th century another major commission followed - that of designing Blenheim Palace in Oxfordshire as the nation's gift to its celebrated general, John Churchill, first Duke of Marlborough. Both Castle Howard and Blenheim are Baroque masterpieces and at both Vanbrugh benefited from the able assistance of another gifted architect, Nicholas Hawksmoor.

Seaton Delaval, on the other hand, is purely Vanbrugh's creation. It was built in the years 1718-28 and construction work was supervised by William Etty of York, an able builder and architect. Admiral Delaval did not live to see the project brought to completion for he died on the estate on 22 June 1723 following a fall from his horse. Vanbrugh also died before his masterpiece was fully realised. He did so in 1726.

It was thus during the days of the admiral's nephew and successor, another naval officer Captain Francis Blake-Delaval, that the house was completed. This gentleman had a large family - the 'gay Delavals' - that acquired a reputation for gaiety, generosity and brilliance in several fields.

One such, was Sir Francis Blake-Delaval, who succeeded his father in 1752. A notable gallant and spendthrift, he had a love of theatrical entertainment that led him to put on lavish displays at Seaton Delaval. Hence, it is said that during this period 'Seaton Delaval was like an Italian palace, and the grounds were a perfect fairyland of light, beauty and music.' He also demonstrated his love of things theatrical in London. On one occasion, for instance, he produced *Othello* at Drury Lane Theatre with himself playing Othello and other members of the family featuring in the cast. The House of Commons adjourned early to enable members to witness the spectacle.

Thrice an MP, he was an authority on Irish legislation and was made a Knight of the Bath in 1761. He went to his grave without legitimate issue in 1771, whereupon headship of the family passed to a brother, Sir John Hussey-Delaval, who had been created a baronet ten years earlier and had added the name of Hussey to his surname after inheriting an estate in Lincolnshire. He had served as MP for Berwick upon Tweed on three occasions and did so again twice after succeeding to Seaton Delaval. Sir John received an Irish peerage in 1783 and was created Baron Delaval of Seaton Delaval three years later.

In 1808 Lord Delaval died at the breakfast table at Seaton Delaval and was buried in St Paul's chapel, Westminster Abbey. As his consumptive heir had predeceased him in 1775 following a hefty kick to the groin by a laundrymaid he was attempting to seduce, his titles died with him. He was succeeded by a brother, Edward Hussey Delaval, a distinguished scientist - he was a Fellow of the Royal Society - and upon whose death in 1814 the Delaval line became extinct.

Seaton Delaval and other property then passed to a baronet, Sir Jacob Astley of Melton Mowbray whose late mother was the eldest child of Francis Blake-Delaval senior, nephew and successor of Admiral George Delaval.

In common with many other country houses, Seaton Delaval has suffered from the ravages of fire. In 1752 the left wing was damaged by one such, while in 1822 a more serious fire destroyed an east wing added around 1770 and gutted most of the interior of the main part of the house itself.

Forty years or so after this disastrous fire, Seaton Delaval was reroofed. During the First World War, the hall was occupied by troops, during which period much damage was done, and was requisitioned again from 1939 to 1948.

Shortly thereafter, Edward Delaval Henry Astley, the twenty-second Lord Hastings, commenced a programme of restoration (which has witnessed several phases over the years) and has saved the house from dereliction. Among other things, restoration work has included renewing the roof and windows and repaving the floors. Of his motivation for the task, Hastings has commented: 'In partially restoring Seaton Delaval and in opening it to the public in 1950 I had three objectives in mind: in the first place the maintenance and improvement of the fabric . . . secondly, the preservation of a monument, architecturally and historically priceless, for the benefit of students of art through the ages; and thirdly, the pleasure and edification I hoped it would afford to many thousands of holidaymakers.'

In 1960, Lord Hastings occupied the restored west wing (not open to the public) which thus became the family home and has remained such.

Description

Seaton Delaval Hall is an imposing, sombre-looking structure, and is orientated north-south, rather than facing east towards the North Sea, for at the time of its construction sea views were little regarded. Although the Palladian style was in vogue at the time the house was built, Seaton Delaval is a much more dramatic structure, defiantly Baroque, and of it Steven Brindle has commented: 'This house alone would confirm Vanbrugh as one of the greatest masters of the Baroque.' For his part, Pevsner declared: 'Here was an architecture for the storm and the driving cloud, for sombre ships and battering sea. Seaton Delaval can never have been a comfortable home - the plan is singularly ruthless - but it is a monument of Baroque grandeur and a passionate power unmatched in England.' He continues, 'No other Vanbrugh house is so mature, so compact and so powerful . . . no one can forget Seaton Delaval. For though it betrays the hand of its master in every detail, it is yet completely individual, with its own unique composition and mood.'

Seaton Delaval consists of a large symmetrical main block, approximately 75 by 75ft (23 by 23m) excluding attached towers and turrets. On either side are arcades that soon turn northward and run along the front of two service wings before ending in small square pavilions that are lower than the service wings which are themselves lower than the house.

Polygonal turrets are located at the corners of the main block, while from the centre of the east and west facades rise oblong stair towers whose exteriors are heavily rusticated for most of their height. The towers ascend higher than the facades and the turrets, and are themselves dominated by a pedimented central attic storey.

The north front is of course the entrance front. Here a broad open staircase rises towards an arched doorway, with groups of three giant Tuscan columns partly adding to the facade's aesthetic impact, as does banded rustication. The south front has the calmest aspect, with a wide flight of steps that rise to an impressive portico with fluted Ionic columns carrying a balustraded balcony.

81. The north front of the main block

The Entrance Hall is a large room, 25ft (7.5m) wide by 44ft (13.4m), with light stone walls and a floor of alternately slate and marble tiles. The hall was originally 30ft (9m) high, but in the centre this was increased by the removal of a separate upper room at second floor level, leading Pevsner to comment that the room is 'of uncomfortably high proportions.' Among other things, at ground floor level there is heavy blank arcading around the walls. Moreover, the east wall has a stone fireplace with male figures carrying the mantelshelf, and the fireplace bears a frieze depicting a Roman wedding march. At first floor level are arched niches with damaged statues by Bagutti, while a gallery runs along the south side of the hall.

Off its south end, the Entrance Hall is connected by vaulted corridors to the stair towers on the east and west sides of the building. Moreover, the corridors open to rooms flanking the Entrance Hall, each of which in turn gives access to a small chamber in one or other of the polygonal turrets at the corners of the house. While the rooms in question off the west corridor are gutted, those off the east corridor are a marked contrast. The main room here - that entered directly from the corridor - escaped the fire of 1822. It is the Mahogany Parlour, so-called because its walls were originally covered with moulded mahogany panelling, of which only two panels now remain: the others were removed when Seaton Delaval was occupied by troops during World War One. In January 1726, the clerk of works wrote that two men were 'sett on to wainscott the North East roome with the Mahoggony wood, which is so well dryed that it works extremely fine.' The walls are adorned with a number of portraits, comprising works by Sir Peter Lely, Francis Cotes, and more recent exponents of portraiture. There are also a number of photographs of the Astley family. The little room in the adjoining turret has pictures and plans of Seaton Delaval.

Off the south end of the Entrance Hall, lies the gutted Saloon, measuring 75 by 30ft (23 by 9.1m). It is in three sections and occupies the entire south front of the house. Originally it had a painted ceiling by Vercelli which is said to have been admirably coloured and exquisitely modelled.

The stairs descend to the basement, where they are linked by an east-west corridor off which are a number of vaulted cellars. Upon ascending the stairs, one comes to the first floor, (beyond which visitors are not permitted to go), and where one room is open to the public. It is in the north-east corner of the house and was repaired and redecorated in 1962: the walls were originally covered with Genoa damask stretched over a timber framework. On display are various documents - charters etc - and a number of paintings.

Turning to the wings, as noted the west wing serves as the residence of Lord Hastings and his family. In contrast, the stables are in the centre of the east wing, where horses ate hay out of arched niches.

Visitors to Seaton Delaval will find strolling around the formal gardens to the west of the house worthwhile. Several fine lead figures by John van Nost and great statues on stone pedestals after the Florentine sculptor, Giovanni Bologna, are a feature of the grounds. To the south-west of the house, moreover, one can see the Church of Our Lady, which mostly dates from the early 12th century and was the Delavals' manorial chapel. Nearby, stood Delaval Castle, a medieval structure that was subsequently enlarged. It was demolished in around 1720 by Admiral George Delaval. In 1813 a visitor to Seaton Delaval wrote: 'The site of the ancient castle was a little to the south-west of the present structure; but its walls have been entirely razed, its ditches levelled, and nothing is left of the first establishments of this family except the chapel - the most purest and perfect specimen of Norman architecture.'

VINDOLANDA ROMAN FORT AND SETTLEMENT

V indolanda is one of the most famous Roman sites in Britain. It lies one mile (1.6km) south of Hadrian's Wall on the line of the Stanegate, the Roman road from Corbridge to Carlisle, and comprises a fort and a civil settlement.

A turf and timber fort was built here in the A.D. 80s during the governorship of Agricola, who pushed the Roman frontier well into Scotland, and was the first of five successive timber forts erected on the site in the late 1st and early 2nd centuries, forts whose remains lie buried well below present ground level.

The First Cohort of Tungrians, a unit of Germanic origin, appears to have formed the first garrison. In around 100, however, by which time the Romans had begun abandoning Scotland, the garrison is known to have been of comparable origin for it consisted of Batavians, mostly or entirely members of the Ninth Cohort of Batavians. But in the early 120s the First Cohort of Tungrians was once again present, although they may well have soon moved to another Roman fort, Housesteads.

At this time, during the reign of Emperor Hadrian, (117-38) the frontier known as Hadrian's Wall was commenced along the Tyne-Solway isthmus. During excavations in 1991-93, a superbly appointed wooden building of Hadrianic date was uncovered at

82. Vindolanda: an aerial photograph showing the site from the west. The photograph was taken before the recent excavation of the commanding officer's residence in the fort (English Heritage)

Vindolanda and it has been plausibly suggested that it was constructed to accommodate the emperor and his immediate retinue when they stayed here in 122.

At some date in the 2nd century a stone fort with an area of approximately 4.15 acres (1.68 hectares) was erected at Vindolanda, though some of its buildings may have been of timber. Then, in the years 208-11 during the reign of Septimus Severus, the fort was demolished to make way for up to 200 small circular stone huts thought to have perhaps housed hostages taken from tribes in southern Scotland during the emperor's Scottish campaigns. An annexe to the west of the former fort accommodated a garrison at this time, evidently part of the Fourth Cohort of Gauls, a unit named on an inscription dating from 213 found at Vindolanda.

Shortly thereafter, in around 215, the Severan arrangements were done away with and in about 220 a new stone fort with an area of 3.6 acres (1.46 hectares) was constructed. It was perhaps garrisoned by the whole of the Fourth Cohort of Gauls, a partly mounted unit approximately 500 strong. But it seems probable that for some years only part of the cohort was present and shared the fort with troops belonging to another unit or units, and that this remained the case until the 230s when the rest of the Fourth Cohort of Gauls likely arrived on the scene. The unit in its entirety is thought to have solely garrisoned Vindolanda from then on until the end of Roman rule in Britain in the early 5th century, save for a break that appears to have occurred around the last quarter of the 3rd century when the fort may have been deserted for some reason before being reconstructed c. 300. Later still, more rebuilding occurred, especially in about 370.

In common with the majority of Roman forts, Vindolanda was associated with a civilian presence. This began in the fort's earliest days, and while some of the civilians lived within the fort others doubtless lived outside in timber structures. During the early 3rd century when the new fort was erected, a substantial civil settlement at least ten acres (4 hectares) in extent was established over and beyond the former Severan annexe. Evidence for industrial activity such as metalworking has been discovered. The buildings were largely of timber resting upon solid stone foundations. The settlement seems to have been abandoned by about 280, though limited occupation doubtless continued on the site for the remainder of the fort's history.

Indeed, there is increasing evidence of post-Roman occupation at Vindolanda. In 1878, for example, a tombstone dating from around 500 was discovered. It is that of a Christian named Brigomaglos, who is thought to have been a warrior chief helping to defend the region against hostile peoples to the north, and who may have worshipped in what is believed to have been a small church recently located within the former fort.

In 1814 and during the early years of the 1830s, the Reverend Anthony Hedley, who built a small house in the fort's vicinity, conducted excavations at Vindolanda. In 1930 a distinguished archaeologist, the late Eric Birley, moved into Hedley's former residence and renewed excavation, work that continued intermittently in subsequent years. 1970 witnessed the establishment of the Vindolanda Trust, (Birley was its first chairman) one of whose objectives is the total excavation of the site, a task that is still in hand.

Before discussing the visible remains of the fort and those of the associated settlement, it is fascinating to note that the excavations have led to the remarkable discovery of a wealth of artifacts such as a large number of leather goods and textiles, as well as the earliest written material ever found in Britain, over 2,000 army documents and personal correspondence.

Most of this written material has been found on ink tablets, that is, specially prepared thin sheets of wood intended to be written on using ink, the first of which were found in March 1973. The tablets date from the timber phases of the fort's existence and some of them had come from far afield, such as London and the Continent.

The tablets were mostly made of alder and birch, and as Robin Birley - who discovered the first tablets - comments, they 'must have been specially dried out and treated to ensure that they could receive ink writing without fear of blotches. No doubt the Roman Army manufactured them in bulk at several establishments.' He also comments: 'The Vindolanda environment in which they lay was perfect for the survival of these delicate sheets of wood, for the old floors and pits had been deliberately sealed with turf and clay by later Roman builders. In effect, there were anaerobic conditions, starving the organic material from oxygen yet keeping it at an even temperature.'

One of the tablets was an invitation by a woman named Claudia Severa to a friend called Sulpicia Lepidina, the wife of the commander of the Ninth Cohort of Batavians, then based at Vindolanda. The body of the letter - which dates from c. A.D. 100 - was written by a professional scribe but Claudia concluded it with farewell greetings in her own unstable hand, the earliest known writing by a woman using Latin.

The letter, addressed, 'Sulpicia Lepidina, wife of Flavius Cerialis, from Severa', reads:

> *Claudia Severa to her Lepidina, greetings.*
> *I send you a warm invitation to come*
> *to us on September 11th, for my birthday celebrations,*
> *to make my day more enjoyable by your presence.*
> *Give my greetings to your Cerialis. My*
> *Aelius greets you and your sons.*
>
> *I will expect you, sister.*
> *Farewell, sister, my dearest soul,*
> *as I hope to prosper, and*
> *greetings.*

How far from Vindolanda Claudia lived is uncertain. She was resident at a fort named Briga, perhaps located at Kirkbride beside the Solway Firth south-west of Carlisle. If so, to attend the birthday party Lepidina would have had to undertake a roundtrip of approximately 70 miles (113km), presumably with a military escort.

Description

Vindolanda fort and settlement are located on a moderately level plateau, with several streams running on lower ground in the vicinity, and are overlooked by Barcombe Hill to the east from where most of the stone used on the site was quarried.

The remains are approached from the west. Visitors first come to the site of wells and water tanks from where water was piped to all the major buildings. It was here that an altar set up by the civilians of Vindolanda, the '*vicani Vindolandesses*' was discovered, dedicated to Vulcan, god of metal workers. Temples are believed to have been located nearby. Beyond, lies the fort's bath house.

83. The bath house

The bath house, whose west wall stands to a height of 7ft (2.13m), is located on the northern edge of the civil settlement. It was constructed in the early 3rd century, evidently at the same time as the second stone fort and, it seems, was mostly built by specialist craftsmen from the VI Legion. It was subsequently enlarged. Evidently its exterior was covered in plaster, (traces of which can be seen on the apse of the hot plunge bath) while internally walls and floors were lined with *opus signinum*, (concrete) some of which survives.

On the east side of the bath house is a long room that served as the changing room and was entered from the south via a porch. From the changing room, bathers moved west into a cool lobby off the south side of which was a cold plunge bath, while to the north was a hypocausted sauna. West of the lobby was a warm room - again with a hypocaust - which led into a hot steam room to the north, off whose west end was an apse containing the hot plunge bath. Two rooms on the north side of the bath house contained the furnaces, while against the extreme north-east of the building one can see the remains of a deep latrine that was flushed using waste water from the baths.

There is evidence that the bath house was used by members of the civil settlement as well as by members of the garrison. This includes bone and silver hairpins lost by females when using the cold plunge bath and recovered by archaeologists from drains in the building.

Only part of the settlement or *vicus* is visible. It is nonetheless the most extensive such site to be seen anywhere in Britain. It mostly consists of long narrow buildings set gable-on to the principal thoroughfare which leads directly to the fort's west gate, (some of the civilian structures on the south side of the road have been removed to allow the examination and display of earlier buildings belonging to the Severan military annexe). In general they appear to have been houses and shops, but some apparent stores buildings have been identified along a side street that runs close to the fort.

On the north side of the main street, close to the bath house, lies what is known as the corridor house, a substantial dwelling with three rooms either side of a central corridor. It was the residence of a person of some substance, perhaps a wealthy merchant. Later it was divided into two separate houses and the corridor became a narrow alleyway.

Virtually opposite this, on the other side of the street, are the remains of what until recently was believed to have been an inn for official visitors and travellers such as merchants. It consisted of a number of rooms opening off an elongated open courtyard. The rooms included a bath-suite and one with a communal latrine that could seat eight people simultaneously. The base of an oven can be seen in the largest room in the west range, presumably the kitchen. The building is now identified as the residence of the commanding officer of the garrison stationed in the military annexe at Vindolanda during the Severan period.

Close to the easternmost buildings of the settlement (3rd century structures that lie over infilled fort ditches) is the fort's west gate. But before entering the fort, some may find making a circuit of its exterior worthwhile. Over half the circuit of the fort wall can be seen and is mostly over 6½ft (2m) in height, rising to 10ft (3m) in many places. Not for nothing does Vindolanda rank among the small group of forts in Britain where very substantial remains of the defensive walls have survived the passage of time. One can see a variety of methods of Roman stone-dressing, partly due to frequent repair work undertaken during the fort's existence: some of the masonry in the west and east walls is thought to survive from the wall of the first stone fort.

84. A section of the fort wall

85. A view from within the fort, looking towards the site of the
west gate and the main street of the civil settlement beyond

The west gate was a single passageway flanked by projecting rectangular towers with guard-chambers. The north gate was of similar design, whereas the east and south gates were simple structures without flanking towers.

Internally, the *principia* or headquarters building and the *praetorium*, the residence of the commanding officer, are the only substantial structures visible. They were part of a central administrative range running across the fort, as were granaries known to have been located to the west of the headquarters. The rest of the fort would have contained structures such as barrack blocks and stables.

The headquarters building faces north and lies on the site of a predecessor which faced in the opposite direction, and the undulating nature of some of the masonry is due to the fact that some of the walls pass over the foundations of the earlier structure.

The headquarters had a front verandah and a central entrance leading to a small court-yard enclosed on three sides by four rooms housing the armouries and arranged asymmet-rically. At the far end of the courtyard and in the usual position, are the remains of the cross-hall whose west end has a fine platform from which the commanding officer briefed his men or gave judgement in judicial matters. Again, typically, off the south side of the hall is a row of five rooms. The centremost was the shrine which housed a statue of the reigning emperor, altars to principal Roman gods, and regimental standards. Behind, in a southerly projection, lay a trench that evidently contained strong-boxes.

The headquarters building experienced modification during its existence. For instance in the early 4th century the rooms overlooking the courtyard were provided with under-floor ventilation channels suggesting that they were converted into stores to hold more perishable supplies such as clothing or food; while the southern row of rooms was converted to domestic use, changes that drastically changed the nature of the building.

Immediately to the east lies the huge commanding officer's residence - with at least 20 rooms ranged around a courtyard: there was an upper floor on the east wing, with the east wall supported by three huge buttresses. Interesting finds made during excavation of the site include three altars dedicated by prefects of the Fourth Cohort of Gauls and the recent discovery of part of the tombstone of Titus Annius, a former commandant 'killed in the war', a conflict thought to have been a revolt in progress when Hadrian became emperor in 117. Moreover, within the courtyard are the remains of what was almost certainly a church erected in the early 5th century. If so, they are the earliest remains of such a building to be seen in Britain. Some of the small stone circular huts mentioned above, predating the commandant's residence, have also been uncovered during the excavations.

More of the huts can be seen near the north-east corner of the fort. In the north-east angle of the perimeter itself, are the remains of a well-preserved latrine which had sewers around three sides (flushed by water that flowed along a drain to the latrine) and two openings that carried the waste through the base of the fort wall. The communal latrine was capable of seating half a dozen people simultaneously and was doubtless supplemented by others elsewhere.

Reconstructions of two representative segments of Hadrian's Wall are appealing features of Vindolanda. They date from the early 1970s, are located to the south-west of the

86. One of the reconstructions of a representative section of Hadrian's Wall

87. The reconstruction of the turf section of the Wall

fort beside two burial tombs - Vindolanda's main cemeteries lay to the north of the Stanegate - and are intended to give an idea of how the Wall may have appeared, although certain details such as the existence of a wall-walk and the crenellated parapet are conjectural: they may not have been features of the genuine Wall. One segment, which incorporates a turret, is built of stone and is 10ft (3m) thick - the original planned thickness of Hadrian's Wall, although only the eastern sections of the Wall were actually built to this gauge as opposed to a narrower one that was adopted from Chesters onward. The other reconstruction (renewed in 1984) is of a section of turf wall, with a timber milecastle gateway, and represents the initial phase of Hadrian's Wall as it existed in Cumbria, where turf was first used before the Wall there was rebuilt in stone.

Furthermore, a collection of full-sized replica Roman buildings can also be seen on lower ground to the east of the fort where they lie amid ornamental gardens. One such is a little temple with wall paintings in the style of those found at Pompeii, Italy. In an adjacent museum are notable displays of the outstanding finds discovered during excavation of the forts and civil settlements. Indeed, the collections of leather goods, textiles, wooden objects and the display of photographs of the writing tablets are the finest of their kind.

WALLINGTON HALL

W allington Hall is one of Northumberland's best known and best loved country houses, a charming residence set in beautiful grounds beside the upper reaches of the River Wansbeck approximately twenty miles (32km) north-west of Newcastle, and famous for its association with scholars, artists, politicians and men of business.

The house dates from the 17th century, but some of the fabric is much older, for the cellars are remnants of a castle that previously existed here, the residence of the Fenwick family. The Fenwicks' association with Wallington began in the early 15th century, when they acquired the property through marriage, and the last of the line to own the estate, Sir John Fenwick, a staunch Jacobite, was beheaded for treason in 1697.

Sir John had lived extravagantly and in 1688 had been forced by debt to sell Wallington. The purchaser was a baronet, Sir William Blackett, a wealthy Newcastle merchant and mine-owner whose family hailed from County Durham. He wrought drastic changes. The castle, and a Tudor house built by the Fenwicks, were demolished and replaced by a residence square in plan - each face was 120ft (36.5m) long - ranged around a courtyard. However, Wallington was not Sir William's principal home: he had an impressive house in Newcastle, amid gardens and orchards. Wallington appears to have served as a glorified shooting lodge.

Sir William died in 1705 and was succeeded by a son who was a Jacobite sympathiser. In

88. Wallington Hall from the south-east

1728, he too, died, whereupon Wallington and other property passed to a 21-year-old nephew, Walter Calverley, a grandson of Sir William and the son and heir of a Yorkshire baronet. It did so on condition that Calverley would marry an illegitimate daughter of his late uncle and assume the arms and name of Blackett.

Sir Walter Calverley Blackett, as he duly became in 1749, proved a significant figure. He was a highly successful businessman, but one noted for his benevolence: among other things he contributed a substantial sum towards the construction of an infirmary in Newcastle. He served as Mayor of Newcastle five times and represented the town in parliament from 1734 until 1777.

89. The Clock Tower: erected at Wallington in the days of Sir Walter Calverley Blackett

At Wallington he made many changes, eager to enhance the estate. For instance, roads and bridges were made, (including a splendid bridge over the Wansbeck by James Paine), labourers' cottages and follies erected, fields created and enclosed, and parks and gardens laid. 'Capability' Brown, who was born near Wallington in 1716, is known to have been involved in some of the landscaping work in the 1760s. Above all, however, Sir Walter employed the architect Daniel Garrett - a leading exponent of the Palladian style in the North East - to transform the house, work that probably began in 1738. Among other things, its roof was heightened, the entrance moved from the south to the east front, the principal rooms remodelled and redecorated, and the size of the courtyard reduced by inserting a staircase hall on the south side and adding corridors along the other sides.

Sir Walter Calverley Blackett died in 1777 without issue and left Wallington to a nephew (the son of his sister), a baronet named Sir John Trevelyan of Nettlecombe in Somerset, a landowner who already possessed 20,000 acres (8,094 hectares) in the West Country and whose landed estate was now substantially increased by the inheritance of Wallington, although he mostly lived on the Nettlecombe estate.

As Wallington is best known for its links with the Trevelyans something should be said about their origin. The family originated in Cornwall and pronounced their name, 'Trevillian.' A member of the line had come to prominence at the court of Henry VI in the 15th century and had married a Raleigh heiress, thereby acquiring large estates in the southwest, including Nettlecombe. Then, in 1662, early in the reign of Charles II, the family had been awarded a baronetcy for its loyalty during the Civil War.

In 1791, upon the marriage of his eldest son, also named John, Sir John Trevelyan handed Wallington over to his heir. In 1828 the latter, an authoritarian character and one of the first members of the Royal Horticultural Society, inherited the title as fifth baronet. He spent much of his time at Nettlecombe whereas his wife, Maria, (from whom he was estranged for a while) was devoted to Wallington. The house is famous for its impressive collection of porcelain and many of the pieces had formed part of her dowry.

In 1846 the baronetcy and estates passed to Sir John and Lady Trevelyan's son, Walter Calverley Trevelyan, who is thought to have owned a total of about 40,000 acres (16,188 hectares). In common with numerous other members of the family, he was academically inclined. Scientists numbered among his friends, as did a pioneering figure in photography, Fox Talbot, with whom he had become acquainted while at Harrow School. Moreover he gained a reputation as a geologist and botanist. His views were generally liberal. For example, he favoured votes for women, the abolition of flogging and capital punishment, and campaigned for state education. On the other hand, he also campaigned for the 'total suppression of all intoxicating beverages.'

By the time he inherited the title, Sir Walter had been married for eleven years. His wife, Pauline, nineteen years his junior and the daughter of a poor Suffolk parson, is likewise an interesting figure. Far more vivacious than her husband, she was high-spirited and possessed 'an ever-flowing spring of most delicious humour'. But like him she found scientific matters - in particular botany - appealing. Indeed, she first met Trevelyan when they were both attending a conference in Cambridge organized by the British Association for the Advancement of Science.

Art also engaged her attention. An accomplished painter, she was especially interested in the work of the Pre-Raphaelites, and numbered Ruskin and Millais among her friends. In June 1853 Ruskin, his wife Effie and Millais, visited Wallington and of the visit Ruskin wrote to his father: 'This is the most beautiful place possible. A large old seventeenth-century stone house in an old English terraced garden, beautifully kept, all the hawthorns still in full blossom . . . undulating country with a peculiar Northumberlandishness about it - a faraway look that Millais enjoys intensely . . . . We are all very happy.'

Meanwhile, Pauline had persuaded her husband to roof over the central courtyard. The architect employed was John Dobson, and the scheme was carried out shortly after Millais and the Ruskins had departed. In March 1856 William Bell Scott, Director of the Newcastle School of Design and described by Rossetti as 'a man of the truest genius', was commissioned to paint large scenes of Northumbrian history to adorn the new Central Hall.

In 1857 Ruskin revisited Wallington, by which time his marriage had ended in divorce and Effie had married Millais. His friendship with the Trevelyans continued in subsequent

90. The house from the south-west

years and when Lady Trevelyan died abroad in 1866, aged fifty, he was by her bedside together with her husband. Of her, Ruskin wrote: 'She was an entirely pure and noble woman, and had nothing to think of that day except other people's interests.'

In 1879 Sir Walter Calverley Trevelyan followed Pauline to the grave and the baronetcy passed to a nephew, Alfred. Although he also inherited the Nettlecombe estate, Wallington was not part of his patrimony. Sir Walter had decided that owning both Nettlecombe and Wallington was too much responsibility for one person. Wallington, to Alfred's great chagrin, was therefore left to a relative, Sir Charles Edward Trevelyan, who had been granted a baronetcy of his own in 1874. Sir Charles had a distinguished political career and was the brother-in-law of Lord Macaulay, the celebrated historian, who described him as 'a man of genius, a man of honour, a man of rigid integrity, and of a very kind heart.'

The next head of the Wallington branch of the family, Sir George Otto Trevelyan (who succeeded to the title upon the death of his father in 1886), had a distinguished political and literary career, serving for example as Secretary of State for Scotland on two occasions and writing acclaimed history books such as his six volume *History of the American Revolution.* He was offered a peerage but declined to accept it.

Sir George married Caroline Philips, a Manchester cotton heiress who duly inherited Welcombe Park, (an estate near Stratford upon Avon) and by whom he had three sons. The eldest, Charles, who inherited the baronetcy in 1928, was keenly interested in politics and successively represented both the Liberal and Labour parties in the House of Commons and, as a member of the latter party, held high office. Strange as it may seem, he was a staunch admirer of the Soviet Union, whose harsh regime he saw through rose-tinted glasses, and was in favour of abolishing the House of Lords. The family was thus ostracised. 'We were absolutely outrés', one of his children recalled, 'we never went anywhere.'

Shortly after taking up residence at Wallington in September 1928, Sir Charles (who had previously lived at nearby Cambo), had the house thoroughly examined by an architect who reported, among other things, that wrought iron girders supporting the roof of the Central Hall were severely cracked. The whole roof was therefore removed and replaced with one with steel girders. Of this time, Pauline Dower (Sir Charles' eldest child) recalled, 'for the first winter, we lived with the central hall roof off and canvas sheeting to keep out the snow; the hall was full of scaffolding, and twenty-seven workmen were busy there all winter. Before the scaffolding was taken down, our whole family climbed up to the top and all wrote our names on the cove of the roof above the south cornice.'

Of Sir Charles' brothers, Robert Calverley Trevelyan was a poet, whereas the youngest brother, George Macaulay Trevelyan, was the most widely read historian of his generation. Born in 1876 and educated at Harrow and Trinity College, Cambridge, he produced his first book, *England in the Age of Wycliffe* in 1899. Notable works that followed include his *History of England*, published in 1926 and an instant success. Of this famous work, Professor J.H. Plumb commented, 'rarely has the craft of narrative been so brilliantly sustained . . . . His book glows with human warmth and some of the best chapters are those in which he recreates the world of ordinary men and women, the medieval peasants, the Tudor yeomen, the Hanoverian squires, the working men of Victorian England . . . . This wise, just book would by itself have secured Trevelyan's place in the great tradition of English historical writing.'

George Macaulay Trevelyan died in 1962, by which time Wallington was no longer owned by the family for in 1958, upon the death of his eldest brother, Wallington Hall and the estate of nearly 12,000 acres (4,856 hectares) had passed into the hands of the National Trust to which Sir Charles had decided to leave the property years earlier. On the radio in March 1937 he had stated his intention of so doing, declaring: 'To me, it is natural and reasonable that a place such as this should come into public ownership, so that the right to use and enjoy it may be for ever secured to the community. As a Socialist, I am not hampered by any sentiment of ownership. I am prompted to act as I am doing by satisfaction at knowing that the place I love will be held in perpetuity for the people of my country.' On this point, however, Merlin Waterson comments: 'Subsequent negotiations with Sir Charles were punctuated with such misunderstanding and back-pedalling that his brother, Professor G.M. Trevelyan, [a leading member of the National Trust] had to be enlisted as arbitrator. What was finally agreed was a Deed of Settlement, signed by Sir Charles in September 1941. This did not immediately transfer ownership but was an irrevocable commitment that on Sir Charles's death Wallington would pass to the National Trust.'

The present head of the Wallington branch of the Trevelyan family is Sir Geoffrey Trevelyan, 5th baronet, born in 1920 and the youngest of Sir Charles' children. He succeeded his brother, Sir George, in 1996 and lives in Hertfordshire.

Description

Wallington Hall is built of honey-coloured sandstone and has an understated exterior. It is two storeys high and its east front overlooks a public road running through the heart of the estate northward to the village of Cambo.

Visitors approach the house from the north, through the Clock Tower, completed in 1754 and attributed to either James Paine or Garrett: the latter had died the previous year but was most likely responsible for the design. It has a central archway flanked by large coupled Tuscan columns and is surmounted by a cupola carried on an open rotunda of columns.

South of the Clock Tower is a grassy courtyard partly enclosed by estate-workers' cottages, and from here a path leads around to the east front of the house. Originally, as noted above, the entrance lay on the south side of the hall but was changed to its present position in the early 1740s during the days of Sir Walter Calverley Blackett.

The house is entered through a pedimented doorway flanked by Tuscan columns which opens to the Entrance Hall. Among paintings hanging here, are portraits of members of the Trevelyan family by Romney and Hoppner and a fine landscape by Pierre-Antoine Patel the younger, (1648-1707). A cabinet against the west wall made for Sir Walter Calverley Trevelyan holds china, including 17th and 18th century Chinese porcelain brought into the family in the late 18th century as part of the dowry of his mother, Maria.

The principal rooms are along the south side of the house. The Dining Room, located at the east end of the front, is a spacious room with a delicate touch and has finely executed plasterwork including a stucco ceiling partly supported by fluted Corinthian columns. Furniture includes mid 18th century mahogany chairs and a late 18th century Sheraton sideboard. At the east end of the room, behind the Corinthian columns, a case contains mostly 18th century porcelain from China and Japan: Wallington's collection of china is one of the finest owned by the National Trust. Among the room's paintings is a portrait by Gainsborough, (dated 1761 on the back of the canvas) of Susanna, the sister of the first Trevelyan to own Wallington.

To the west, the Dining Room is adjoined by the loftier and more imposing Saloon, located in the middle of the south front. Described by Geoffrey Tyack as 'one of the best rooms of its date in England', it has a pronounced coved ceiling whose wonderful Rococo decoration - plasterwork of winged sphinxes, garlands and bowls of fruit - dates from 1741 and is by Italian *stuccatori* led by Pietro Lafranchini who were also responsible for the stuccowork in the Dining Room, executed the previous year. On the north wall, oval recesses on either side of the fireplace contain 17th and 18th century Chinese and Japanese porcelain. On the east wall, hangs a fine full-length portrait by Romney of Sir John Trevelyan who inherited Wallington in 1777. It was brought to the house in 1991, having previously hung at Nettlecombe. Opposite it, at the far end of the room, is another full-length portrait, in this case of Sir Walter Calverley Blackett, painted in or about 1760 by Sir Joshua Reynolds, the foremost English portraitist of his day.

Beyond the Saloon, and occupying the west end of the south front, is the Library, again with plasterwork by Lafranchini, albeit more modest. Originally a drawing room, it was transformed into a library in 1853 and among its collection of books are ones that belonged to Lord Macaulay, some of which lie open in a showcase to display pencilled comments he made in the margins, a habit shared by other members of the family. Over the doors are large early 18th century Japanese Imari dishes, while busts of ancient philosophers, acquired by Sir George Otto Trevelyan in the 1890s, are on the bookcases.

From the Library one enters the groin-vaulted west corridor, off which lie three rooms occupying the west range: the Study, Lady Trevelyan's Parlour and the Writing Room. Originally the staircase was located in the first of the rooms, but was removed in 1743 by

91. The Central Hall (Andreas von Einsiedel, © The National Trust)

Garrett who transformed the room into an ante-room serving the main bedchamber, now Lady Trevelyan's Parlour. It was later used as a study by Sir George Otto Trevelyan and his successor and contains Macaulay and Trevelyan memorabilia as well as other objects of interest.

The Parlour was first used as a sitting-room by Caroline, Lady Trevelyan, (who was responsible for the Morris wallpaper of 1897), and contains portraits by William Bell Scott of Sir Walter Calverley Trevelyan and his wife, Pauline, as well as a satirical watercolour by Scott of Ruskin, whom he disliked. Also noteworthy is a needlework panel over the chimneypiece embroidered between 1910 and 1933 by Mary, Lady Trevelyan, portraying a legendary member of the family, the 'first' Trevelyan, coming ashore near St Michael's Mount, Cornwall, wearing armour and mounted on a white charger. Continental porcelain, including Meissen can also be seen in a Sheraton case: some of the Meissen dates from around 1740, but the earliest piece was made before 1720.

The Writing Room functioned as the estate office for a number of years, (originally the southern part of the room served as a bed closet to the principal bedchamber) and has been arranged to provide visitors with a place to sit and rest or write if they wish. In the centre of the room is the desk at which Macaulay wrote his celebrated *History of England* which enchanted so many Victorian readers. Present, too, are a number of estate maps charting Wallington's development from 1728 to the 20th century as well as number of items belonging to the house's collection of architectural drawings.

Opposite the three rooms just mentioned, lies the Central Hall, created in 1853-4 when the central courtyard was roofed in by Dobson and provided with arcades carried by square piers, and above which is an arched gallery at first floor level. The piers of the ground floor arcades are decorated with paintings of plants by several artists including Pauline, Lady Trevelyan, and Ruskin: in 1857 the latter was persuaded by her to paint a group of wild oats, wheat, cornflowers and yarrow on the pier in the south-west corner of the Central Hall. The spandrels of the arcades have medallions bearing portraits by William Bell Scott of celebrated figures in the region's history or, at gallery level, scenes of the Battle of Otterburn.

The most notable feature of the Central Hall is eight large Pre-Raphaelite canvases by William Bell Scott which, at ground floor level, fill the north and south arcades and vibrantly depict events in the region's history such as the building of Hadrian's Wall, and the death of Bede while the final work - considered by some to be the finest - depicts industrial Tyneside and is entitled 'The Northumbrian shows the world what can be done with Iron and Coal.'

On the west side of the Central Hall is a marble sculpture by Thomas Woolner, who was introduced to the Trevelyans by William Bell Scott. Entitled 'Civilisation', it comprises a mother teaching her infant child the Lord's Prayer, with the naked little boy standing on a plinth which bears carved depictions of pagan barbarism. Opposite this notable work are plaster figures by Alexander Munro of lovers from Dante's *Inferno*, Paolo and Francesca.

At ground floor level in the north range the two principal rooms open to the public are the Common Room (formerly the servants' hall) and the Kitchen: both are entered from the north corridor which contains a collection of model lead soldiers acquired in the early 1880s. The Common Room, where the original glass and wide glazing bars can be seen in the windows, contains a collection of predominantly 19th century dolls' houses, mostly fairly recent acquisitions or gifts. The largest, Hammond House, a 36 room mansion with 77 dolls, dates from around 1886, has rooms lit by electricity, and running water in the scullery and bathroom.

92. The Walled Garden

The Kitchen, located in the north-east corner of the house, has been arranged by the National Trust to look as it did around 1900, although some of the objects on display would normally have been in a pantry or larder. Pauline Bower relates that in 1938 a large hotel Aga cooker was installed 'in place of the old range, which had had to be stoked with two shovelfuls of coal every ten minutes throughout the day.'

From the Kitchen, one heads along the east corridor, which contains a number of interesting works of art such as *The Madonna and Child* by the Italian Renaissance artist Francesco Francia, who died in 1517, and *The Pilgrim at the Gate of Idleness* by the Victorian painter, Edward Burne-Jones.

After ascending the staircase, located in the Staircase Hall along the south side of the Central Hall, several rooms are open to the public. Among such are the Trevelyan Bedroom (in the south-east corner of the first floor) which among other things contains a 19th century four-poster that belonged to Lord Macaulay and an 18th century Dutch mahogany wardrobe, and the Needlework Room on the east side of the house, which contains ten panels of needlework executed by the mother of Sir Walter Calverley Blackett in the early 18th century. The most notable room however, is the Museum or Curiosity Room above the Saloon. It dates from the 1820s and contains an assortment of objects of scientific and antiquarian interest, some of which came to Wallington through Maria, the wife of Sir John Trevelyan, the fifth baronet, for Maria's mother, a pioneer coleopterist, had amassed a large private museum that eventually passed to the Trevelyans.

The grounds of Wallington contain much of interest, including woodland walks and ornamental ponds. Particularly charming is the Walled Garden, located in a sheltered position half a mile (0.8km) to the east of the house and of which Raleigh Trevelyan has commented, 'No garden lover can fail to be delighted and amazed.' Although originally created in the 1760s by Sir Walter Calverley Blackett, its present appearance owes much to Sir George Otto Trevelyan, who for instance provided a rockery and also erected the conservatory which contains enormous fuschias, geraniums, bougainvillaea and an assortment of exotic climbing plants.

WARKWORTH CASTLE

Warkworth Castle stands on the neck of a peninsula formed by a loop of the Coquet near where the river joins the North Sea, and dominates the attractive village of Warkworth occupying the rest of the peninsula.

The castle is best known for its connections with the Percy family, which has been associated with Warkworth since the 14th century. However, the castle existed long before this for it was apparently founded as a motte and bailey in about 1150 by Henry, Earl of Northumberland, the son of David I of Scotland, a king in whose realm the county of Northumberland then lay.

In 1157 England's formidable young ruler, Henry II, regained control of Northumberland for the English Crown and the following year granted Warkworth to Roger fitzRichard, whose descendants remained lords of Warkworth until the early 14th century, by which time they had assumed the surname of Clavering. Roger seems to have begun rebuilding the castle in stone. Despite such work, when the Scots invaded the north of England in 1173, Warkworth's defences were deemed by him to be inadequate to resist them and so he abandoned the castle and withdrew towards Newcastle, leaving the Scots to take possession of the stronghold.

In 1178, he was succeeded by his son, Robert fitzRoger, who is known to have strengthened Warkworth's defences, using money acquired while serving King John in the early

93. Warkworth Castle from the south-west, with the Coquet in the foreground

94. The south side of the castle, with the remains of the
Carrickfergus Tower on the left and the gatehouse on the right

years of the 13th century. Further building work ensued and in 1249 the chronicler Matthew Paris was able to describe Warkworth as a noble castle.

In 1292 Edward I is known to have spent a night here. Four years later, his reign witnessed the commencement of war with Scotland, and Anglo-Scottish conflict was to be a marked feature of life for Northumberland's inhabitants for much of the 14th century. In 1319, Warkworth is known to have had a garrison of 24 men accompanied by a support staff of cooks, servants and armourers, half of whom were being paid by the Crown, for in 1311 the then lord of Warkworth, John de Clavering, had made a deal with Edward II in which he would subsequently hand over Warkworth and his other properties in Northumberland to the Crown in return for estates in the south of England, a deal that only became fully effective in 1332.

In the latter year, Warkworth, (which had been twice unsuccessfully besieged by the Scots in 1327), was granted by Edward III to Henry de Percy II, lord of nearby Alnwick, who had been a member of the regency appointed to govern England during the young king's minority. Furthermore, in addition to serving against the Scots, Percy also fought abroad. In 1340, during the early years of the Hundred Years War, he participated in the great naval battle of Sluys in which an English fleet annihilated that of France; two years later he was at the siege of Nantes, and in 1347 fought in France under the Black Prince. He died at Warkworth unexpectedly on 27 February 1352.

Evidently, as the 14th century drew to a close, Henry de Percy IV (who became head of the family in 1368 and was created Earl of Northumberland in 1377), built the splendid keep that is Warkworth's crowning glory, very possibly employing the services of John Lewyn, the most able English military architect of the late Middle Ages.

In the early years of the 15th century, the first earl and other members of the Percy family unsuccessfully rose in rebellion against Henry IV, and it is interesting to note that some of the scenes in Shakespeare's play, *Henry IV*, are set in Warkworth Castle which is erroneously described as a 'worm-eaten hold of ragged stone.' In 1405 the king granted the castle to one of his young sons, John, the future Duke of Bedford, after employing artillery against its walls to bring about its submission - the garrison had surrendered on 1 July.

Bedford regularly resided at Warkworth. But in 1416, early in the reign of his elder brother Henry V, the forfeited Percy lands and castles were mostly restored to the late first earl's grandson. If his grandfather had not already done so, the second Earl of Northumberland began founding a collegiate church in Warkworth Castle intending it to serve as a family mausoleum where a number of clergy, (a 'college'), would pray for the souls of deceased members of the family. However, it was never finished.

The second earl was killed in 1455 at the First Battle of St Albans - the start of the Wars of

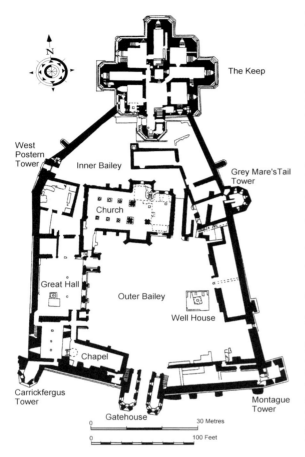

N

The Keep

West
Postern
Tower

Inner Bailey

Grey Mare'sTail
Tower

Church

Great Hall

Outer Bailey

Well House

Chapel

Carrickfergus
Tower

Montague
Tower

Gatehouse

0   30 Metres

0   100 Feet

95. A plan of Warkworth Castle (after English Heritage)

the Roses - while fighting on behalf of Henry V's weak son and successor, Henry VI. In 1461, the third earl likewise perished in the same cause. He did so at Towton in Yorkshire, whereupon the Percy estates were again declared forfeit and a Yorkist, John Neville, Lord Montague (the brother of Warwick the Kingmaker), was subsequently installed at Warkworth. Warwick himself resided at the castle in the early 1460s when engaged in crushing Lancastrian support in Northumberland by besieging the castles of Alnwick, Bamburgh and Dunstanburgh. On 10 December 1462 a member of the Paston family wrote as follows in Newcastle, 'My lord of Warwyk lythe at the castyll of Warcorthe . . . and he rydyth dayly to all these castelys for to overse the segys.'

In 1470 the Percies regained Warkworth when the third earl's young son, Henry, was granted the forfeited estates by Edward IV. The fourth earl may have completed a tower at Warkworth begun by John Neville, and is known to have hunted opposite the castle in a park on the west side of the Coquet. He was present at Bosworth in 1485 on the side of Richard III but for one reason or another remained aloof from the fighting, and was subsequently murdered by a mob near Thirsk in Yorkshire in 1489 when helping to raise an unpopular tax.

His son and successor preferred residing in Yorkshire than in Northumberland, but nevertheless sometimes spent money on repair work at Warkworth. In contrast, the sixth earl frequently stayed in the castle for prolonged periods in line with the general practice of his forebears (generations of the family often spent the winter months at Warkworth) and rebuilt a section of the curtain wall. He died in 1537, without a son to succeed him, and left all his possessions to Henry VIII. Hence royal officers sometimes resided at Warkworth - whose great days were over - until 1557 when the castle was restored to the sixth earl's nephew during the reign of Mary Tudor.

A staunch Catholic, the seventh earl subsequently took part in a rebellion against Protestant Queen Elizabeth. The revolt occurred in 1569 and proved a failure. Northumberland paid for his involvement in the debacle by losing his head in 1572, by which time Warkworth Castle had been thoroughly ransacked by men loyal to the queen.

In 1574, Elizabeth restored the earldom of Northumberland to the Percies, but in the years that followed Warkworth suffered from neglect. Indeed, in 1617 when James I inspected Warkworth (at which time the head of the Percy family was a prisoner in the Tower of London) goats and sheep were found in almost every room.

Warkworth was occupied by both the Scots and parliamentary forces in the 1640s during the Civil Wars, and when parliament's troops left the castle they did as much damage to it as they could. Its descent into a ruinous state continued when, in 1672, the widow of the eleventh earl granted building materials from the castle to one of the estate auditors, John Clarke. Hence 272 wagon-loads of lead and timber were carted off for other purposes and the keep was left a shell.

During the days of Algernon Percy, fourth Duke of Northumberland, (1847-65), excavation work was undertaken at Warkworth which uncovered the remains of the collegiate church mentioned above. The duke, who wrought significant changes at nearby Alnwick Castle, whose keep he transformed into a magnificent series of state rooms, also employed the architect Anthony Salvin to work on the keep at Warkworth, apparently intending to have manor courts held in it, although this plan was dropped. Among other things, Salvin refaced the keep's entrance and reroofed the chambers of the uppermost floor, rooms that were used for picnics by the duke and his companions when they visited Warkworth from Alnwick.

In 1922, the eighth Duke of Northumberland entrusted Warkworth Castle to the Office of Works.

Description

96. The imposing gatehouse

'Warkworth Castle is one of the most impressive examples in Britain of an aristocratic fortified residence.' So comments Henry Summerson, and with good reason, for the castle amply testifies to the wealth and power of its former baronial masters and of the high standard of life that they were able to enjoy in the castle's heyday.

It occupies an elevated position and is entered from the south through an imposing gatehouse, approached by crossing a bridge (originally a draw-bridge) over a deep dry moat. The gatehouse, which has experienced significant alterations over the years, presumably dates from the days of Robert fitzRoger. It projects boldly on either side of the entrance and has cruciform arrow loops, some of which enabled defenders to fire at anyone trying to approach the south curtain wall either side of the gatehouse. Among other things, further protection was afforded by machicolations above the entrance arch and by a portcullis, the grooves of which can still be seen. The gate passage has a pointed tunnel-vault and is flanked by guardrooms, while stairs on either side of the passage, and entered from the north, lead straight up to a chamber above the gate passage that housed the portcullis machinery.

West of the gatehouse, and running along the inside of the south curtain wall, are the remains of a chapel of mostly early 14th century date: the ground floor was used by members of the garrison, while a gallery at the west end was used by the lord and his family to hear and observe services below.

The west end of the chapel adjoined a range of buildings running north along the inner face of the west curtain wall. Prior to the construction of the late 14th century keep, this range formed the heart of the castle. At its southern end was a cellar, with the lord's solar above, while to the north lay the Great Hall and service rooms. A straight stair in the thickness of the curtain wall led up from the hall to the solar.

Both the cellar and the solar had access to the Carrickfergus Tower, in the south-west angle of the defences. The tower, a well-lit structure with a fireplace on each floor, appears to have served as an extension of the solar for the lord of Warkworth and his family.

97. The southernmost of the towers located on the east side of the hall range

From the solar, moreover, they would also have had access to the gallery at the west end of the chapel.

Access to the hall range from the outer bailey was, in time, provided by entrances in two towers (likely both the work of the first Percy Earl of Northumberland, although the fourth earl heightened the northern most tower) located on the east side of the range. The southernmost tower, crowned by a graceful pinnacle, has a west doorway at ground level that gives access to the former cellar: another doorway at the same level in the tower opened southward to the chapel, while a third gave entry to the south end of the Great Hall: a door at first floor level opened to the solar. The second tower is known as the Lion Tower, on account of the Percy lion in high relief above the entrance arch. The entrance here served as the state

98. The Lion Tower

entrance to the Great Hall for important guests: lesser folk entered the hall through the doorway mentioned above.

The Great Hall, whose earliest masonry dates from the mid 12th century, was evidently originally on an east-west alignment with the lord's dais at the west end so that he sat with his back to the curtain wall, and with a fireplace in the south wall. Subsequently, and likely early in the 13th century, the hall was realigned to have a north-south axis in which the dais was located at the south end with warmth provided by a fire burning in front of it. Furthermore, the new hall had an aisle down its east side. Off the north end of the hall were the buttery, pantry, larder and kitchen. The latter, the northernmost, contains the remains of a bread oven beside a fireplace, both made of brick.

Just beyond the kitchen lies the west postern gate. In addition to serving a military function, the postern is thought to have acted as a tradesmen's entrance through which goods from the village and the lord's estates were delivered to the service rooms such as the buttery and pantry.

Adjoining the north-east end of the hall range, and stretching eastward are the foundations of the unfinished collegiate church, planned to have an aisled nave of four bays, transepts, a tower above the crossing, and a two-bay aisled choir. Crypts were provided beneath the north transept and the choir, while a passage beneath the east end of the church was built to lead from the outer bailey to the inner bailey and keep.

In close proximity to the east end of the church stands the Grey Mare's Tail Tower, located along the east curtain wall. Of 13th or early 14th century date, it perhaps owes its name to its position near the stables, built just to the south along the inner face of the curtain wall. On entering, one can see to the left of the entrance at ground level, a double latrine in the angle between the curtain wall and the tower's north wall. Also noteworthy are deep embrasures, two in each of the tower's five faces, with one embrasure above the other. These enabled longbows or crossbows to be fired through a single long slit in each face.

Just in front of the low remains of the stables, are the remnants of a well house that housed a well at least 60ft (18.3m) deep. On the other hand, just south of the stables is the east postern in the curtain wall. The wall itself terminates at the Montague Tower in the south-east corner of the defences, begun and perhaps completed in the 1460s by John Neville, Lord Montague. In addition to a defensive role, on its three well appointed upper floors the tower also provided accommodation, no doubt for important guests. The curtain wall between the tower and the gatehouse is a modern reconstruction on a 13th century foundation.

Having discussed the buildings and defences enclosing the outer bailey, attention needs to be turned to the inner bailey and the keep. The former is substantially smaller than the outer bailey and housed what was probably the brewhouse, built into the south slope of the motte.

On the motte stands the keep, by far the most imposing and fascinating part of Warkworth and a structure that in effect served as a castle within a castle. Of it, Pevsner has commented, 'Here is one of the rare cases where the military engineer happened to be a great architect . . .[it] is a work of architecture in the sense that both its mass and its inner spaces are beautiful as well as useful.'

It is three storeys high and basically 80ft (24m) square in plan, with a tower-like projection c.25 by 15ft (7.6 by 4.6m) roughly in the centre of each face. The lower courses of masonry are earlier than the rest of the fabric and probably date from the 13th century. The date of the present keep's construction is disputed. It has been attributed to either the days of the first or second Earls of Northumberland, and, recently, to as late as the early 16th century by one architectural historian. However, as Malcolm Hislop comments: 'The documentary evidence is on the whole supportive of the generally accepted attribution to the first earl.' Hislop further plausibly suggests that the keep was most probably erected in the 1390s.

The entrance, reached via modern steps, is located in the west wall of the south-facing projection and was defended by a portcullis. If by any chance enemy troops managed to make their way beyond this point, the floor immediately through the entrance lay above a pit and could be made to collapse beneath them by the removal of a bolt.

To the left after entering, is the entrance hall located in the body of the keep. Most of the rooms off this were storerooms containing such items as beer and wine that could be transported to floors above by one or other of several flights of stairs, (the wine was bought in Newcastle), and such provisions were brought into the keep via a postern in the west wall. However, the first room off the west side of the entrance hall was a guardroom - beneath whose floor is a dungeon - and the bowl of a stone font can be seen here, having for some reason been left on the guardroom floor. All the ground floor rooms are tunnel-vaulted.

Almost exactly in the centre of the keep, and extending through all the floors up to and beyond the roof itself, is a lightwell. It is open to the sky and pierced by windows admitting air and some light to the tower. Additionally, rainwater that descended to the foot of the lightwell was either discharged into a large tank and used for purposes such as washing floors or cleaning out drains, or more often than not was directed into a pipe to flush out the shafts of latrines on the floors above. All in all, the keep would thus have smelt less than was the case in many other castles.

A grand flight of stone steps located in the south projection leads up from the south-east corner of the entrance hall to a lobby on the first floor. The lobby has a fireplace and windows with window seats providing fine views. Here, visitors would have waited until being admitted to the lord's presence.

Just to the north of the lobby is the Great Hall, occupying the south-east part of the keep. A well-lit room measuring 40 by 25ft (12.2 by 7.6m), the hall rose to the roof of the keep and had a minstrels' gallery at the east end. The largest window - the largest in the keep - faces south and is so high that it has two transoms. Moreover, the east wall contains stairs up which wine was brought to the hall from the wine cellars on the floor beneath.

At the west end of the hall are three doorways opening to the pantry, the buttery, (connected to the beer cellar below by stairs) and the kitchen. The latter, by far the largest of the rooms in question, occupies the north-west part of the tower and really contains two kitchens, one smaller than the other. The former has a fireplace with a bread oven on the left and a place for a cauldron on the right. The larger kitchen, open to the roof, has two huge fireplaces while in the north-west corner of the room are stairs up which provisions were brought from a storeroom beneath.

North of the Great Hall, the east side of the first floor contains the chapel, whose altar stood on a dais, the floor of which comprised glazed tiles. The chapel extended into the east projection (where light was provided by a three-light window) and contained painted stone statues in niches and hangings on the walls. In 1532 one is known to have portrayed the twelve prophets, another the apostles. The Percies did not attend services at first floor level. They did so from a gallery above the chapel's west end.

99. The keep

Beyond the chapel, and connected to the Great Hall by a passage, is the great chamber in the north-east part of the first floor, a well appointed room designed to provide the Percies with both privacy and comfort. The south wall has a fireplace while the north and east walls have windows, the former providing views of the hustle and bustle of life down in the neighbouring village below; the other of the coast and the North Sea.

At the north-west end of the great chamber is a doorway. Upon progressing through this one sees, to the right, a small passage leading to a latrine. On the other hand, directly ahead and located in the projection on the keep's north face, is a bedroom with a fireplace on its west side and its own latrine, reached via a passage in the east wall. The keep's second floor is not open to the public.

Warkworth Castle is owned by the Duke of Northumberland, but is in the care of English Heritage.

Some Other Sites of Interest

Alnwick: St Michael's Church

Undoubtedly the finest Perpendicular church in Northumberland, St Michael's stands at the west end of the town, dates from a complete reconstruction carried out after 1464 (it was partly restored in the 19th century), and is a rare example in the county of a church dating from the late Middle Ages. In plan, it is a fully aisled parallelogram. Among other things, there is a variety of tracery forms, while the arcade piers of the chancel have richly carved capitals.

Berwick-upon-Tweed Barracks

Located in the north-east part of Berwick, the barracks were begun in 1717, shortly after the suppression of Jacobite risings in England and Scotland. They were the first barracks built in Britain and were occupied in 1721. Although often attributed to Vanbrugh, they were actually designed by Nicholas Hawksmoor. Ranged round three sides of a quadrangle - the fourth side is bounded by a high wall with a gatehouse - they consist of three separate buildings. That facing the gatehouse is known as the Clock Block - it was erected in 1739 on the site of a gunpowder magazine - and contains the Borough Museum and Art Gallery. The barracks also contain a museum dedicated to the King's Own Scottish Borderers.

Berwick-upon-Tweed Castle

Berwick Castle, first mentioned in 1160 but rebuilt by Edward I following his capture of Berwick in 1296, lay outside the north-west angle of the medieval town and changed hands on several occasions during the period of Anglo-Scottish conflict. In June 1318, for instance, it was retaken by the Scots after an eleven week siege (after being in English hands since its capture by Edward I) and remained under Scottish control until 1333 when it once again passed to the English.

From the early 17th century onward, the castle was abandoned. It was later used as a quarry for building material by the town's inhabitants, while in the mid 19th century further destruction was wrought by the building of a railway station on part of the site. Nonetheless, substantial sections of fabric survive. The most important remains are the south-east angle tower, known as the Constable Tower, and a stretch of adjoining curtain wall, as well as the castle's north-west wall which has a tall tower at its north end. The Constable Tower is polygonal and has masonry of exceptionally good ashlar.

Blanchland Abbey

In 1165 Walter de Bolbec III, lord of Styford, founded a house for canons of the Premonstratensian Order here, beside the River Derwent, which lasted until the Dissolution of the Monasteries in the reign of Henry VIII.

The 15th century monastic gatehouse has survived, while the west range of claustral buildings is now incorporated in the Lord Crewe Arms Hotel. In the mid 18th century the church, which had become ruinous, was rebuilt incorporating a substantial amount of surviving medieval fabric (mostly 13th century) and further rebuilding occurred in the 19th century. The most conspicuous surviving parts of the medieval church include a tower adjoining the north end of the north transept, and the transept's west wall: the tower is of three stages, the two lowest date from the 13th century whereas the uppermost is mid 14th century. The transept's west wall has tall two-light lancets with Y-tracery dating from around 1300.

Bolam: St Andrew's Church

St Andrew's has a late Saxon west tower (perhaps built in two stages in view of a change in the masonry at mid-point), while the quoins of the nave and its west wall are likewise Saxon. The rest of the church is essentially Norman, although some fabric is later. The chancel, for instance, was extended in the 13th century. An early 14th century effigy of a knight in the church is almost certainly that of Robert de Reymes I (died 1324), who built Aydon Castle near Corbridge, several miles to the south-west.

Bywell Castle and the churches of St Andrew and St Peter

Built on the north bank of the River Tyne in the early 15th century by Ralph Neville, second Earl of Westmorland, Bywell Castle is a large three-storey rectangular gatehouse tower. The roof has gone, but the shell is virtually complete. The gatehouse, which faces south, was planned to be part of a large enclosure but this scheme was evidently not

100. St. Andrew's Church, Bywell

completed, although some of the curtain wall is known to have been erected.

In addition to the castle, the village of Bywell boasts two important churches located a short distance apart. St Andrew's is a small cruciform structure celebrated for its excellent late Saxon west tower, the finest in the county, while St Peter's likewise contains Saxon material. The north wall of the nave, and the west parts of the side walls of the chancel, are now generally held to be surviving fabric from a large church perhaps erected as early as the 8th century and in which Bishop Egbert of Lindisfarne was perhaps consecrated in 802.

Cherryburn: Birthplace of Thomas Bewick

Thomas Bewick, Northumbria's celebrated artist, wood engraver and naturalist, was born here in 1753 and visitors can see an exhibition of his life and works, as well as demonstrations of wood engraving, bookbinding and printing. Cherryburn is located between Hexham and Newcastle.

Chipchase Castle

Chipchase Castle, in upper Tynedale, consists of a mid 14th century tower-house and an attached Jacobean mansion. The tower, with an entrance defended by a wooden portcullis, consists of a vaulted basement and three upper storeys (the Great Hall was on the second floor) and is crowned by four circular bartizans. The three-storey Jacobean house faces south-east and was added in 1621. Although it experienced some alterations and additions in Georgian and Victorian times, it is nevertheless the finest structure of its period in the county. A garden surrounds the castle and there is also a walled nursery specialising in unusual hardy plants.

Corbridge: St Andrew's Church and Vicar's Pele

St Andrew's Church has fabric dating from several periods and was first built in the Saxon era, likely before 786, and has been described by Pevsner as the 'most important surviving Saxon monument in Northumberland' after the crypt at Hexham. An arch giving access from the west porch into the nave is believed to have been reused from the nearby Roman site of *Coriosopitum* or *Corstopitum* as it is more widely known. In the Middle Ages the church housed an anchorite in a 13th century addition off the west end of the north aisle of the nave.

The Vicar's Pele lies on the south side of the churchyard. It is a small tower-house, built of Roman stones in around 1300 or perhaps as late as the mid 14th century. It was first mentioned in 1415 when it was described as owned by the vicar, and was restored and reroofed in 1910. It is a three-storey structure whose ground floor is tunnel-vaulted, and has a parapet with machicolation at each of the four angles.

Edlingham Castle

Edlingham Castle, described by Pevsner as 'one of the most interesting in the county', lies in a beautiful valley south-west of Alnwick. The ruins date from the 13th to the 15th century. A barbican of c.1400 leads southward to the remains of a gatehouse erected c.1340, and beyond which lies a courtyard whose south side was enclosed by a hall house erected c.1295-1300 by Sir William Felton. The most notable feature of the castle is a mid 14th century three-storey solar tower off the south side of the hall house. Built in about 1340, it stands up to 33ft (10m) high,

101. Edlingham Castle

has a good selection of masons' marks, evidence of a former lofty rib-vault and a spectacular fireplace.

Hulne Priory

Picturesquely situated in an historic park on the western outskirts of Alnwick, Hulne Priory, one of the earliest Carmelite houses in England, was founded in 1265 by the lord of Alnwick, John de Vescy. He granted the friars various rights, such as permission to take timber for building from the park, honey and wax from wild bees in the woods, and broom to thatch their buildings. The priory survived until the Dissolution of the Monasteries.

The ruins lie within a 15th century curtain wall, with a square gatehouse tower near the centre of the south wall. Much of the church has survived. Little remains of the west and south claustral ranges, but the east range has been rather more fortunate. The dominant feature of the site is a large rectangular tower built in 1488 by the fourth Earl of Northumberland to serve as a hunting lodge. In addition to the priory, Hulne Park contains enchanting walks and is home to herds of red, roe and fallow deer.

Langley Castle

Langley Castle, in upper Tynedale, is a large tower-house that currently serves as an hotel and restaurant. It appears to be the result of a mid 14th century remodelling of an earlier structure by Thomas de Lucy, lord of Langley, who died in 1365. A prominent owner of the castle was Henry Percy, first Earl of Northumberland, who acquired it through marriage and unsuccessfully rebelled against Henry IV in the early 15th century. In 1882 the castle, which appears to have been ruinous since 1405, was purchased by the Northumbrian historian Cadwallader Bates who undertook substantial restoration work and rendered it habitable.

The castle comprises a four-storey main block, with five-storey corner towers and a rectangular forebuilding against the east face. A unique series of latrines, arranged above each other in three groups of four, exists in the south-west tower, leading Pevsner to comment, 'the arrangement is uncommonly lavish.'

Mitford Castle

Occupying the summit of a rocky knoll overlooking the River Wansbeck a short distance upstream from Morpeth, Mitford Castle was a motte and bailey fortress founded in the 12th century by the Bertram family, lords of Mitford, and was subsequently rebuilt in stone. During John's reign the head of the family sided with the king's opponents and the castle was captured by John in late 1215. It

102. Mitford Castle

was restored to the Bertrams five years later and remained in Bertram hands until the late 13th century. In 1297, the castle was captured and largely destroyed by Scottish troops who were homeward bound after invading the North. Later still, in 1317, it served as the base of a gang of outlaws led by Sir Gilbert de Middleton, who was seized at Mitford, and executed in London in 1318.

The castle comprises a motte and two baileys. The former is partly enclosed by a wall with an entrance in the east side and has the remains of a five-sided 13th century keep, as well as the foundations of another structure. The south bailey is enclosed by the remains of a curtain wall, whereas the north bailey, on slightly lower ground, evidently had a wooden palisade rather than a wall.

Newcastle: Bessie Surtees House

Bessie Surtees House lies on Newcastle upon Tyne's Quayside and consists of two stately timber-framed merchants' houses dating from the 16th and 17th centuries, though one of the houses was enlarged and provided with a brick frontage in about 1741. Its companion is a remarkable and rare example of 17th century domestic architecture. In all, three rooms are open to the public, enabling visitors to view dark carved oak panelling, ornate chimney-pieces, and a 'Jacobean' plaster ceiling dating from the 1930s. One can also learn about the story of the elopement of Bessie Surtees herself, which occurred on 18 November 1772 when she ran away with John Scott, (the future Lord Eldon) and was married in Scotland the following day.

Newcastle: Cathedral of St Nicholas

Until 1882, when the diocese of Newcastle was created, St Nicholas was Newcastle's principal parish church. It measures 245ft (75m), and mostly belongs to the 14th and 15th centuries, although there is a small amount of earlier fabric. Its exterior is dominated by a west tower and spire rising to a total of 193½ft, (59m), while inside an interesting characteristic is the presence of octagonal piers without capitals and carrying chamfered arches that simply die into them.

Norham: St Cuthbert's Church

Although most of the church dates from 1846-52, important Norman work survives. This comprises the south arcade of the nave and the chancel. The former, aptly described by Pevsner as 'truly majestic for a parish church', has huge circular piers whose capitals are ornamented with waterleaf and support richly moulded arches. The chief feature of the chancel is its south wall, an impressive composition with ornate windows.

Warkworth Hermitage

A lovely walk along the south side of the Coquet leads from Warkworth to the hermitage, an enchanting site located about half a mile (0.8km) upstream. Here, a boat carries one across the river to the hermitage which is cut deep into the rock of a cliff on the north bank and comprises a chapel and several other rooms. The hermitage dates from the medieval period but who the first hermit was is unknown, as is the date when the hermitage began.

103. The church of St Lawrence, Warkworth

Warkworth: St Lawrence's Church

St Lawrence's Church lies on the northern fringe of Warkworth near a medieval bridge across the River Coquet: the south side of the bridge is protected by a tower, a rare feature in Britain. The church is the finest and most complete Norman church in Northumberland. Particularly remarkable is its rib-vaulted chancel - few 12th century parish churches have vaulted chancels - which owes much to Durham Cathedral. The west tower was added around 1200 and carries a spire believed to date from the 14th century. The south aisle of the nave is likewise late medieval.

Wylam: George Stephenson's Cottage

The cottage, in which George Stephenson was born in 1781, was built around 1760 and has been furnished to reflect the time period of his birth. Wylam lies in the Tyne valley near Prudhoe.

GLOSSARY

AISLE: passage alongside a nave, transept etc. of a church or the main body of some other building, separated from it by columns etc.

ACANTHUS: formalized leaf ornament with thick veins and a frilled edge.

APSE: in churches, a semicircular or polygonal end to a chancel, aisle, etc.

ARCADE: a series of arches supported by piers. *Blank* or *blind arcade* - series of arches supported by piers attached to the surface of a wall.

ASHLAR: squared blocks of masonry laid in regular courses.

BAILEY: defended enclosure or courtyard of a castle.

BALUSTERS: vertical supports for a handrail or coping.

BARBICAN: outer fortification defending a gateway.

BAROQUE: an exuberant style of architecture of the 17th and part of the 18th centuries, characterized by curving forms, extravagant decoration and spatially complex compositions. The style was first used in this country in the latter half of the 17th century.

BARREL-VAULT: see 'Vault'

BARTIZAN: a square or round corbelled turret frequently at the corner of a tower etc.

BAYS: divisions of a building defined by regular vertical features such as buttresses.

BEAKHEAD: Romanesque ornamental motif comprising a row of bird or beast heads.

BLANK (or BLIND) ARCADE: see 'Arcade'

BLANK TRACERY: purely decorative tracery applied to a surface without glazing or openings.

BOSS: an enriched ornamental block usually covering the intersections of ribs in a vault.

BUTTRESS: projecting mass of masonry or brickwork supporting a wall, or resisting the lateral thrust of a vault, arch or roof.

CAPITAL: head of a column etc; it is normally decorated.

CARYATID: a female figure supporting a capital etc.

CHAMFER: a surface formed by cutting of a square edge, usually at an angle of 45 degrees.

CHANCEL: the part of the east end of a church in which the principal altar is located. Also often applied to the entire east limb of a church.

CHAPTER HOUSE: room where monks etc. met daily to hear a chapter of the monastic Rule and to discuss business.

CHEVRON: zigzag Norman ornament of the 12th century.

CLAUSTRAL: pertaining to the cloister.

CLERESTORY: the upper stage of a church elevation and pierced by windows.

CLOISTER: in a monastic establishment, a covered walkway around an open quadrangle (garth).

COFFERED: a ceiling decorated with sunken square or polygonal ornamental panels.

COLONNADE: a row of columns set at regular intervals, and usually supporting a series of arches, an entablature etc.

COLUMN: a vertical structural member typically consisting of a shaft with a base and a capital.

COMPOUND PIER: a pier consisting of a solid core surrounded by attached or detached shafts, or consisting of a bundle of shafts.

CORBEL: a projecting stone or piece of timber to support a weight.

COURSE: continuous layer of bricks etc. in a wall.

COVED CEILING: one which has a pronounced concave curve joining the walls to a flat central area.

CRENELLATED: a battlemented wall.

CROSSING: in a church, the space at the junction of the nave, transepts and chancel.

CRYPT: a subterranean chamber, usually at the east end of a church, and used as a burial place etc.

CUPOLA: term usually applied to a small dome on a circular or polygonal base crowning a turret etc.

CURTAIN WALL: the outer wall of a castle and often punctuated by towers.

CUSHION CAPITAL: a Romanesque capital, basically cubic in form, but with the lower parts rounded away to fit the circular column whose head the capital forms.

DECORATED: historical division of English Gothic architecture c.1290 to c.1340. A sumptuous style characterized by among other things rich decoration of surfaces, flowing and reticulated tracery, and lofty spires.

DIAPER: surface decoration consisting of repetitive patterns of diamonds or squares, and either carved or painted.

DOGTOOTH: typical Early English decoration consisting of a series of pyramidal flowers of four petals.

EARLY ENGLISH: term applied to the style of English Gothic architecture of c.1190 to c.1290. An essentially refined style, chiefly characterized by lancet windows, which are often grouped together. Other motifs include columns surrounded by marble shafts, and dogtooth and stiff-leaf ornament.

ENTABLATURE: in Classical architecture, the horizontal members above a column.

FLUTING: series of concave grooves.

FOIL: Leaf-like ornamentation in windows etc. Trefoil, quatrefoil, cinquefoil etc. express the number of lobes in a shape.

FOLIATED: ornamented with representations of foliage.

FOREBUILDING: defensive structure protecting the entrance to a keep or other building.

GABLE: area of wall - often triangular - at the end of a double pitched roof.

GARDEROBE: individual lavatory in a medieval building.

GOTHIC: a general term used for the architecture of western Europe c.1140 to c.1530. The style appeared in England in the third quarter of the 12th century at places such as Canterbury. Gothic buildings have less massively built walls, larger windows and more lofty proportions than the earlier Romanesque style and characteristic features are rib-vaults, pointed arches, flying buttresses, window tracery and spires. English Gothic architecture is usually divided into three phases: Early English, Decorated and Perpendicular.

HERRINGBONE WORK: masonry or brickwork in zigzag courses.

HOODMOULD: projecting moulding over an arch or lintel to throw off water.

HYPOCAUST: Roman underfloor heating system.

INGLENOOK: a recess for a hearth with provision for seating.

JAMB: one of the straight sides of a doorway, window, etc.

KEEL-MOULDING: moulding shaped like the keel of a ship.

KEEP: the main tower of a castle. Also sometimes known as a donjon. *Shell keep* - a keep with a circular, oval or polygonal wall forming an enclosure, with the living accommodation built against the inner face of the wall, and with an open courtyard in the centre.

LANCET WINDOW: slender window with a pointed arch.

LAVATORIUM: trough with running water where monks etc. washed their hands before meals.

LIGHT: architectural term for a compartment of a window.

LOOPHOLE: a small or narrow opening in a wall through which arrows etc. could be fired.

LOUVRE: opening in the roof of a room to let smoke escape.

MACHICOLATIONS: openings between the corbels of a projecting parapet through which boiling water etc. could be dropped on assailants.

MOTTE AND BAILEY: a castle comprising an earth mound (motte) surmounted by a tower, and an attached enclosure (bailey) at a lower level, and defended by a ditch and palisade.

MOULDING: a decorative band or edge.

MULLION: a vertical bar dividing a window into lights.

NAVE: the main part of a church and where the congregation assembles: often flanked by aisles.

NEWEL STAIR: one ascending round a central supporting post (newel).

NIGHT STAIR: a stair by which canons etc. entered the church from their dormitory to celebrate night services.

NORMAN: see 'Romanesque'

NUTMEG MOULDING: ornament consisting of a chain of tiny triangles placed obliquely.

ORDER: one of a series of concentric stages - shafts for instance - receding towards the opening of a doorway etc.

PALLADIAN: a style of architecture based on the work of the Italian architect, Andrea Palladio, (1508-80), and introduced into England in the first quarter of the 17th century, although the style only started becoming fashionable in c.1715. It is far less exuberant than Baroque and is characterized by good taste, harmonious proportions, and self-restraint.

PARAPET: a low wall for protection at any sudden drop.

PEDIMENT: in Classical architecture, a formalized gable over a portico etc.

PERPENDICULAR: the final phase of English Gothic architecture c.1340 to c.1530, and a marked contrast to the richness and great variety of the preceding Decorated phase. It is characterized by emphasis on straight verticals and horizontals. Among other characteristics are subdued window tracery and a fondness for lofty towers.

PIER: a strong vertical support for arches etc.

PILASTER: shallow pier attached to a wall.

PLINTH: a projecting band of masonry at the base of a wall.

PORTICO: a porch which is open on at least one side, and is enclosed by columns which support the roof and often a pediment.

POSTERN: a small secondary entrance or gateway.

QUATREFOIL: see 'Foil'

QUOINS: stones at the angles of a building.

REREDORTER: a building containing monastic latrines.

RESPOND: a half-pier bonded into a wall and supporting one end of an arch.

ROCOCO: the last phase of the Baroque style. It originated in France c.1720 and was current in Britain and on the continent until c.1760. It is characterized by its elegant refinement of plasterwork etc.

ROOD SCREEN: screen below a crucifix, usually at the west end of a chancel.

ROMANESQUE: a term applied to the style of architecture which is often called Norman in England, and was current in the 11th and 12th centuries. It is characterized by massively built walls, round arches, small windows, zigzag ornament, very robust columns, and clearly defined spatial units.

RUSTICATION: masonry consisting of blocks with recessed joints and, in many cases, an artificially roughened surface. It is intended to give the impression of strength.

SACRISTY: room for keeping vessels and vestments.

SCAGLIOLA: plasterwork imitating marble.

SHAFT: a slender column.

SOLAR: first floor private chamber or withdrawing room of a medieval residence.

SPANDREL: triangular space between two arches or between an arch and its containing rectangle.

SPLAY: a sloping chamfered surface cut into a wall. A splayed loophole, for instance, is much wider internally than externally.

SPRINGING: level at which an arch or vault rises from its supports.

STIFF-LEAF: Early English foliage ornamentation consisting of many lobed shapes.

STRING-COURSE: a horizontal band of masonry along the face of a wall from which it usually projects.

TRACERY: ornamental work in the head of a window (and elsewhere such as on blank arcading) and usually formed by the curving and interlacing of bars of stone. *Geometrical tracery* was in vogue in the latter half of the 13th century and the early years of the 14th, and consists of circles or foils within circles.

TRANSEPTS: the transverse portions of a cross-shaped church.

TRANSITIONAL: the term applied to the architecture of c.1175-c.1190 during the transition from Romanesque to Early English.

TRANSOM: a horizontal bar across the lights of a window.

TRANSVERSE ARCH: in vaulting, an arch which divides one compartment of vaulting from another.

TREFOIL: see 'Foil'

TRIFORIUM: an arcaded gallery between the main arcade and the clerestory.

TUNNEL-VAULT: see 'Vault'

UNDERCROFT: a vaulted room - sometimes below ground - beneath the principal upper room.

VAULT: an arched stone ceiling, sometimes imitated in wood or plaster. *Barrel-* or *Tunnel-Vault* - one that looks like a continuous circular arch: the most basic vault. *Groin-vault* - one composed of two tunnel-vaults intersecting at right-angles. *Rib-vault*: a more attractive vault consisting of arched ribs and cells or compartments of masonry between the ribs. In a quadripartite vault, for instance, each bay of vaulting is divided into four sections by ribs springing from the corners of the bay. Rib-vaults can be very ornate, depending on the number of ribs employed.

VAULTING-SHAFT: a shaft supporting a transverse arch etc. of a vault.

VOUSSOIRS: wedge-shaped stones forming an arch.

WALL-WALK: a walkway along the top of a wall, especially a curtain wall.

WARMING HOUSE: the only room in a monastery - with the exception of the infirmary and kitchen - where a fire was allowed.

WATERLEAF: a broad, leaf-shaped motif with a tied-ribbon effect at the top. Often used to ornament capitals in the latter half of the 12th century.

WHEEL WINDOW: a circular window with radiating shafts like the spokes of a wheel.

BIBLIOGRAPHY

Abbreviations

AA 1,2,3, etc, *Archaeologia Aeliana* series 1,2,3, etc.
AJ, *Archaeological Journal*
DAJ, *Durham Archaeological Journal*
NH, *Northern History*

Apart from standard reference works on Northumberland, the following have been used.

Allibone, J., 'Alnwick Castle', AJ 133, 1976
Amery, C., *Lindisfarne Castle: an illustrated souvenir*, 1982.
Ayris, I., *A City of Palaces: Richard Grainger and the making of Newcastle upon Tyne*, 1997
Batho, G.R., 'The Percies and Alnwick Castle 1557-1632', AA 4 vol. 35, 1957
Batho, G.R., 'The State of Alnwick Castle 1557-1632', AA 4 vol. 36, 1958
Bean, J.M.W., 'The Percies' Acquisition of Alnwick' AA 4 vol. 32, 1954
Bean, J.M.W., *The Estates of the Percy Family, 1416-1537*, 1958
Bennett, J., 'The Roman Frontier from Wallsend to Rudchester Burn Reviewed', AA 5, vol. 26, 1998
Bidwell, P., *The Roman Fort of Vindolanda*, 1985
Bidwell, P., *Roman Forts in Britain*, 1997
Birley, R., *Vindolanda: a Roman Frontier Post on Hadrian's Wall*, 1977
Bishop, M., and Dore, J., *Corbridge: Excavations of the Roman Fort and Town*, 1988
Bishop, M.C., 'An old Corbridge Bath-house Revisited.' AA 5 vol. 26, 1998
Blair, C.H.H., 'The Early Castles of Northumberland', AA 4 vol. 22, 1944
Blair, C.H.H., and Honeyman, H.L., 'Norham Castle', 1966
Blair, J., 'The Early Churches at Lindisfarne', AA 5, vol. 19, 1991
Cambridge, E., 'C.C. Hodges and the nave of Hexham Abbey', AA 5, vol. 7, 1979
Cambridge, E., *Lindisfarne Priory and Holy Island*, 1988
Cambridge, E., and Williams, A., 'Hexham Abbey: a review of recent work and its implications',
        AA 5, vol. 23, 1995.
Clark, A.B.E., *Brinkburn Priory*, 1992
Clay, C.T., 'The Ancestry of the early Lords of Warkworth', AA 4 vol. 32, 1954.
Crow, J., *Housesteads Roman Fort*, 1989
Crow, J., *Housesteads*, 1995
Curnow, P., 'Warkworth Castle', AJ 133, 1976,
Dallison, C.N., *Hexham Abbey*
Dixon, P., and Marshall, P., 'The Great Tower in the Twelfth Century: the Case of Norham Castle',
        AJ 150, 1993
Dixon, P., *Aydon Castle*, 1988
Dore, J.N., *Corbridge Roman Site*, 1989
Dower, P., *Living at Wallington*, 1984
Ellison, M., 'Excavation at Aydon Castle, Northumberland 1975', AA 5 vol. 4, 1976
Ellison, M., and Harbottle, B., 'The Excavation of a 17th-century Bastion in the Castle of Newcastle upon
        Tyne, 1976-81', AA 5, vol. 11, 1983
Embleton, R. and Graham, F., *Hadrian's Wall in the days of the Romans*, 1984.
Fairclough, G.J., 'Brinkburn Priory: a structural analysis of the manor house', AA 5 vol. 8, 1980
Fraser, C., and Emsley, K., *Northumbria*, 1989
Gradidge, R., *Edwin Lutyens: Architect Laureate*, 1981
Grierson, E., *The Companion Guide to Northumbria*, 1976
Harbottle, B., et al, 'Excavations at the South Curtain Wall of the Castle, Newcastle upon Tyne, 1960-61',
        AA 4 vol. 44, 1966
Harbottle, B., 'An Excavation at Warkworth Castle, Northumberland, 1966', AA 4 vol. 45, 1967

Harbottle, B., *The Castle of Newcastle upon Tyne*, 1977

Harbottle, B., and Ellison, M., 'An Excavation in the Castle Ditch, Newcastle upon Tyne, 1974-6', AA 5 vol. 9, 1981

Harbottle, B., and Fraser, R., 'Black Friars, Newcastle upon Tyne, after the Dissolution of the Monasteries', AA 5 vol. 15, 1987

Heslop, D.H., McCombie, G., and Thomson, C., 'Bessie Surtees House - Two Merchant Houses in Sandhill, Newcastle upon Tyne', AA 5 vol. 22, 1994

Hewlings, R., and Anderton, S., *Belsay Hall, Castle and Garden*, 1994

Higham, N., *The Northern Counties to AD 1000*, 1986

Higham, N., *The Kingdom of Northumbria AD 350-1100*, 1993

Hislop, M., 'The Date of the Warkworth Donjon', AA 5 vol. 19, 1991

Hislop, M., 'John of Gaunt's building works at Dunstanburgh Castle', AA 5 vol. 23, 1995.

Hodges, C.C., 'The Conventual Buildings of Hexham Priory', AA 3 vol. 21, 1924

Honeyman, H.L., 'The Cathedral Church of St Nicholas, Newcastle upon Tyne', AA 4 vol .9, 1932

Johnson, J.S., *Chesters Roman Fort*, 1990

Johnson, S., *Hadrian's Wall*, 1989

Kirby, D.P., (ed.) *Saint Wilfrid at Hexham*, 1974

Knowles, W.H., 'The Gatehouse and Barbican at Alnwick Castle', AA 3 vol. 5, 1909.

Knowles, W.H., 'The Castle, Newcastle upon Tyne', AA 4 vol. 2, 1926

Lomas, R., *County of Conflict: Northumberland from Conquest to Civil War*, 1996

Longstaffe, W.H.D., 'The New Castle upon Tyne', AA New Series, vol. 4, 1860.

Mann, J.C., 'The Housesteads Latrine', AA 5 vol. 17, 1989

Mann, J.C., 'The Function of Hadrian's Wall', AA 5 vol. 18, 1990.

Mather, J.Y., 'Bamburgh Castle', Tyne and Tweed no. 45, 1990

McAleer, J.P., 'The upper nave elevation and high vaults of Lindisfarne Priory', DAJ vol. 2, 1986

McNamee, C.J., 'William Wallace's Invasion of Northern England in 1297', NH, 1990

Nelson, I.S., *Etal Castle*, (third edition), 1994

Nolan, J., 'The Castle of Newcastle upon Tyne after 1600', AA 5 vol. 18, 1990

O'Sullivan, D., and Young, R., *English Heritage Book of Lindisfarne: Holy Island*, 1995

Pevsner, N., et al, *The Buildings of England: Northumberland*, 1992

Raimes, F., 'Robert de Reymes of Bolam, Shortflatt and Aydon Castle, and his connection with Suffolk', AA 3 vol. 4, 1908

Reavell, G., 'Warkworth Castle: notes on discoveries made during the Office of Work's operations ending 1931', AA 4 vol. 9, 1932

Saint, A., et al, *Cragside*, 1992

Saunders, A., *Prudhoe Castle*, 1993

Sherlock, D., 'Aydon Castle Kitchen and its Roof', AA 5, vol. 25, 1997

Shrimpton, C., *Alnwick Castle*, 1999

Simpson, W.D., 'Warkworth, A Castle of Livery and Maintenance', AA 4 vol. 15, 1938

Simpson, W.D., 'Dunstanburgh Castle', AA 4 vol. 16, 1939

Simpson, W.D., 'Belsay Castle and the Scottish Tower-houses', AA 4 vol. 17, 1940

Simpson, W.D., 'The Warkworth Donjon and its Architect', AA 4 vol. 19, 1941

Simpson, W.D., 'Further Notes on Dunstanburgh Castle', AA 4 vol. 27, 1949

St. Joseph, J.K., 'Castles of Northumberland from the Air', AA 4 vol. 28, 1950

Stranks, C.J., 'John Sharp at Bamburgh Castle 1758-1792', AA 5 vol. 6, 1978

Summerson, H., *Dunstanburgh Castle*, 1993

Summerson, H., *Warkworth Castle*, 1995

Trevelyan, C., *Wallington, its history and treasures*, 1939

Trevelyan, R., *Wallington, Northumberland*, 1994

Waddington, C., 'A Review of "Pit Alignments" and a tentative interpretation of the Milfield Complex', DAJ 13, 1997

Waddington, C., 'Coupland: the earliest henge-type monument in Britain', AA 5 vol. 25, 1997

Waterson., M., *The National Trust: the first hundred years*, 1994

Woolliscroft, D.J., 'Signalling and the Design of Hadrian's Wall', AA 5 vol. 17, 1989